The Perfectibility of Human Nature in Eastern and Western Thought

SUNY series in Religious Studies

Harold Coward, *editor*

The Perfectibility of Human Nature in Eastern and Western Thought

Harold Coward

STATE UNIVERSITY OF NEW YORK PRESS

Published by
State University of New York Press, Albany

For information, contact State University of New York Press, Albany, NY
www.sunypress.edu

Production by Diane Ganeles
Marketing by Fran Keneston

Library of Congress Cataloging-in-Publication Data

Coward, Harold G.
   The perfectibility of human nature in eastern and western thought /
Harold Coward.
        p. cm. — (SUNY series in religious studies)
   Includes bibliographical references and index.
   ISBN 978-0-7914-7335-1 (hardcover : alk. paper)
   ISBN 978-0-7914-7336-8 (pbk. : alk. paper)
   1. Perfection.   2. Perfection—Religious aspects.   3. Philosophical
anthropology.   I. Title.

BD233.C69 2007
128—dc22   2007016826

10 9 8 7 6 5 4 3 2 1

To my granddaughter, Annie,
who stood at my elbow
watching me write this book

Contents

Acknowledgments

I wish to thank Nancy Ellegate of SUNY Press for encouraging me to write this book. June Thomson gave me valuable assistance in library research and Vicki Simmons in preparation of the manuscript. Thanks are due to several colleagues who kindly read draft chapters and offered suggestions for revision: Elizer Segal, David Hawkin, Andrew Rippin, Anatanand Rambachan, David Loy, and Robert Florida. Helpful suggestions were also received from Roland Miller, Hanna Kassis and Fred Denny.

To make this volume as accessible as possible to readers who do not know the sacred languages, diacriticals have been omitted from Hebrew, Arabic, and Sanskrit words.

Finally a word of special appreciation to my wife, Rachel, who lovingly supported me in the writing of this and all my previous books.

Chapter 1

Introduction

How perfectible is human nature as understood in Eastern* and Western philosophy, psychology, and religion? For me this question goes
back to early childhood experiences. I remember one day as a young
child of perhaps five or six years being sent to my room by my mother
for an afternoon nap. Lying there in silence, my mind was suddenly
overwhelmed with questions: "Why am I here?" "What is the meaning
of it all?" Questions like these imply a goal or purpose that each of us
has to achieve. Later, as a young man being brought up in the Christian tradition, I resonated strongly with Paul when he cried out in
Romans 7: "I do not do what I want, but I do the very thing I
hate. . . . Wretched man that I am. Who will rescue me from this
body of death?" It is these or similar questions that poets, philosophers, psychologists, and the world's spiritual traditions have sought
to answer.

The poet T. S. Eliot in his poem *Burnt Norton* puts the question
this way:

---

*I recognize that the use of terms such as "Eastern" and "Hinduism" have become
problematized by feminist, subaltern, and other contemporary theoretical perspectives.
Yet for an interdisciplinary volume such as this that bridges philosophy, psychology, and
religious studies, the terms "Eastern thought" and "Western thought," along with the
names most widely used for the great religious traditions (e.g., "Judaism," "Christianity,"
"Islam," "Hinduism," "Buddhism"), seem to me to be the most accessible ones for a wide,
nonspecialist, and interdisciplinary audience. As for geographical limitations, although
my title "Eastern and Western Thought" suggests a very broad scope that could include
areas such as China, Japan, Africa, the Caribbean, and Native America, I have restricted
myself under "Eastern" to the great traditions of philosophy, psychology, and religion that
are grounded in India—my area of expertise. I leave others to take on the task of
examining human nature and its perfectibility in other traditions, such as Confucianism,
Taoism, Shintoism, and the African and Aboriginal traditions.

> At the still point of the turning world. Neither
>   flesh nor fleshless;
> Neither from nor towards, at the still point,
>   there the dance is,
> But neither arrest nor movement. And do not
>   call it fixity,
> Where past and future are gathered.[1]

Reading these lines as a young university undergraduate awakened within me a fondness for speculation about the goal to be achieved as "the still point of the turning world"—the still point from which the pattern of the universe and one's place in it could be seen. Some years later while studying Hindu and Buddhist philosophy, speculation on the "still point" and one's place in it was revived in a debate over its nature. For the Hindu, the perfect "still point" to be achieved is consciousness shorn of its changing mental states—the mind calmed until it becomes still like an unrippled mountain lake that perfectly reflects reality. For the Buddhist, however, the "still point" that is left when our self-centered desirous thought ceases is just the steady flow of pure consciousness, like a clear, constantly moving mountain stream in which the world is perfectly reflected. The Hindu-Buddhist debate over the nature of the goal to be achieved is revisited in some of the Western philosophers and theologians in their discussion about the nature of the goal to be reached and the degree to which it can be realized.

In human religious experience the quest for the "still point" of human perfection and its place within the pattern of the universe is seen in the search for full human realization within the world's philosophies and religious traditions. This book examines the sometimes quite different answers offered. In Western thought, human nature is often understood as finite, flawed, and not perfectible (which in Western religion means that God's grace is required to reach the goal). By contrast, Eastern thought arising in India frequently sees human nature to be perfectible and presumes that we will be reborn until we realize that goal (and the various yoga psychologies, philosophies, and religions are the paths by which one may perfect oneself and realize release from rebirth). This rather striking difference in the assessment of how perfectible our human natures are forms the comparative focus of this book.

There is a wide range of views about human nature, about what human beings essentially are, and about their proper goal in the universe in which they live. Keith Ward groups these views into two main categories: the first sees all human selves as essentially pure spirits; the second views humans as embodied souls born from the material world.[2] At one extreme of the pure spirits category is the view that human beings are essentially spiritual and only appear to have individual souls and bodies. Indeed, their bodies are not seen as essential to them, and ultimately their individuality proves to be unreal. An example of this approach to human nature is the Advaita Vedanta school of Hindu thought, which teaches that Brahman, the divine self, is the only ultimate reality and the apparent existence of each of us as separate individuals is superimposed on it. Spiritual practice involves overcoming the illusion of separateness and realizing our true state as one with the divine Brahman defined as *sat-cit-ananda* (pure being, pure consciousness, pure bliss). This realization that we are really nothing but the universal pure spirit of the divine Brahman frees us from the illusion that we are distinct embodied individuals filled with worldly desires. Views like this Advaita Vedanta teaching that we are all ultimately nothing but pure divine spirit are found in some Indian religious traditions as well as "in Plato and in some strands of slightly heterodox Western religious thought which have Neoplatonic roots."[3] The Yoga school of Indian philosophical psychology offers a different interpretation in which each human is ultimately seen to be only pure spirit, but a pure spirit or self (*purusa*) that is never absorbed into a universal Self. While we may first experience ourselves as being trapped in a real material body filled with egoistic desires (*prakrti*), spiritual practice involves disciplined meditation to control our bodies and minds until the materialistic and egoistic desires are purged—leaving only the pure spirit of our individual consciousness shining like a star in the star-filled sky.[4] In these Indian Hindu traditions there is agreement that human nature is first experienced by us as being in bondage to ignorance and desire, and that our goal in life is to realize release from this bondage into a state of perfect freedom and bliss. Spiritual practice (which the Indian traditions refer to as *yoga*) involves knowledge and actions, including disciplined meditation, that enable one to realize that goal—although it may take many lifetimes to so perfect oneself.

India is also the source of another group of "pure spirit" views of human nature—the various schools of Buddhism. In the Buddhist approach it is the misperception of ourselves as permanently existing individual egos with selfish desires that keeps us trapped in ignorance and suffering (*dukkha*). However, by rigorous spiritual discipline including ethical practices, along with mental and physical training in meditation, one seeks to eliminate egoism and selfish desire, and cultivate mindfulness, compassion, and equanimity. One's everyday thought and action becomes less focused on the gratification of personal desires.

The goal is to transcend the sense of self and the attachment it spawns and to realize one's true nature as part of the harmonious, compassionate, and interdependent reality that is the universe (sometimes referred to as the "Buddha Nature"). This is the perfected state of realization that Buddhists call *nirvana*. Because we are so deeply attached to experiencing ourselves as separate individuals with our own desires (built up through repeated lifetimes), it may well take many lifetimes of dedicated Buddhist practice to overcome our attachments to egoistic desires. But, especially in the Mahayana traditions, when these ignorant desires are purged, then we are freed to realize our true selves in a state of pure knowledge and compassionate action dedicated to the welfare of all sentient beings. This is the bodhisattva state of perfection.

What is of fundamental importance for these Indian views of human nature is that the imperfections with which we begin life can be purged through rigorous and disciplined spiritual practice. This may include ritual activity, meditation, and/or devotion to gods or gurus. Such training is seen as continuing until all ignorance and egoistic desires are purged and only pure spirit (which has been one's true nature all along) remains. This may take many lifetimes. Indeed, in Indian thought, one is reborn until one is perfected and one's true state of pure spirit is realized. Such a realization is very different from our usual sense of ourselves as individuals with personal consciousness. It is not so much cancellation of our ordinary experience of human nature as an expansion of our personal consciousness into a better state of "no-self," "pure consciousness," or "pure bliss." Individual human nature, to the extent that it survives, is understood as a manifestation of spiritual being. To realize such states of perfection, human limitations such as egoistic thought and action along with illusory notions of the self have had to be overcome completely. Such is the Hindu and Buddhist idea of the perfectibility of human nature.

Whereas the traditions of India tend to think of human nature as essentially pure spirit, the Semitic traditions of the West view humans as embodied souls born from the material world. Unlike in the Hindu and Buddhist traditions, such souls have had no previous lives, but they may have a resurrected existence beyond this life. Such a resurrected life would not be purely spiritual. "It will be either in a reassembled material universe or in a different form of existence in which both individuality and community will be retained. Such views may take a dualistic form, insisting on the distinctness of the spiritual and the material elements of human nature, even though they are intimately related to one another," says Ward.[5] These approaches stress that human beings are essentially embodied parts of the material universe;

however, "they may have other forms of embodiment in other forms of space-time. These views are characteristic of orthodox strands of Judaism, Christianity, and Islam. . . ."[6] Although these Semitic views stress the embodied nature of human souls, they also maintain that human beings depend upon God for their existence at every moment of their lives. The religious practices of these traditions help humans to recognize and remember this through prayer, intellectual study of revealed scriptures, and various forms of contemplation. Through such activities the individual induces attitudes of reverence, humility, gratitude, repentance, and compassionate action that characterize authentic human life in these traditions. Ward describes the goal as follows:

> For these traditions, human beings are parts of the material order, not separate from it. But what is important about them is that they are enlivened with the Spirit of God, given the possibility of relating in understanding, creativity and love to the Creator and to one another, and the responsibility of nurturing the material order of which they are a part. In this context, the material realm itself is seen, not as an inert, purposeless realm of impersonal laws, but as a dynamic and developing expression of the divine glory, containing already in its primal origin and constitution the potential for self-understanding and creative self-realization in a holistic and conscious community of being. Human beings are one growing point in the development of the material towards fully conscious life, attracted and empowered by the absolute value of the divine Being.[7]

From the above perspective of the Semitic religions, humans are embodied selves—fully and unequivocally material beings but related to the goal to be achieved in somewhat different ways. Christianity emphasizes the flawed aspect of human nature through its doctrines of original sin and the need for atonement. Humans are understood to be created from material dust in order to bring the universe into being a perfect expression of God's glory. Judaism and Islam reject the Christian ideas of original sin and atonement. But they agree with Christianity "in seeing humans as created from dust in order to bring the material universe to a perfect expression of God's glory."[8] Judaism has little interest in the soul after death but seeks to achieve the goal by bringing in a perfected society—the future messianic kingdom. Islam, unlike Judaism, focuses on the experience human beings can look forward to after death: the Last Judgment and the resurrection of the dead. The goal for Islam is not found in the future of this earth but in its hope for a new creation in the life to come. In the chapters that follow we will examine how each religious tradition understands human nature, the goal to be achieved, and the means of perfecting human nature toward the achievement or realization of that goal. We will also sample how human nature and its perfectibility is dealt with in Indian and Western philosophy and psychology. In part 1 we will begin with Western thought before moving on to Eastern ideas in part 2.

Part I

The Perfectibility of Human Nature in Western Thought

Chapter 2

The Perfectibility of Human Nature
in Western Philosophy
and Psychology

PERFECTIBILITY IN WESTERN PHILOSOPHY

John Passmore begins his classic book on the topic of the perfectibility
by distinguishing between "technical perfection" and the perfectibility
of a human being.[1] Technical perfection occurs when a person is deemed
to be excellent or perfect at performing a particular task or role. In this
sense we may talk about a perfect secretary, lawyer, or accountant, suggesting that such persons achieve the highest possible standards in
their professional work. But this does not imply that they are perfect in
their performance of the other tasks and roles of life. Passmore points
out that Plato in his *Republic* allows for technical perfection by allocating to each person that task to perform in which the person's talents
and skills will enable a perfect performance of the task. But that same
person might be a failure as a parent; and so, in Plato's *Republic* he or
she would not be allowed to be a parent. The parent role would be
reserved for someone else whose talents enabled him or her to perfectly perform the task of raising children. But Plato distinguishes such
technical perfection from the perfection of human nature evidenced
by the special class of persons who are rulers of the Republic. These
"philosopher-kings," as he calls them, are not perfect because they rule
perfectly; they are perfect because they have seen "the form of the
good" and rule in accordance with it. Passmore comments, "in the end,
the whole structure of Plato's republic rests on there being a variety of
perfection over and above technical perfection—a perfection which
consists in, or arises out of, man's relationship to the ideal."[2] Passmore
goes on to point out that other Western thinkers including Luther,

9

Calvin, and Duns Scotus follow Plato in talking about technical perfection in terms of one's vocation or calling. But the perfecting of oneself in the performance of the role in life to which one is called is not sufficient by itself to ensure one's perfection as a human being.

A more philosophically complex idea of perfection is Aristotle's idea of "teleological perfection," which in the West has often been taken as the test of human perfectibility. Aristotle argues that every form of activity is directed toward reaching its natural end. Sculpting, for example, has as its end the depiction of the human form. The art of medicine has health as its end. But the overall natural end for humans is "happiness" or "well-being." Humans are perfectible, according to Aristotle, only if they are able to achieve happiness or well-being. Passmore notes that Aquinas took over Aristotle's analysis of perfection and gave it systematic Christian development. According to Aquinas, everything moves toward a particular condition in which it can rest. That condition is the thing's perfection. The perfection of human nature, according to Aquinas, comes with the realization of the vision of God. But humans cannot achieve that end by their own efforts, through their own talents and skills. In the view of Aquinas, the vision of God is both our natural end or goal as human beings and a gift to us from God. As humans we cannot achieve our end by the exercise of our own talents no matter how perfectly we might do that—we can achieve our end only by the gift of God's grace. As humans, then, we may reach technical perfection without achieving our final goal of teleological perfection. Passmore puts it as follows: one "can perform perfectly his religious and moral duties, so far as that involves the skilled use of his abilities, he can make himself expert in ritual and in Christian knowledge, without being vouchsafed the vision of God, and he can attain to that perfection without being technically perfect."[3]

The teleological approach of Aristotle and Aquinas assumes that humans, like all other things, have a natural end ("happiness" or "the vision of God") in which they can realize perfection. But another way of presenting this metaphysical assumption is to think of one's natural end or goal in terms of having unrealized potentialities. In this way of thinking, "becoming perfect" consists in actualizing one's inherent potentialities. Kant adopts this approach in his *Critique of Judgment.* A thing perfects itself, says Kant, "only when it attains an end inherent in the thing itself, what it has in itself to be, not merely an end which someone has chosen to set up as its objective."[4] From the teleological perspective, the end to be actualized cannot be negative (such as becoming a perfect scoundrel), but must be for good (such as becoming a perfect saint). In answering our question as to whether human nature is perfectible, we do not want to allow that a person is perfectible by actualizing a negative potentiality such as becoming a perfect liar. To be perfected must imply becoming better, and in the teleological view all the potentialities to be actualized must be for the good. How then do we deal with negative behavior such as lying, stealing, or bigotry? Augustine solves the problem by arguing that "evil has no positive nature; what we call evil is merely the lack of something good."[5] Negative behaviors such as lying, no matter how developed in a person, are not the actualization of one's true potentialities but rather the result of their absence. Passmore groups Descartes and Leibniz together with Augustine in their understanding of evil as a lack of good. Passmore summarizes by saying: "On this view, then, the bigot does not actualize a human potentiality, he does not 'realize his nature,' by his bigotry. Rather, he fails to realize his nature, since he is deprived of some good which is potential in it. All potentialities, then, are for good. . . . If Augustine and Descartes and Leibniz are correct, all such judgements [i.e., that a person is potentially a criminal] are mistaken: criminality is not a potentiality, capable of being actualized, but only a defect, the imperfect actualization of a potentiality."[6] In addition to technical and teleological perfection, says Passmore, there is a third variety of human perfection—namely, "obedientiary perfection," which involves obeying the commands of a higher authority (God, or a member of the elite). All three have a concept of a function, a task, and an end to be achieved.[7]

Plato seems to have started it all as far as Western philosophy is concerned. By introducing the idea of a metaphysical good as the ideal to be achieved, he also evoked the idea of evil or the lack of good, and the tension between the two. They are related to the terms "perfect" or "perfection" in the sense of an end or goal that is completed (the Greek *telos* [end], and the Latin *perficere* [to complete]).[8] Thus, human nature attempts to perfect itself by actualizing the end (the "good," in Plato's thought) that is inherent in it. Insodoing it "completes" itself. Another approach to perfection in Western thought is to define it as that which has no flaw in it. By focusing on "flaws," our consideration of the perfectibility of human nature is cut loose from any consideration of "ends." A perfect person is simply one who is free from flaws. But what counts as a flaw? From a Christian perspective, sin has traditionally been judged to be an absolute moral flaw. Consequently, humans are seen from this religious perspective as having human natures that are fatally flawed by sin and made perfect or completed only through the gift of God's grace (see chapter 4 for more detail). Another approach purposes the setting up of a perfect human being (e.g., Socrates for the Stoics, Jesus for the Christians) as the ideal to be emulated.

Kant has rejected this idea by pointing out that every example such as Jesus or Socrates must itself be judged with reference to our ideal of moral perfection to see if it is fit to serve as an original example.[9] But if we are in possession of our own ideal of perfection we should judge our own conduct by direct reference to it rather than to an example. Spinoza raises a further difficulty. What if we have competing ideals of moral perfection from different schools of thought? As there is, in Spinoza's view, no higher ideal in relation to which competing views of perfection may be compared and judged, any appeal to an ideal is arbitrary. When we judge perfectibility in this way we must ask, "[I]n relation to whose ideal of perfection?"[10]

However, says Passmore, neither Plato nor Kant agree that ideals are arbitrary. "For Plato . . . ideals have an independent reality. Indeed, only the ideal is fully real. . . . Kant is not prepared, as he himself puts it, 'to soar so high.' Ideals, he grants, do not have objective reality. But they nonetheless have, he says, 'practical power.' They provide us with what he calls on 'archetype,' to 'form' the basis of the possible perfection of certain actions.' "[11] Passmore goes on to describe the complexities present in Plato. Plato does not argue that there is an ideal within us that we should seek to emulate in our pursuit of perfection. Instead, in the *Theaetetus*, Plato sets up God, not an ideal humanity, as the pattern on which humans must model themselves. To be perfect, therefore, is to be like God. Aquinas followed Plato in adopting God as the metaphysical ideal of perfection. But in other dialogues, says Passmore, Plato identifies perfection with harmony and order. For example, in the *Republic*, Plato thinks of the soul as having parts. The perfection of the soul can then "be taken to consist in each of these parts harmoniously contributing to the production of the soul as a whole, playing its particular role in an ordered system."[12] In a similar way Plato defines the ideal state as one that is harmonious, orderly, stable, and unified, and in which the ideal citizen by performing the tasks allotted to him or her contributes to the total social harmony.

Passmore summarizes the various classical views of the perfectibility of human nature as follows:

(1) there is some task in which each and every man can perfect himself technically;

(2) he is capable of wholly subordinating himself to God's will;

(3) he can attain to his natural end;

(4) he can be entirely free of any moral defect;

(5) he can make of himself a being who is metaphysically perfect;

(6) he can make of himself a being who is harmonious and orderly;

(7) he can live in the manner of an ideally perfect human being;

(8) he can become godlike.[13]

In early Western attempts to answer the questions "Are humans perfectible?" certain ambiguities were present. For the Greek perfectibilists, only an elite group endowed with exceptional talents could attain perfection. For Christian thinkers a distinction was made between earthly and heavenly life. Perfectibility was often denied as a possibility for all persons in their earthly lives, but not necessarily in their heavenly lives. More will be said about this in chapter 4 on Christianity.

   In later Western thought the role of society in enabling humans to perfect themselves is examined. In the Christian view, progress toward perfection is dependent upon God's grace, which opens it as a possibility to all people. For Plato, by contrast, perfection is open only to a few persons with certain talents and education—the elite. Although in the Christian view God's grace was open to all, it was generally held that not even God's grace made people perfect, even though God had the power to do this. As Augustine put it, God has simply chosen to bestow so much grace on humans in this life.[14] As we shall see in chapter 4 there was one Christian thinker, Pelagius, who disagreed with Augustine and held that a person could perfect himself or herself by the exercise of free will. But Pelagius was condemned as a heretic, so few followed his thinking. Between Pelagius and Augustine lay the two extremes between which Christian thought fluctuated: perfection is open to all through the self-effort of free will and perfection is possible only by the infusion of God's grace. However, Passmore notes that in the seventeenth century a third possibility began to be considered, a possibility that cut across the old quarrel between Pelagius and Augustine. In this new approach, says Passmore, humans "could be perfected not by God, nor by the exercise of their own free will, nor even by some combination of the two, but by the deliberate intervention of their fellow men."[15] To pursue this third possibility one needed to imagine that Plato would give up the idea that perfection required the contemplation of the form of the good or that Aristotle had described life in the purely secular terms of scientific investigation, with no reference to the theoretical life. Then, says Passmore, perfection could be conceived in wholly nonmetaphysical terms "as the attainment of the maximum possible civic goodness together, perhaps, with such a degree of philosophical goodness as education could ensure."[16] From the fourteenth century, civic humanists extolled the active life, rather than the contemplative life, and "identified it with the 'civically good' life of free, enterprising, community-minded citizens. . . . On the other side, the 'contemplative' life gradually came to be identified not with the life of the monk or the hermit, withdrawn in silence from the ways of men, but with the vigorous, inquiring life of the scholar, the philosopher, the scientist, typified by Leonardo da Vinci, but no less manifest in the burning, inexhaustible goal of the Renaissance classicist."[17] The focus shifted from the contemplative quiet of the countryside to cities like Florence with their amalgam of businessmen, scholars, statesmen, artists, and scientists, cities that ushered in notions that humans and human society could be perfected.

An early move in this direction is made by John Locke. In his book *Some Thoughts Concerning Education*, published in 1693 Locke argues that education, as distinct from God's grace, is capable of leading persons toward moral virtue and perfection.[18] Human nature, according to Locke, is composed of a mind that is like a tabula rasa or blank tablet at birth. One's intellect is, he thought, a passive thing that acquires "content and structure only through the impact of sensation and the criss-cross of associations."[19] In his view there can be nothing in the mind that was not first in the senses. With these assumptions as his starting points, Locke is clearly rejecting the Christian doctrine of original sin strongly maintained by the followers of Augustine. In Locke's view, "Men are born with one and only one natural impulse—the morally neutral impulse to pursue what gives them pleasure and avoid what gives them pain. Apart from that one natural tendency their minds are entirely devoid of any impulse whatsoever."[20] The role of education is simply to furnish the empty room of the young child's mind with good habits that will produce a moral character and lead them to love the ways of virtue. The tools education uses to create these good habits are, according to Locke, shame and concern for one's reputation in society. What are the implications of all of this for human perfectibility? First, Locke maintains there is nothing in human nature (no original sin, for example), to prevent one from being morally improved. Second, through the secular processes of education (and the use of the pleasures of reputation and the pains of blame), good habits will be instilled, leading to the life of virtue. In this way Locke establishes in principle "the possibility of perfecting men by the application of readily intelligible, humanly controllable, mechanisms. All that is required is that there should be an educator, or a social group, able and willing to teach the child what to pursue and what to avoid."[21]

Jean-Jacques Rousseau, in his publication of *Emile* in 1762, also studied the role of education in relation of the perfectibility of human nature. Unlike Locke's tabula rasa view of human nature, Rousseau was convinced that original human nature is good.[22] In *Emile* Rousseau suggests that the innate potentialities of the child's good human nature need to be freely allowed to flower rather than being forced into a predetermined mold. "Each individual," says Rousseau, "brings with him at birth a distinctive temperament, which determines his spirit and character. There is no question of changing or putting a restraint upon this temperament, only of training it and bringing it to perfection."[23] This education toward perfection takes place in *Emile* by raising the child in a natural environment away from the corrupting influences of society. In Rousseau's view, vice and error are alien to the child's nature and are introduced into the child from a society corrupted by its fixation on self-interest and personal fame. This can be avoided if the child is surrounded by nature and given the freedom to have direct contact with the physical world; he or she will learn through the processes of trial and error. Rousseau sees all of nature and the universe as having been created by God with an inherent goodness, unity, and order, just as human nature was. Humans need no mediator such as a priest or the church between themselves and God. God's goodness can be directly experienced by each individual in nature. It is then up to each person to work out salvation by his or her own efforts. Humans are, however, drawn toward God by the spiritual order implicit in the physical world with which one forms a bond. The process of education plays a key role in using sense perception and reason to develop a deep "feeling for nature." Added to this is a strong inner conscience—a "divine instinct" or "voice of the soul"—which, Rousseau believed, guides our human qualities of reason and free will in making moral decisions. As Rousseau put it, to aid us in perfecting ourselves, God gave us "conscience to love the good, reason to know it and freedom to choose it."[24] Only through the harmonious development of all these potentialities of human nature do persons come to a full realization of themselves and the place allotted to them by God in the natural order. Through this process persons also learn to ground their relationships with other people on the innate feeling of compassion that leads us to "extend our being." Through the educational process, there is a growth of sensibility, reason, and imagination. This leads the child to leave "the self-sufficiency of the primitive stage for a fuller life involving relations with the physical realm of nature and the world of human beings."[25]

An implication of Rousseau's ideas about perfectibility is that humans are naturally good and naturally free, and that the institutions of society are the source of all corruption. As Passmore points out, these ideas influenced other European thinkers following Rousseau. For example, the British anarchist William Goodwin argued that "[i]t was not by legislation that men were to be perfected, but rather by the unfettered exercise of their reason, its liberation from the restrictions now imposed on it by government, private property and marriage."[26] Only as individuals become more enlightened and more rational will they reform their social institutions, leading to a gradual improvement and eventually to paradise on earth, where individual intellectual excellence and moral excellence reign supreme. For Locke, Rousseau, and many who came after them, perfectibility meant the possibility for unlimited individual improvement and social progress, rather than the realization of some vision of God or union with the divine. But for this to be achieved, the existing corrupt and corrupting state of society needed to be reformed either by revolution or by peaceful means. As we will see shortly, the new discipline of psychology focused on how this reformation could be achieved through the education and training of the individual. Other thinkers focused on changes needed in society to parallel the changes required in education. Joseph Priestley, for example, argues that the progress of the species toward perfection occurs when government acts as the agent of divine providence.[27] Jeremy Bentham follows Priestley, but gives up ideas of a guiding divine providence. Bentham puts his faith in a code of laws that an ideal government or legislator would enforce. Bentham equates perfection with "perfect happiness" but denies that it lies within human reach. Bentham saw a definite limit to the power of legislation to perfect human nature. Moral vices cannot be legislated out of existence. As Passmore puts it, for Bentham legislation "cannot equalize talents and should not try to equalize possessions; envy, jealousy, and hatred, therefore, it cannot destroy."[28] However, in Bentham's view the limits of legislation can at least be partially overcome by the positive role played by commerce. As commerce grows, individuals find themselves having to live more and more of their lives in public in a manner that is subject to the moral pressures of their fellow human beings. Thus, they are led to become more virtuous day by day. Priestly agreed and argued that commerce brings people into contact with other places and people, expands the mind, removes harmful prejudices, and encourages positive practices such as the love of peace, justice, and honor. Thus, large-scale commerce is a powerful influence for the good.[29]

Faith in large-scale commerce as a force for progress toward perfection and good is challenged by socialists such as Karl Marx. Writing in the nineteenth century, Marx rejected Locke's view that humans at birth are like a blank slate on which culture writes its text. Marx maintained that inherent in each person is a set of fixed human drives such as hunger and the sexual urge. These drives, which comprise the essence of human nature, can be changed only in their form and the direction they take in various cultures. In addition, there are some "relative needs" that are not an integral part of human nature but owe their origin to certain social structures and certain conditions of production and communication. Marx says, in his *Economic and Philosophical Manuscripts*, that the need for money is the need created by the modern economy of the capitalist society and the only need it creates.[30] According to Marx, human potential is seen in the way humans transform and develop themselves in the course of human history. History is the record of human self-realization. History is nothing but the self-creation of humans through the process of their work and their production. Marx saw perfectibility not in terms of the classical idea of the perfectibility of an individual but rather in terms of a society or state progressively moving from lower to higher forms of the self-realization of history. Marx saw this in class struggles arising at particular historical phases in the development of production until the goal of the abolition of all classes was achieved, and a classless society resulted.[31] In that society humans would be free from the oppression of being treated as mere labor for the production of others. Positively, society "will be so organized that men can express their own nature in their labour and in their social relationships. Social organization will become the freely chosen act of humans themselves rather than something seemingly decreed by nature and history. Historical progress is the ascent of man from the kingdom of necessity to the kingdom of freedom."[32] In this kingdom of freedom in a creative intellectual and artistic society, the possibility for improvement seems endless.

Marx imagined this kingdom of freedom as "a progressive national society with no wages, no money, no social classes, and, eventually, no state."[33] If Marx rejects the classical ideal of a final perfection, he does seem committed to the Phoenix myth, "the myth of a fresh start, a 'breaking through' which will carry men if not to perfection then at least to a condition which permits of unlimited improvement."[34]

Our sampling of the variety of views in Western philosophy regarding the perfectibility of human nature concludes with the idea that through scientific progress humans will be perfected. Against the view that human nature can only be perfected by God's grace, Locke and Bentham among others argued that human nature is *in principle* perfectible by natural as distinct from supernatural means. All of this suggests that humans can look forward to an endless history of constant improvement. While Marx argued that such improvement depended on a fundamental change from a capitalist to a classless society, others looked to a change in the genetic makeup of human beings as a way of reaching perfection. The idea that by careful breeding humans might improve the moral character of their descendants has a long history in Western thought from Plato's ideal Republic to more recent utopian proposals. Eugenic controls were often proposed so that in an ideal society males and females of the best natures would be selected by scientific rules to produce children. In 1869, for example, Francis Galton published his *Hereditary Genius*, in which he argues for improvement by social engineering. "There is nothing either in the history of domestic animals or in that of evolution," he wrote, "to make us doubt that a race of sane men may be formed, who shall be much superior mentally and morally. . . ."[35] In Galton's time two methods were proposed for achieving this goal: negative eugenics to breed out defects by sterilization, and positive eugenics by which human nature would be improved by matching the best males and females according to some scientific principle. Today, however, with modern genetic methods and the mapping of the human genome complete, it is suggested that intelligence along with other human traits can be directly modified by genetic engineering. Now it seems that genetic manipulation rather than mystical contemplation may make it possible for humans to achieve perfection and become godlike.

However, even if such scientific methods for perfecting human nature become possible, one great problem remains: who shall do the controlling? "As Rousseau pointed out and as we have all come more and more to recognize, men may be degraded by the same means which could be used to elevate them," says Passmore.[36] If education, social, or genetic engineering is as effective as its proposers maintain, then these means could be used to degrade and enslave human nature rather than to perfect and free it. These worries recur among some of the Western psychologists to whom we shall now turn.

PERFECTIBILITY IN WESTERN PSYCHOLOGY

Gordon Allport, in his seminal book *Becoming: Basic Considerations for a Psychology of Personality*, points out that Locke's tabula rasa or "blank slate" view of human nature has been foundational for much of modern scientific psychology.[37] As the human mind is held to be a tabula rasa in nature, it is not the person but what happens to the person from outside that is fundamental. Thus the approach of conditioning discovered by Pavlov in Russia but rapidly adopted by American psychologists; in it "learning is regarded as the substitution of one effective stimulus for another or of one response for another."[38] By controlling the stimuli a person receives it was thought that he or she could be conditioned to develop in desired directions. Little attention was given to what happened inside the mind, since, on Locke's approach, it was assumed to be a passive tabula rasa. Additionally, Locke had proposed that "simple ideas" were more fundamental than "complex ideas." This paved the way for a reductionist approach in modern psychology. The leader of stimulus-response psychology in North America was John B. Watson. He wrote his textbook *Behaviour: An Introduction to Comparative Psychology* in 1914.[39] His approach came to be known as "behaviorism." According to Watson, all humans are born equal as "blank slates" to be furnished with behavioral responses. It is what happens after birth that makes one person a diplomat, another a thief. Moral defects originate not from innate instincts but from habit systems formed as children and carried over into adult life. These habit systems can be changed by deconditioning. Watson believed that one day we would have hospitals devoted to helping us change our personality just as surgeons can alter the shape of our nose. Human nature, in his view, is quite perfectible in the sense of allowing unlimited improvement. Passmore quotes Watson saying, "I wish I could picture for you what a rich and wonderful individual we could make of every healthy child . . . if only we could let it shape itself properly and then provide for it a universe . . . unshackled by legendary folklore, unhampered by disgraceful political history, free of foolish customs and conventions which have no significance in themselves, yet which hem the individual in like taut steel bands."[40]

Following Watson, B. F. Skinner was perhaps the most widely known American behaviourist. In 1938 he published *The Behavior of Organisms* in which he argued for a stimulus-response psychology that ignored anything that happened within the person—which he viewed as an "empty organism."[41] Skinner applied his views to the perfectibility of human nature in a widely read Utopia written in the form of science fiction, *Walden Two*. Assuming a Locke-Watson view of human nature, Skinner allows that while there are innate differences in intelligence, persons are made good or bad, wise or foolish, by the environment in which they grow up.[42] Rejecting philosophies of innate goodness or evil, Skinner has no doubt that we have it in our power to change human behavior for the better. Skinner admits that experiment is still needed to determine exactly how the social environment needs to be modified to ensure that children can be conditioned to grow up good rather than bad—but thinks that is just a matter of time. Skinner has no doubt that under the right conditions positive reinforcement is all that is needed to achieve the desired ideal result.[43] Experiment, suggests Skinner, can also serve to improve the state so that the society can provide the right conditions for perfecting the child. Passmore observes that Skinner in *Walden Two* "conjoins a boundless confidence in experiment with the Lockean belief in the malleability of man in order to construct a Utopia which is not, on his view, an impractical ideal but a realizable society."[44] Unlike the classical ideal of perfection as a static state to be achieved, modern psychologists, like Skinner, view human nature as open to infinite improvement through the use of appropriate social, educational, and psychological procedures. The new science of psychology is believed to hold open the opportunities of such achievement to modern humans.

In opposition to the above views of human nature as passive (the Lockean tradition), Gordon Allport identifies a stream of psychology that sees human nature active. This he calls the Leibnizian tradition.[45] Aristotle's teleological view of human nature anticipated Leibniz's idea that every created thing must eventually actualize the perfections it potentially contains. According to Leibniz, Passmore says, "the universe as a whole must display a 'perpetual and very free progress . . . such that it advances always to still greater improvement,' as one thing after another attains to its individual perfection."[46] However, the universe would never reach a static state of absolute perfection in which all its potentialities had been actualized. New perfections will always remain to be unfolded, and progress will never cease. Leibniz's dynamic view of human nature was taken over and developed by Kant, who said that "all the capacities implanted in the creature by nature, are destined to unfold themselves, completely and comfortably to their end in the course of time."[47] Kant grounds his thinking in this regard on our sense of duty. "It is morally necessary," he says, "that we should believe in the perfectibility of human society, since to believe otherwise would weaken our moral efforts."[48] For Kant the perfectibility of human nature and society is a "regulative idea" that must govern our behavior. However, it is not individuals who will be perfected as a result of their moral efforts, but human society as a whole. Nor can this be achieved by human effort alone. In his *Religion within the Limits of Reason Alone*, Kant concludes that individual humans and the society they produce can be perfected only with the help of God's grace.[49] Kant's view of inherent categories of the forms of thought was opposed to the passive tabula rasa idea of Locke. The stress on the active purposeful mind of Leibniz and Kant was picked up in the European psychology of Wilhelm Wundt in the late nineteenth century. Wundt, with his theory of creative apperceptive synthesis, stressed the active and changing nature of the mind.[50] These ideas are taken up and developed by gestalt psychology, which focuses almost entirely on dynamic principles of cognition. In late nineteenth-century European psychology, Franz Brentano held that at every moment in time the human mind is active and pointed in its judging, comprehending, loving, desiring, and avoiding activities. He brought the thinking of Aristotle into modern psychology. Brentano built on the foundation established by Wundt and influenced the young Sigmund Freud.[51]

Following in the Leibnizian tradition, Freud understood the inherent activity of human nature in terms of instincts. Freud defined instincts such as the need for food and sex as inborn conditions that impart direction to psychological processes. For example, the sex instinct directs one's processes of perceiving, remembering, and thinking toward the goal of sexual consummation. "An instinct has a *source*, an *aim*, an *object*, and an *impetus*. The principal sources of instinctual energy are bodily needs or impulses. A need or impulse is an excitatory process in some tissue or organ of the body which releases energy that is stored in the body."[52] When hunger activates the hunger instinct by providing it with energy, this energy then gives direction to one's processes of perception, memory, and thought. One looks for food, and remembers where it has been found and the way it has been obtained before. The goal is to satisfy the bodily need, a satisfaction that also produces pleasure. In Freud's view of human nature, the ideal is achieved when there is an immediate gratification of an instinctual need that arises. But because there is scarcity (e.g., food is not always available when one becomes hungry) the psychological mechanism of repression is used by the ego to control one's desires, and this is the foundation of human civilization. Without the need to delay gratification through repression, humans would not work, produce, or create art. Instinctual repression makes possible the transition from a gratification-seeking animal governed by what Freud calls "the pleasure principle" into a reasonable, civilized human being.[53] In Freud's view, then, repression and scarcity are the foundations of human civilization. Nevertheless, notes Passmore, by their very nature "they limit and warp the 'humanity' they make possible. Perfection is not to be expected. The repressed always returns, whether as a nightmare to trouble the repose of civilized man or a war which destroys his illusions of peaceful, perpetual, progress."[54] Thus, for Freud, our inherent psychological makeup and the conditions of scarcity under which humans necessarily live create a fatal flaw that effectively prevents the perfecting of human nature. A civilization that keeps our aggressive instincts in check by repression is the best we can hope for.[55]

Carl Jung was a student of Sigmund Freud. While he accepted much of Freud's view of human nature, he made some important additions. In addition to the basic instincts, Jung argued that each human was born with a set of archetypes within. Archetypes, thought Jung, were basic forms of instinct formed from characteristic modes of functioning in key human situations and established within the psyche by earlier generations.[56] The archetype may be thought of as an a priori conditioning factor in the human psyche, comparable to a biological pattern of behaviour—a disposition that starts functioning at a given moment in the development of the human mind and arranges the material of consciousness into definite patterns. Jung identified, among others, archetypes for our experiences as child, mother, father, hero, self, shadow, and wise old man. Such archetypes provide an inherent form of human behavior present in the collective unconscious that each of us has to actualize or individuate for ourselves.[57] Unlike Freud, Jung sees a positive role for religion. Indeed, it is through the individuation of the God archetype that the opposing instinctual forces manifested through the various archetypes are integrated.[58] In developing this line of thinking, Jung was influenced by gnostic thought in the West and the traditional Yoga psychology of India. The gnostics caught Jung's eye because they were one group in classical Western thought that did differentiate between basic types of psychological functioning and stressed the individual development of the personality even to the point of perfection.[59] As we shall see in part 2, this notion of the perfectibility of human nature is also found in yoga psychology. Although yoga psychology influenced Jung, this is an idea that Jung never accepted. In one of his letters Jung makes clear that in his view humans are not perfectible in that the problem of suffering will never be resolved. "The Oriental wants to get rid of suffering by casting it off. Western man tries to suppress suffering with drugs. But suffering has to be overcome and the only way to overcome it is to endure it."[60] As Allport concludes, although Jung defines personality as the ideal state of integration to which the individual is tending (the God or Self archetype), it is never fully achieved.[61]

The American psychologist William James accepted Freud's idea that human nature contained an unconscious dimension. James also followed the notion of Leibniz that the mind is active—an ever-flowing stream of consciousness.[62] In his 1901 Gifford Lectures entitled *The Varieties of Religious Experience*, William James calls the ideal that the personality strives to realize "saintliness."[63] James relates saintliness to a person's religion, which he defines as "the feelings, acts and experiences of individual men in their solitude, so far as they apprehend themselves to stand in relation to whatever they may consider the divine."[64] The direct experience of the divine is described by James as follows: "It is as if there were in the human consciousness a sense of reality, a feeling of objective presence, a perception of what we way call 'something there.' . . ."[65] Saintliness is the ideal response of the individual to this experience of the divine in one's life. James discusses saintliness in terms of its fruits as seen in the great saints of the world's religions—the Buddha, St. Paul, St. Francis, and Martin Luther, spiritual heroes whom everyone acknowledges. Everyone immediately perceives their strength and stature. "Their sense of mystery in things, their passion, their goodness, irradiate about them and enlarge their outlines while they soften them."[66] Such saints offer us ideal images of the perfectibility of human nature against which to measure our success or failure. They also inspire us. So, concludes James, "let us be saints, then, if we can, whether or not we succeed visibly and temporally."[67] Consistent with his view of human nature as a constantly changing stream of consciousness, James does not offer a static picture of sainthood as the criterion that everyone must achieve. Rather, says James, "in our Father's house are many mansions, and each of us must discover for himself the kind of religion and the amount of saintship which best comport with what he believes to be his powers and feels to be his truest mission and vocation."[68] Human perfectibility is both a path and a possibility that each of us must discover for himself or herself.

James individual psychological approach to perfectibility is picked up by his successor Gordon Allport. Allport talks of the mature mind and comprehensive philosophy of life needed to enable one to approach perfection. "The hurly-burly of the world," says Allport, "must be brought into some kind of order. And the facts calling for order are not only material, they must include emotions, values, and man's strange propensity to seek his own perfection."[69] While secular causes can motivate and unify the mind toward the realization of some idea, for Allport only a mature religious sentiment is able to integrate the whole personality of an individual with all of nature and all of existence in an ideal fashion.[70] The life so created must not only be comprehensive, it must also compose a harmonious pattern. And while admitting that much experience seems determined, the integrated mature person maintains that there is also freedom of will—"that there are doors that may be opened that lead to a fuller realization of values he will explore, discover, enter. A well-differentiated religious sentiment engenders freedom simply because the possessor of such a sentiment finds that obdurate though nature and habit be, still there are regions where aspiration, effort, and prayer are efficacious."[71] By contrast, if one believes life to be predetermined, such a person will not exert effort to improve his or her lot. Allport's final attribute of a mature religious sentiment is that it is heuristic in nature. One's religious ideal is heuristic in that it is held tentatively until it is confirmed or until it leads one to a more valid belief. One's faith, says Allport, is one's working hypothesis. A mature mind knows that doubt concerning one's belief or ideal is always theoretically possible, yet one can still act wholeheartedly. Allport quotes Cardinal Newman's statement that although in religion certainty is impossible, "the commitment one makes—a fusion of probability, faith and love—engenders sufficient certitude for the guidance of one's life."[72] Perfection, on this view, is not a set goal to be achieved, but an ever progressing oscillation between faith and doubt leading one ever deeper into the divine.

Abraham Maslow is a leading name in another stream of North American psychology—namely, humanistic psychology. Humanistic psychology focuses on needs such as emotional needs, sexual needs, self-esteem needs, and spiritual needs. Maslow has become widely known for his arranging of needs into a hierarchy within which humans pursue "self-actualization" culminating in "peak-experiences." The human nature being actualized ranges on Maslow's hierarchy from "deficiency-needs" at one end of the scale to "being needs" at the other end.[73] Our current concern focuses on the question of how close these ideas of Maslow are to the classical idea of perfectibility. Maslow describes a peak experience as "a coming into the realization that 'what ought to be' is, in a way that requires no longing, and suggests no straining, to make it so."[74] Such an experience becomes the ordering principle for a hierarchy of meanings and involves a merging of subjectivity and objectivity into what seems an infinite extension. It is the goal to be realized for those individuals who have fully actualized the inner potential of their human natures—who have become fully human.[75] Maslow says that the self-actualizing process involves persons in a cause outside of themselves, a calling in the old vocational sense.[76] Their lives are devoted to a search for ultimate values that are intrinsic and provide one's meaning of life. The search for and actualization of these ultimate values is called a "metaneed" by Maslow. Many people do not recognize that they have these metaneeds. It is the role of counselors and spiritual directors to help people become aware of their "metaneed" to actualize these ultimate values. As to how one goes about the actualization of ultimate values, Maslow identifies several key kinds of behavior. First, self-actualization requires experiencing things fully, vividly, and selflessly, with full consciousness and total absorption. Second, one learns to think of life as a process of choices, one after the other. In self-actualization one learns to progress by making the growth choice and by rejecting the fear or safety choice that would end in regression. Third, one must discover that there is an inner self that needs to emerge. One is not a tabula rasa, a blank slate, but rather has a temperament, a physical nature, a self that is struggling to be heard above the voices of parents, society, or tradition telling us what we ought to be. Self-actualization involves finding and trusting in one's self, one's own judgment, one's own voice. Fourth, when in doubt, one must be honest rather than not. One must not respond to doubt by posturing and pretending to be or think something one is not. Rather, one must take responsibility and honestly look within to actualize the self. Fifth, such honesty about who one is and what one thinks, involves daring to be different, unpopular, and perhaps a nonconformist. It takes courage. Sixth, self-actualization is not only an end state but also the process of actualizing one's potentialities, and this involves hard work and self discipline. Realizing one's possibilities often means going through an arduous and demanding period of preparation in order to do well the thing one wants to do. Seventh, peak experiences are transient moments of high self-actualization that cannot be bought or even sought. One must be, as C. S. Lewis wrote, "surprised by joy."[77] But one can make peak experiences more likely by getting rid of conditions that make them less likely—one can break up illusions, get rid of false notions, learn what one is not good at. Practically everyone, says Maslow, does have peak experiences, small mystical experiences, but often they are not recognized as such. The counselor or spiritual director's role is to help a person recognize these experiences for what they are. Eighth, finally self-actualizing to the level of peak experiences requires that we open up to ourselves, recognize the defense mechanisms that we use, and find the courage to give them up. Freud has taught us that repression and rationalization, for example, are not always good ways of solving problems. One defense mechanism that Maslow thinks is especially damaging to young people today is "desacralizing." It occurs when young people mistrust the possibility of actualizing key values or virtues because they are not lived or taught by their parents or society. Young people then reduce the person to nothing but his or her lowest biological needs. Says Maslow, "Our kids have desacralized sex, for example. Sex is nothing, it is a natural thing, and they have made it so natural that it has lost its poetic qualities in many instances, which means that it has lost practically everything. Self-actualization means giving up this defence mechanism and learning or being taught to resacralize."[78]

Resacralizing means being willing to see the sacred, the eternal, and the symbolic in ourselves and actualizing it. Self-actualization, however, is never fully complete. It is a matter of degree, "of little accessions accumulated one by one."[79] As with Allport and Jung, perfecting oneself involves endless progress toward a constantly moving horizon. It is this limitation of never being able to fully perfect one's nature that is challenged by the transpersonal psychologists, to whom we now turn.

Transpersonal psychologists are often influenced by the yoga psychology of Eastern thought to extend the degree to which human nature can be fully perfected. Unlike Freud, who focuses on the role of the individual ego, the transpersonalists maintain that the ego needs to be transcended for the full realization of human potential. Michael Washburn, for example, sets forth a new paradigm for psychological development that bridges Freud and Jung and draws on both Eastern and Western religions.[80] Washburn's thesis is that "the ego, as ordinarily constituted, can be transcended and that a higher, trans-egoic plane or stage of life is possible."[81] This higher state is reached when the ego is properly rooted in its "Dynamic Ground," which for Washburn is the psychological locus of the divine. Washburn has simplified Freud's id, ego, and superego by removing the superego and reinterpreting the id (one's basic instincts) by adding to it positive elements of the divine, like Jung's God archetype. For Washburn, personality development begins in a period of dialectical conflict between the Dynamic Ground (symbolized as the Great Mother and the Oedipal Father) and the weak ego, which is attempting to strengthen and grow. This the weak ego does by dissociating itself, through repression, from its Dynamic Ground so as to create a stronger ego. Although freed from domination by the Dynamic Ground, the mental ego experiences the existential anguish of alienation, guilt, and despair. Washburn sees this as a necessary but passing phase that sets the stage for the growth of self through the regression of the mental ego to its true foundation in the Dynamic Ground. At this point, Washburn is strongly influenced by Jung's notion of the individuation of the God archetype as being the height of personality development. When it comes to the crucial question of the degree to which transcendence of the ego is possible, Washburn remains resolutely Western and rooted in a Jewish or Christian position. Through "regression in the service of transcendence" the mental ego gives up its autonomy and opens itself by regression to recover its roots in the Dynamic Ground. This leads to integration of the instincts, the body, and the external world in experiences of awe, ecstasy, blessedness, and bliss. However, it is clear for Washburn that human nature is limited. Transcendence reaches its height in the degree to which the ego by surrendering its autonomy is infused and illuminated by the divine spirit of the Dynamic Ground. But the ego itself can never be completely transcended.

Back in the 1970s a series of books established a new movement in the field of psychology called "transpersonal psychology." This movement was very concerned with integrating Yoga and modern Western psychology, as well as with exploring the limits of human nature. During the decade of the 1970s, Charles Tart was the leading figure in this group of thinkers, and his book *Transpersonal Psychologies* is their key statement.[82] In many ways they were more open to Yoga and its challenge to Western views of human limitations than thinkers such as Jung and Washburn. So it will be of interest to see how far the transpersonalists were willing to push the limits of the West in opening up to the claims of Yoga psychology.

Tart begins by positioning transpersonal psychology within modern psychological thought as follows: "transpersonal psychology," says Tart, "is the title given to an emerging force in the psychology field by a group of psychologists . . . who are interested in those ultimate human capacities and potentialities that have no systematic place in behaviouristic theory . . . classical psychoanalytic theory . . . or humanistic psychology."[83] States such as mystical or unitive experiences, awe, bliss, and transcendence of the self are pointed to as the contents to be studied by transpersonal psychology. A leading transpersonal psychologist, Robert Ornstein, in his book *The Nature of Human Consciousness* argues for the asking of such fundamental questions as "Is consciousness individual or cosmic?" and "What means are there to extend human consciousness?"[84] To answer these questions, Ornstein suggests, modern Western psychology needs to link up with the esoteric psychologies of other cultures (e.g. the Yoga psychology of Patanjali). Tart attempts a beginning to such answers in his *Transpersonal Psychologies* by treating modern Western psychology as just one among many psychologies. So after outlining the assumptions of modern Western empirical psychology in his chapter 2, he goes on to include what he calls the traditional or esoteric "spiritual psychologies" in succeeding chapters— including Buddhist, Sufi, Christian ones, and Hindu Yoga.

In the Yoga chapter, written by Haridas Chaudhuri, the development of the personality from infancy is described as punctuated by changing patterns of self-image or self-identity.

When the growing male infant becomes aware of himself as an individual entity separate from the mother, he identifies himself with the body. This is his material self (*anamaya purusa*). Next, he identifies himself with his vital nature—that is, with various impulses, passions, and desires. This is his vital self (*pranamaya purusa*). Next he identifies himself with his mental nature as a sentient percipient being (*manomaya purusa*). This is his aesthetic nature. Next he identifies himself with his rational nature and perceives himself as a thinking, deliberating, choosing being (*vijnanamaya purusa*). Finally, through a bold meditative breakthrough in consciousness he discovers the transcendental level of existence and finds his true self there (*anandamaya purusa*).[85]

It is this final "bold breakthrough" that is questioned by Western psychologists as stretching the limits of human nature beyond the possible. Yet it is just that breakthrough of ego limitations to transcendent consciousness that is taken to be the goal of life by Yoga and other Eastern psychologies/religions. Yoga describes this "transcendent consciousness" as a deeper level beyond the subject-object dichotomy and beyond the limitations of a filtering individual ego—a level of pure transcendence experienced as the great Silence, as the unutterable Peace that passeth understanding. "The dichotomy of subject and object, spectator and spectacle, witness and his field of observation, is entirely dissolved. The silent Self shines as the absolute (*kevala*)."[86] Here Chaudhuri is describing the *nirvikalpa samadhi* state of Patanjali's Yoga (see chapter 6). The question is whether such a state of altered consciousness is, in reality, the goal to be achieved by all of us—through repeated rebirths until it is realized (the Yoga claim)—or whether Eastern intuition has overreached itself and is suggesting a goal that may be imagined but is not realizable (as Jung, Washburn, Passmore and other Western thinkers have claimed).

CONCLUSION

In this chapter we have surveyed some of the views of human nature and its perfectibility in Western philosophy and psychology. While there is considerable diversity in the understanding of human nature, there is general agreement that while progress may be made toward perfection, the limitations inherent within us make the full realization of perfection unlikely. Let us now turn to the religions of Judaism, Christianity, and Islam and examine their understandings of human nature and its perfectibility.

Chapter 3

The Perfectibility of Human Nature in Jewish Thought

Jews see humans as having been created in the image of God. Unlike classical Greek philosophy and its dualistic view of human nature as composed of body and soul, in the biblical view persons are seen as a psychosomatic unity composed of many parts. Overall, the biblical Hebrews "conceived of man as an animated body, not as an incarnated soul. . . . There is, in man, no immortal part which can survive death on its own account."[1] Later Jewish thinkers, such as Maimonides, were significantly influenced by Greek thought—especially that of Plato and Aristotle. Being created in God's image and being called to be like God means, in the Jewish view, to be God's partner in carrying forward God's work of making just order in the world. Humans can descend to great depths but are not by nature irretrievably sinful. Their task is to hallow life, to raise the workaday world in which one eats, labors, and loves, to its highest level so that our every act and thought reflects the divine unity of all being.[2]

In Jewish thought there is no single answer to the question as to how perfectible we are as human beings. The different strands within Judaism offer different approaches to the question: for the priests it is through holiness that perfection can be best understood and practiced; for the prophets, it is through righteousness; for the rabbis it comes via observance of the commandments and study of the Torah; for the philosophers it is by knowledge of God; and for the kabbalists it is through the restoration of harmony among the *sefirot* (divine emanations). In this chapter we will briefly survey these views. Underlying all of these approaches is a basic confidence that humans are capable of considerable progress toward perfection "through the life of the Torah, the ongoing possibility of repentance, and a lot of assistance from a merciful God."[3] We will begin by examining biblical thought and then

29

proceed to look at the thought of the rabbis, philosophers, and the kabbalists or mystics.

BIBLICAL THOUGHT

The biblical period in Hebrew thought runs from the exodus of the Jews from Egypt and God's establishing of a covenant with Moses in 1447 BCE to the destruction of Jerusalem and the Second Temple by the Romans in 70 CE.[4] In biblical thought scholars identify four basic notions about human nature.[5] First, a person is regarded as a living body with various qualities, but with no sharp distinction between body and soul. The Hebrew word meaning "flesh" is often used for humankind in general or human nature in particular. For example, in Genesis the idea of all humankind as a collective is expressed by "all flesh" and by the word *adam* (man). Second, consciousness was not centralized in the brain, as it is in modern thought. For the Hebrews, human consciousness, with its ethical qualities, was thought to be diffused through the whole body, so that the flesh and bones, as well as the mouth, eye, ear, hand, and so on, had a quasiconsciousness of their own. Third, these "separate consciousnesses" are thought of as being easily accessible to all kinds of outside influences, from possession by demons (as in the case of a toothache) to invasion and control by God's Spirit (as in the case of the prophets). Fourth, there is also the idea of a ghost or double (not necessarily to be identified with the soul)—a faint and shadowy replica of the self, such as the ghost of Samuel described by the "witch of Endor" (1 Sam. 28:14) as "an old man," wrapped in the ghostly counterpart of the familiar cloak of life. This fainter self or "shade," as the Hebrews called it, can be detached even from the living and is seen by others in their dreams, while after death it passes to the cave of Sheol under the earth.

In addition to these four basic notions, biblical Hebrew uses certain key terms to describe human nature. The Hebrew word *nephesh* is usually translated into English as "soul" but this is inadequate and misleading. Literary analysis of the usage of nephesh in the Hebrew Bible shows three distinct meanings. First, nephesh is commonly the principle of life, with breath as the underlying meaning—for example, in 2 Kings 1:13 the Israelite captain, threatened with death, says to the prophet Elijah, "Let my *nephesh* and the *nephesh* of these fifty servants be precious in thy sight." Here the best translation is simply "life." Second, nephesh is "self" or "person," as in Psalm 3:2 "Many are saying of my *nephesh* [self], there is no deliverance for him in God." Here there is no reference to the psalmist's inner life as distinct from his outer body, and therefore "soul" is a wrong translation.[6] Third, nephesh is also used to denote "human consciousness" in its full extent, as in Job 16:4: "I could speak like you if your *nephesh* were instead of my *nephesh*." Here Job is speaking to God. Of these three usages, the most common would seem to have been nephesh as "breath-soul" or the "life principle." This "breath-soul" is considered to be the animating principle of human life and its essential constituent. Death is understood as the departure of nephesh or breath-soul from the body. Momentary unconsciousness is described in the same way, as a brief loss of nephesh. And life is described as being returned to someone thought dead by breathing in nephesh. For example, in 2 Kings 4:34 we are told that Elisha stretches himself over a dead boy's body and places his mouth to the boy's mouth to breath life into it. Throughout the biblical usage nephesh is strongly identified with the body, its organs, especially the heart, and its blood as the animating principle of life.

Ruach is a second key Hebrew term. It is especially important for the biblical understanding of how God communicates with the prophets. Wheeler Robinson notes that ruach has three main usages in the Hebrew Bible. First, ruach is "wind," either the natural wind or the "wind of God"—God's energy or angry breath. In Hosea 13:15 we are told that the Lord's ruach comes up out of the desert and dries everything up. Second, ruach is "inspirational wind," the spirit of God. In his activity as a prophet, Jeremiah is infused with God's ruach, which speaks through him. And in Ezekiel, chapter 37, it is the ruach of the Lord that gives new psychical and physical life to the dry bones of the valley in Ezekiel's vision. Finally, in biblical thought after the exile in Babylon (c. 598–515 BCE), ruach becomes almost equated with nephesh as the principle of life in humans and animals, but it also signals an origination of life from God. Whereas nephesh is sometimes translated as "soul," ruach is translated as "spirit," which connotes a sense of divine energy acting on human nature from without—implying that the life of humans or animals is drawn from God.

Robinson warns we must not be swayed by the body-soul dualism of Greek thought. For the biblical Hebrew, nephesh (breath-soul), ruach (spirit), and *basar* (flesh) are together conceived of as a psychophysical unity—the human personality as an animated body.[7] This includes one's central organs, to which the Hebrews ascribed psychical functions. The heart (*leb*), for example, is identified with mental rather than emotional activities—the opposite of the way it is often used today when it is contrasted with the mind. In its biblical use, special emphasis is placed upon the volitional role of the heart.[8] This is important, since the will is primary in Hebrew ethics—one chooses with one's heart. Other organs, such as the kidneys, are also given psychophysical function. Emotion that urges the heart to action is seen to be located in the kidneys. Robinson points out that this attribution of psychical functions to parts of the body is not restricted to organs such as the heart, liver, and kidneys, but also extends to the ear, eye, mouth, hand, and so forth. The eye, for example, is described in Psalm 131:1 as having the qualities of "pride" or "humility." Ancient thought lacked knowledge of a central nervous system, and the biblical Hebrews (like others of their day) distributed the psychic powers we localize in the mind to various parts of the body, including all aspects of "flesh" and "bone." So the psalmist says "All my bones shall say, Yahweh [Lord], who is like thee?" (Ps. 35:9–10). Robinson concludes that for the biblical Hebrews, human nature is understood as a complex of parts drawing their life and activity from a nephesh/ruach, which has no existence apart from the body. The most important aspect of human nature, other than its psychosomatic unity, is its constant openness to "spiritual" influence from without.[9]

But in the Bible human nature also has an inherent telos. The underlying conception of personality in these texts is a unity of body animated by the breath-soul (*nephesh*) and with a higher nature (*ruach*) that may be possessed by the Spirit (*ruach*) of God.[10] The Hebrew Bible knows nothing of autonomous human beings. "Man's nature is determined entirely by his relation to God, a relationship which preserves the distance between God and man, between Creator and creature. The belief that man was created in the divine image defines his relation both to God and to the rest of nature."[11] Humans cannot claim divine descent, but they are created for a unique fellowship with God that requires obedience to God's will. Because humans are created in God's image, they can be given authority and responsibility. This is true for humanity as a whole, with no distinction of race or nation, which in the biblical view has a collective unity. Israel, however, is understood to have a special role and responsibility, not due to any inherent superiority, but simply due to God's choice. This special role is understood in the covenant established by God with Moses at Mount Sinai and later reaffirmed by God speaking through the prophets and calling Israel to account. In these instances it is the Spirit (*ruach*) of the Lord that invades human spirit or ruach and speaks God's word. In biblical understanding, God is not just there, but is turned toward humankind and calling for their cooperative response.[12] God's speaking to humanity was especially experienced by the Israelites who understood themselves as having a special responsibility because they had been chosen as representative humans by God. Consequently, the way for them toward perfection was simple and clear—namely, to completely fulfill their covenant agreement with God. Thus, when the defeated Israelites were carried off into Babylonian exile (587–538 BCE), this was understood as God's punishment of Israel for its conscious neglect of the covenant.[13] This failure to obey revealed other aspects of human nature—namely, its frailty and sinfulness that obstruct perfectibility. Unlike in Christianity, in the Hebrew Bible sinfulness is not part of the essential definition of human nature. As Genesis 3:11 shows, humans sin because they vainly attempt to assert their autonomy vis-à-vis God. This is exemplified by Adam and Eve, Cain, Lamech, and the builders of the Tower of Babel. The prophets especially brought home the fact of sin to the conscience of Israel and highlighted the nature of sin as an estrangement from and rebellion against God. Human arrogance, self-assertion, and pride, when indulged in by Adam and Eve and the builders of the Tower of Babel, led them to attempt to be like God. This disobedience blocked their ability to fulfill their telos of being coworkers and cocreators with God.[14]

Frailty is another characteristic built into human nature that limits perfectibility. In the Bible, the psalmist puts it this way, "He [God] knows our frame; he remembers that we are dust" (Ps. 103:13–16). In Genesis 18:27 humans are described as "dust and ashes." Human frailty shows itself in liability to disease, in loss of strength with age, and in eventual death. As a result of this frailty, humans in the biblical texts experience anxiety and fear, which can obstruct one's progress on the path of perfectibility through obedience to God. Frailty, together with sinfulness, prevents the actualization of the image of God within. But the Bible also teaches that in spite of these human limitations there is always the presence of God's mercy, which makes possible continued progress toward a perfect covenant relationship between God, humans, and all of creation. That would be the consummation of God's plan for the whole of creation, toward which Israel and individual humans are called as their destiny.[15] Yet how to reach that goal produced different responses within biblical thought—some of which we will now sample.

The Shema, the morning and evening daily prayer said by Jews, speaks of how God has revealed his plan for creation through the Torah, the scripture given through Moses to his people Israel. As Neusner puts it, "The covenant made at Sinai, a contract on Israel's side to do and hear the Torah, on God's side to be the God of Israel—that covenant is . . . confirmed by the deeds and devotion of men."[16] And this is where the problem occurs, for as individuals and as a group the people of Israel inevitably, because of their human limitations, seem to fall short of what God, in the covenant agreement, asks of them. Thus, the Shema also speaks of God as the redeemer and deliverer who helps pious people overcome their failures. From the Jewish perspective people are trapped between what the Torah lays out for them as their path to perfection and what they are actually able to achieve. When God's will is done by the people of Israel, then all people will recognize that the unique destiny of Israel is intended for everyone—that Israel's hope for redemption is ultimately the hope of everyone. This is the biblical vision of the goal to be realized if perfection is to be achieved.

An early biblical response as to how to achieve perfection comes from priests. The priesthood in biblical thought represents Israel's ideal union with God through which human perfection is achieved by holiness. Under God's covenant with Moses, the whole nation is to be a "kingdom of priests" and hence a holy people (Exod. 19:6; Lev. 11:44ff.). Perfect holiness as required by the covenant is symbolized in the priesthood. Holiness (qedushah) signifies the attainment of moral purity and perfection by imitating the holiness of God. Originally, however, holiness was not an ethical term but rather signified "separateness"—the divine attribute of being apart from that which is not divine. "As a result of the covenant with God, Israel, too, became 'separate' (Exodus 19:6) and accepted a state of holiness . . . by remaining separate from contaminating things but still living in their presence."[17] Israel is separated as a holy people, the priests are separated as a holy group responsible for the temple ritual, and the Sabbath is separated as a holy day. "The obligation of holiness falls on the individual as a part of the holy people, and any shortcomings on the part of the individual reflect on the entire people."[18] Because holiness was lacking in the people, the priests took on the role of symbolizing holiness—the state of sanctity and purity necessary for the service of God. "The result was twofold: first the true requirements of serving God were continually kept before the eyes of the covenant people, and second, the overall relationship with God was vicariously maintained by the priesthood on behalf of the nation as a whole."[19]

While the priests focused on ceremonial holiness, the biblical covenant also required holiness in the ethical sense of right conduct in the actualization of the divine image within human nature. The prophets clashed with the priesthood over the lack of ethical behavior in the practice of holiness. The prophets did not negate ceremonial holiness but proclaimed it to be meaningless without accompanying ethical holiness. Thus, the emphasis by the prophets on "righteousness" as the path to perfection. Righteousness is identified with such traits as mercy, love of neighbor and compassion for the poor and weak. The righteous person is free of avarice, violence, envy, and oppression. Judges who are righteous must show equity, especially in their dealings with widows and orphans, and reject bribery. In addition to its ethical aspects, righteousness requires ritual conformity in practices such as temple offerings, tithes, pilgrimages, and the avoidance of forbidden foods and of idolatry. Certain individuals are described in biblical sources as outstanding for their righteousness: Abraham, Moses, David, Solomon, and Elijah. Israel, as a nation, is sometimes described as a righteous people.[20]

The prophets, more than other biblical writers, emphasize righteousness as the path to perfection. What the Torah requires from people is not just religious observance but also moral behavior—both morality and religion form a unity in the teaching of the Torah as they do in the nature of God. The prophets condemned not only idolatry but also injustice and oppression in any form, especially poverty resulting from social evil. Anyone more favored in personal attainments or material wealth has a greater responsibility to help others. As the prophet Jeremiah puts it, "Let not the wise man glory in his wisdom, neither let the mighty man glory in his might, neither let the rich man glory in his riches. But let him that glorieth glory in this that he understands and knoweth Me, that I am the Lord who exercises mercy, justice and righteousness in the earth" (Jer. 9:23–24). God is active in history and in daily life, and he calls people, through Torah, to work in doing away with poverty and injustice. The prophets offer a vision of perfection in which the world is filled with harmony and all people reverence the one God. The culmination of this vision was called "the day of the Lord" and symbolized the rule of universal righteousness on earth.[21] It would come to Israel, said Jeremiah, as a new covenant that would enforce the covenant made with Israel at Sinai in the giving of the Torah. While the Torah had communicated an understanding of God's wishes, the people of Israel continued to act in deceitful and stubborn ways. To overcome this failure, a new covenant, "the Torah of Sinai[,] would be engraved in the very heart of the people and operate with a power of instinctive and instantaneous response to the demands of God. . . . Thus shall the knowledge of God become the common possession of all Israel and through Israel all the nations of the world."[22] All people will worship and serve God through the practice of righteousness, and redemption will be universal.

The prophets taught that to reach this universal goal of perfection, a new and righteous earth must begin with the individual. One should not rely on the priests, temple, or sacrifices to save the whole of Israel. Rather, each person must choose to be delivered from sin and through confession and service to others create a new spirit within. Then God will respond: "A new heart also, I will give you, a new spirit

I will put within you" (Ezek. 26:26). God's Spirit (*ruach*) will infuse and renew our personality (*nephesh*) and our heart (*leb*). Through personal relationship with God the individual is reconciled, redeemed from sin, and placed on the path of righteousness.

RABBINIC THOUGHT

While the prophets viewed righteousness as the path to perfection, for the rabbis perfection is to be reached through observance of the commandments and study of the Torah. The term "rabbi" means a master or teacher learned in the law of Moses' covenant with God. Rabbinic Judaism arose in the first century CE. For modern Judaism, the rabbi is an ordained leader of a congregation. Let us begin by examining the view of human nature adopted by the rabbis. According to Urbach, the rabbis assume the biblical view of human nature outlined above. Humans are not composed of two elements but are a psychosomatic unity of flesh and spirit called a nephesh or "breath-soul." "The *nephesh* is in actuality the living person, and hence nephesh is also used in place of the word *adam*.[23] Similarly ruach, or spirit, as we have seen, becomes synonymous with nephesh. Urbach makes a slight distinction by saying that "*ruach* is not the centre of *nephesh* but the power that moves it, the force that acts on the centre of *nephesh* and thrusts it forward in a given direction. Every organ of the body serves as a substitute for the entire body. Thus the heart (*leb*) stands for the whole body. Nephesh, *guf* [body], and *ruach* form an indivisible entity, and it may be said that man is a psycho-physical organism."[24] In their thinking about human nature, the rabbis adopted and added to this biblical view. In their contemplation of the paradoxes of human existence, of being and nothingness, they probed deeply into the creation and formation of humans. The rabbis found a basic principle in the biblical teaching that humans were created "in the image of God." Rabbi Akiba's student Ben Azzai called this teaching the great principle of the Torah. In its light, the purpose of humans is to know the acts of God and follow them. One starts with God, not humans. "In the way that man was created and in the form that the Creator gave him, two principles find expression— that of human unity and that of the individual worth of each man."[25] Humans are to be mindful that they came last in the order of creation; even the gnat came before them, yet humans are the crown of creation. As the psalmist puts it, "What is man that Thou art mindful of him. . . . Yet Thou hast made him a little less than the angels" (Ps. 7:5 [4]–7 [5]), capturing both the greatness and nothingness of humans.

The rabbis speculated that while the first human was created entirely by God, all others are born from parents who contribute various parts: "The white is from the male, out of which brain and bones and sinews are formed; and the red is from the female, out of which the skin and the flesh and the blood are made; and the spirit and the life and the soul are from the Holy One [God], blessed be He."[26] At death God takes back his share and leaves the portion of the parents. Because the father and mother had a share, with God, in creating the child, so parents are to be honored. This idea of humans as constituted by three parts opened the way for the Hebrew psychosomatic view of human nature to begin to more closely approximate the Greek body/soul dualistic understanding. For example, Rabbi Simai suggests that in the creation of a human, the soul is drawn from heaven and the body from the earth. And Philo, following Plato, describes human nature as having three parts: "the body that is from clay, the animal vitality that is linked to the body, and the mind that is instilled in the soul, that being the Divine mind."[27] Humans are thus a synthesis of earthly parts and the Spirit of God. The human soul, composed from God's spirit, includes the mind and is the immortal part. Trapped within the body, the soul experiences the miseries that arise from the human failings of frailty and sin. But the soul also inspires and directs the body toward perfection. Ultimately, however, the soul requires release from the body. This is Philo's view, and it is dualistic and Greek in nature. The rabbis reject such an extreme move and view the relationship between the earthly parts (from the parents) and the divine part of human nature more positively. For the Greeks the ultimate goal is the release of the soul from the body, but for the rabbis, human perfectibility and ascent are achieved by following the laws of the Torah and by the performance of good deeds.[28] With this understanding of human nature in mind, let us now focus on the rabbis' view as to how this goal of study and observance of Torah is to be achieved.

God's first revelation to humans in the Bible is marked by commandments and the need to be observant. In Genesis 2:16–17 God commands Adam, saying, "Of every tree of the garden thou mayest freely eat; but of the tree of the knowledge of good and evil, thou shalt not eat of it; for in the day that thou eatest thereof thou shalt die." God reveals himself to be a commanding god who permits and forbids. The man is allowed to choose whether he will observe the precept or not, but to transgress it spells death. In Exodus, after Moses had received the Ten Commandments from God, the response of the people to the divine revelation was, "All that the Lord hath spoken will we do and obey" (Exod. 24:7). Rabbinic Judaism is especially concerned with the human response to God's commandments and the human tendency toward evil that leads to sin. As creator, God is seen to have some responsibility in this regard. Yet the rabbis fully embrace human freedom and responsibility for sin, even as they lament conflicts between good and evil in human life. The complexity of the rabbinic analysis is seen in Tractate Berakot 9:5:

> A person is bound to bless [God] for the evil even as he blesses for the good, as scripture says, "You shall love the Lord your God with all your heart and with all your soul and with all your strength" (Deuteronomy 6:5). "With all your heart" means with both your impulses, with the good impulse and the evil impulse; "with all your soul" means even if [God] takes away your soul; "with all your strength" means with all your wealth. Another explanation: "with all your strength" means with whatever measure [God] measures out to you, give thanks to him greatly.[29]

Here the condition of human nature is compressed into three experiences: (1) humans experience good and evil in life because the human heart (the seat of thought, emotion, and will) is divided between tendencies to good and evil; (2) evil constantly threatens the soul (the principle of life) with death; and (3) to maintain life and resist evil and temptation requires more than human resources—namely, strength from God for help in perfecting oneself.

For the rabbis, God remains the source and giver of the commandments. But even the person who does good, says Urbach, because he or she "regards it as a precept and law, is allowed to determine his own ways of fulfilling the observance, so that he may achieve perfection through them and also introduce innovations and augment them."[30] Observance of God's commandments is not only a path to perfection but also an act of cocreation with God. For example, the rabbis extended the range and number of the commandments that humans were to observe. According to Urbach, the rabbinic use of the term "precept" came to include not only the positive and negative commandments explicitly mentioned in the Torah; every verse of the Torah is called a precept. Further, the concept of precept is extended beyond the Torah to include, for example, human actions related to a person's bodily needs. This idea is attributed to Hillel the Elder. When Hillel went anywhere and was asked where he was going, he would reply, "I go to perform a precept." When asked what precept, Hillel would reply, "I am going to the bathhouse." When asked "Is this then a precept?"

Hillel replied, "Yes, in order to cleanse the body. . . ."[31] Because humans were created in the image of God, it is judged to be a holy requirement to care for one's body. Through such elaboration, the rabbis interpreted all actions on life's path as precepts to be observed if one is to achieve perfection. As Urbach concludes, the Israelites were encompassed every moment by precepts so that it seemed that the Lord "[l]eft nothing in the world unendowed by a precept."[32]

Following the destruction of the Second Temple by the Romans in 70 CE, the immediate response from many was to attempt to rebuild the temple and proclaim that the Messiah would soon come. But, notes Urbach, rabbis of the day such as Johanan b. Zakkai began immediately "reconstructing the life of Torah and precept, and although he did this in the hope that the Sanctuary would be rebuilt and the people redeemed, he realized that these things could not happen in the near future."[33] Debate among the rabbis ensues over how people are to be redeemed and over an emphasis on repentance. Rabbi Eliezer b. Hycranus argued that repentance comes first, then redemption. Rabbi Joshua adds that should Israel not repent, the Messiah will come and bring Israel back to the right path. This allows for speculation as to when the Messiah will come. Rabbi Eliezer taught that people should occupy themselves with the practice of perfection through the study of Torah and by doing acts of benevolence. Doing repentance in this way would bring redemption without having to wait for the intervention of the Messiah or the coming of the end time.[34] Rabbi Akiba, a student of Rabbi Joshua, adopted his teacher's view that the repentance and redemption of Israel are linked to the Messiah and the end time. But Rabbi Akiba elaborates this position by relating it to the political events of the day—the revolt against Rome led by Bar Kokhba whom Akiba suggested was the Messiah.[35] Other rabbis of the day, however, strongly disagreed with Akiba's identification of Bar Kokhba as the Messiah.

Following the failure of Bar Kokhba's revolt and the religious persecutions and dispersal of the Jews that followed, the thinking of the rabbis focused on the challenges of how to live the path of perfection so as to achieve redemption in the farflung diaspora. Toward the end of the second century CE a kind of "competition" developed between the rabbis residing in Babylon and those still living in Israel. The competition arose over depictions of the disintegration of the world and the coming of the Messiah. Rabbi Johanan, the leading rabbi in Israel, said that a generation of continual decline and wickedness would bring on the Messiah.[36] This was a complete reversal of Akiba's earlier interpretation that it was the achievement of virtue and perfection of a generation that would usher in the Messiah. Other rabbis attempted to calculate exactly when the end would come. According to Urbach, however, when all the views are taken into account, there is till in the end a return to the dictum of Rabbi Eliezer that "if they do not repent, they will not be redeemed."[37] Or, in the view attributed to Rabbi Joshua b. Levi, the place of the Messiah is dependent upon the merits and deeds, the practice of perfection, of the people of Israel.[38]

THE PHILOSOPHERS

Jewish philosophy arose and flourished as Jews participated in the philosophical speculation of the cultures around them—especially the Greek philosophical tradition. Various biblical verses contain the antecedents of the philosophers' views of human nature. The verses "See, I have set before thee this day life and good, and death and evil . . . therefore choose life, that thou mayest live . . ." (Deut. 30:15–19) were quoted to support the contention that humans possess freedom of choice. That the essential part of human nature is reason was derived from the biblical verse, "Let us make man in our image . . ." (Gen. 1:26). Some philosophers supported their view that the path to perfection is via the knowledge of God by quoting the verses: "Know this day, and lay it to thy heart, that the Lord, He is God in heaven above and upon the earth beneath . . ." (Deut. 4:29) and "Know ye that the Lord he is God" (Psalm 100:3).[39] As Jewish philosophy began in the Diaspora in the Hellenistic world from the second century BCE to the first century CE, it is not surprising that the philosophers view of human nature and its perfectibility was influenced by Greek thought. This is especially seen in the works of Philo of Alexandria (20 BCE–50 CE), who wrote in Greek, presented his views in a series of commentaries on biblical passages, and was influenced by Platonic and Stoic ideas.[40] Let us briefly outline Philo's views on human nature and its perfectibility.

It has been suggested that Philo arrived at his view of human nature by holding the book of Genesis in one hand and Plato's *Timaeus* in the other.[41] Following Plato, Philo makes the cause of the world's creation God's goodness. God creates by bringing order out of the chaos of preexisting matter. God does this by first creating the ideal world—an ideal eternal world of forms discerned by reason. These forms are the divine patterns for ordering the material world. Philo identifies the biblical image of God within human nature as its ideal form. However, this image of God is not in one's corporeal body; it is in one's mind.[42] From there it contemplates heaven and the physical world around, reaching out to discover the patterns and original forms of the things it sees. Here the language of Philo approaches a mystical goal just as Plato does in the *Republic.*

Philo makes use of dualistic terminology in describing human nature as composed of body and soul. The body is formed out of earth, the soul is a detached portion of God's nature and includes reason, emotions, and desires. Philo further subdivides the soul into two parts: the rational part and the part that has to do with emotions and desires. In their rational souls humans are akin to God and the angels. In the irrational part of their souls relating to emotions and desires, humans are akin to the animals.[43] Following Greek thought, Philo refers to the body as a prison or tomb of the soul—a corpse to which the soul is tied. In Philo's view, for the wicked person who is animated by desire and sensual pleasure the body is alive, while for the virtuous person the body is dead. The body, by being a corpse, works against the soul's higher good. The ultimate goal of the religious life is to free one's soul from the body's entrapping and corrupting influences.[44] For Philo, this is the path to perfection. It involves two goals: the harmony of the soul and the union of the soul with the divine. The harmony of the soul results from the complete control of the lower mind and the senses by reason. This Philo calls the virtuous man and cites Noah, who had expelled from his soul all passions, as an example. However, for Philo this is only the intermediate goal of the religious life. It is only a means to the ultimate goal of complete perfection—a mystic vision of God in which the soul passes beyond the realm of the body altogether. For this ideal, Philo is indebted to Plato's theory of forms and to his own Jewish mysticism. Philo cites Moses as an example of someone who achieved this ideal vision of God. On Mount Sinai, says Philo, Moses entered "into the darkness where God was, that is, into the unseen, invisible, incorporeal and archetypal essence of existing things. In so doing, he was 'changed into the divine.' "[45] Moses' song of praise to God was displayed for all to see—an ideal model of perfection to be copied. However, the vision of God Moses attained cannot be reached by reason alone; it must be achieved through mystic experience. Such mystic experience comes as a result of years of faithful religious practice in response to God's commands, and again Philo offers Moses as the ideal example to be emulated.[46] Upon death the human soul, which is immortal, may ascend to the realm of the angels and come to rest near God. This immortal mystical experience is God's gift to the perfected person.[47] When thinking of Philo, however, it should be noted that his thought was not preserved or known by subsequent Jewish thinkers.

Saadiah Gaon (882–942 CE) differs from Philo in offering a traditional supernatural approach. Saadiah was the first major Jewish philosopher of the Middle Ages and headed the rabbinical academy of Sura (near Baghdad). He follows the thinking of earlier Talmudic schol- ars but is also influenced by Platonic, Aristotelian, and Stoic ideas. In Gaon's view, God's kindness toward humans requires that he provide them with a law, the Torah. This law contains commandments of two kinds: rational ones, such as the prohibitions against murder and theft, which reason can discover on its own; and traditional ones, such as the Sabbath and dietary laws, which must be revealed by God. The human soul "originates at the time of the formation of the body, and its place of origin is the human heart. The substance of the human soul is akin to that of the celestial sphere."[48] God creates the world out of goodness, with humans as its ultimate purpose. Humans, although created finite by God, are to reach knowledge of God from the Torah, and through that knowledge attain redemption from their finite condition and achieve immortality. But this final perfection occurs in the messianic age and the world to come. Saadiah accepts the biblical doctrine of the resur- rection of the body—that is, of the individual's psychosomatic person- ality. This resurrection will take place only after Israel is redeemed.

While Saadiah's approach is based on the Torah, Maimonides in his *Guide of the Perplexed* shows stronger influence by Aristotelian and Neoplatonic concepts. Unlike the rabbis with their biblical view of human nature, Maimonides views are dualistic, with the soul as being separate from the body. According to Maimonides the creation of the universe comes from God as a series of emanations during which humans and their world are created out of matter. Everything created from matter is good but finite in nature. Thus, humans are finite, and to make progress toward perfection and redemption they must overcome their finite material natures. This is accomplished through metaphysical and scientific studies, which give one an acquired intellect. "The acquired intellect enables man to gain ascendancy over his material desires during the life of his body, and at the time of death gives him immortality, since the acquired intellect exists separate from the body and is unaf- fected by its states or finity."[49] Maimonides understands human perfec- tion to be a complex combination of contemplative life and a life of socially oriented activity. In his book *Maimonides' Political Thought*, Howard Kreisel carefully explores this understanding.[50]

Kreisel shows how Maimonides is strongly influenced by Aristotle in his view of human nature and its perfectibility.[51] Maimonides distin- guishes two types of intellect: the theoretical intellect (the human ra- tional faculty) and the active intellect (which is acquired when the rational faculty apprehends the intelligible). In his *Guide of the Perplexed*, Maimonides defines the ultimate perfection as having a fully active or actualized intellect—knowing everything that it is within the capacity of a human to know. The key problem upon which Maimonides focuses is the nature of the intellect and its relation to the human soul and body, on the one hand, and its relation to God and the active intellect, on the other. God is defined by Maimonides as a self-intellecting intellect, wholly transcendent, and the cause of all existence. To perfect themselves humans must attempt to follow the commandment in Deuteronomy 28:9 to "walk in God's ways" by imitating God. Moses offers an example to follow. Although he was denied knowledge of God's essence, he gained knowledge of God's actions, which we humans are to follow. For Maimonides, following Moses' example means translating the knowledge of physics and metaphysics into a set of rules and directives for human society—and this requires the perfection of one's intellect. "Intellection, for Maimonides, no less than for Aristotle, is what characterizes divinity."[52] Perfection involves drawing our human intellect near to God's Intellect through knowledge ("theoretical perfection") and the action ("practical perfection") such knowledge requires from us. The tension between these two requirements of "withdrawal or ascent into contemplation" and "descent into action" is seen to be resolved by Maimonides in the biblical prophet. Here Maimonides' key idea is the notion of God's divine "overflow" or "emanation," which functions something like ruach or divine Spirit of biblical thought. In the *Guide of the Perplexed* Maimonides says, "Know that the true reality and quality of prophecy consists in its being an overflow overflowing from God . . . through the intermediation of the Active Intellect, toward the rational faculty in the first place and thereafter toward the imaginative faculty."[53] From this analysis of the prophet's experience, human perfection may be understood as an "overflowing" of God's perfection. The rational faculty of the soul achieves its own perfection and affects that which is beneath it, such as the imagination. This may manifest in two kinds of human behavior: the private and the public. Sometimes the "overflow" renders one perfect and has no other effect— perfection is experienced in solitude. Sometimes, however, the "overflow" not only renders one perfect but also compels one to address the people, to teach them, and to let one's own perfection overflow toward them. This would be the situation of a biblical prophet or Plato's philosopher-king. Human perfection, however, is to be understood as "perfection of the intellect," with the teaching and ethical leadership seen as a practical "overflow" or consequence of the intellectual perfection.[54]

But what does Maimondes' conception of "overflow" mean in the context of human experience and the practice of perfection? One may live one's life so that a balance is achieved between contemplation and practical activity, but one side always tends to overbalance the other. Maimonides stresses that perfection requires total devotion to God and the constant employment of intellectual thought in loving God—mostly achieved in solitude. Yet while contemplating God one is to be simultaneously engaging in physical activity as directed by the commandments of the Torah. Maimonides ascribes this kind of perfection to Moses and the patriarchs, whom we are to emulate. One is required to live on two levels at the same time. One's intellect is engaged in constant contemplation, while at the same time, as an embodied person, one engages in physical activity. As Maimonides puts it, "[T]here may be a human individual who, through his apprehension of the true realities . . . achieves a state in which he talks with people and is occupied with bodily necessities while his intellect is totally turned toward [God] . . . so that in his heart he is always in His presence . . . while outwardly he is with people."[55] As to what happens at death, Maimonides in his *Guide to the Perplexed* offers a description of the perfected individual while in a state of contemplation. When death approaches, the perfected person's apprehension of God powerfully increases along with an increase of joy and love for God until the soul, including the intellect, is separated from the body. Then one no longer feels the sufferings of embodied existence, for one has attained immortality. Maimonides offers as examples Moses, Aaron, and Miriam, all of whom died by "the kiss of God" while in a state of contemplative ecstasy. Such a death is, in his view, really a salvation from death. Having reached this perfected state of immortality, the intellect portion of one's soul remains permanently in a state of intense joy that transcends all states of bodily pleasure.[56] What is clear in Maimonides view is that in embodied human life, perfection can be approached but never attained in full. In life there will always be times when contemplation and action seem to conflict. The person who approaches intellectual perfection will minimize such conflict and will instinctively avoid all wrongdoing. This person will have freed himself or herself from the pursuit of imaginary materialistic goals and the subjection to bodily desires that foster evil actions. Any actions performed will be noble ones. Yet the perfected person's existence as a separate intellect will never be complete until the body drops off at death.[57]

THE KABBALISTS—PERFECTIBILITY IN JEWISH MYSTICISM

The kabbalah, the major esoteric tradition of Judaism, developed alongside Jewish philosophy during the medieval period. The thinking and practice of kabbalah began in the south of present-day France around 1150 CE and spread over the Pyrenees into Spain in the thirteenth century. The basic idea of the kabbalists is that the universe proceeds by means of a link between the hierarchical orders of the created world and the roots of all beings implanted in the world of the sefirot. Variously described as the internal powers of the divine, as hierarchically ordered intermediaries between the infinite or the finite, or simply as instruments of divine activity, the ten sefirot are listed as follows:[58]

1. *keter elyon* The Supreme Crown (perhaps identified with the En Sof, the infinite unknowable deity)

2. *hokhma*   Wisdom, the location of primordial ideas in God

3. *bina*   Intelligence, the organizing principle of the universe

4. *hesed*   Love, the attribute of goodness

5. *gevura*   Might, the attribute of severity

6. *tiferet*   Beauty, the mediating principle between goodness and severity

7. *netzah*   Eternity

8. *hod*   Majesty

9. *yesod*   Foundation of all the powers active in God

10. *malkhut*   Kingship, identified with Shekinah, the divine "Presence"

The basic idea of the kabbalists is that the unity of God's good creation, symbolized in the ten sefirot, has been broken apart by human sin represented by the exile. The achievement of human perfection comes with the restoration of unity and harmony among the sefirot.

For kabbalist thought, the exile represents a state of creation in which human sinfulness has caused a fissure in the Godhead so that the sefirot are no longer joined in divine unity. "The return of the people of Israel to its land at the time of redemption symbolizes the inner process of return of the 'Congregation of Israel' or the shekhinah (the 'Matron') to a continuous attachment to her husband."[59] The symbolism used represents the exile as a temporary separation between a king and a queen—between God and his Shekinah. Redemption and perfection are exposed as the restoration of their union as the united Godhead. Kabbalistic writers also employ the symbols of the Garden of Eden from the book of Genesis. The "Tree of the Knowledge of Good and Evil" was originally one but was separated into two by the sin of Adam, who disobeyed God, bringing sin and separation from God into being. These two trees symbolize exile (as did the earlier image of the king and his queen) as the experience of separation from God. Thus, during exile there are separate spheres of good and evil, holiness and impurity.[60] In the major kabbalist text, the *Zohar*, attributed by Gershom Scholem to Moses de Leon (ca. 1240–1305),[61] the idea is developed that humans, by observing the biblical and rabbinical commandments in their slightest details, make an indispensable contribution to unifying the spheres of good and evil and to reestablishing universal harmony.[62] Perfection is achieved when one incorporates evil, even experience of the demonic side of life, into one's spiritual path. "One can achieve holiness only through the unholy . . . one can see the light only through darkness."[63] According to the *Zohar*, the ideal state is one in which good and evil are contained together as one in both the individual and the cosmos. Job's fatal flaw was that he separated good and evil instead of containing them together. The sin of Job is referred to in the *Zohar* as not including the evil and the good together. Had Job offered a sacrifice in which he included evil with the good, rather than attempting to separate out the evil, he would have then been able to ascend to the good and achieve perfection.[64]

After the *Zohar* the most important further development of kabbalistic thought was provided by Isaac Luria (1534–72). Central to Luria's thinking is that prior to creation, God, the Infinite (En Sof), engaged in an act of self-limitation to make room for the universe. Into the dark vacuum thus created, God projected divine light and "vessels" to receive the light. But some of the vessels were unable to withstand the inrush of light from the Divine (En Sof) and broke apart. The breaking of the vessels caused a deterioration in the worlds above and chaos in the world below. Instead of being uniformly diffused, the divine light was broken into sparks illuminating only certain parts of the world. Thus did light and darkness, good and evil, begin to compete with each other for dominance in the world. As Epstein puts it, "The Divine harmony was disrupted and the *Shechinah* exiled. At the same time, scattered hither and thither, the sparks of Divine Light intersected everywhere the darkness, with the result that evil and good become so mixed that there is no evil that does not contain an element of good, nor is there a good entirely free from evil."[65] The "breaking of the vessels" resulted in a state for all of creation of something like a "general exile," a disruption of the state of harmony God intended for the universe. Perfection, for Luria, is the restoration of a state in which the breaking of the vessels is completely mended and the originally intended harmony of the sefirot is realized. The history of the people of Israel, together with the history of all creation, is seen as a part of the process through which universal harmony will be restored.[66]

Luria also refers back to Adam. All souls, he suggests, were created with Adam, although not all of the same quality. Some were superior to others, but all were good and in complete harmony. But when Adam sinned they all became tainted in varying degrees, resulting in a rupture of their harmony into a state of confusion among them. "The superior souls intermingled with the inferior, good with evil, so that the best souls received some admixture of the evil infesting the inferior souls, and the worst an admixture of good from the superior."[67] Thus, although there is everywhere some impulse toward evil, this will come to an end with the coming of the Messiah sent by God to restore the original harmony to the souls of people and to all creation. But it is up to humans to take the lead in restoring this initial harmony and state of perfection. To take the lead includes the possibility of being reborn on earth to help others who are weaker to get rid of their evil.[68] Luria also suggests that the dispersion of the Jews into the Diaspora around the world has helped the souls of other peoples to rid themselves of evil and realize perfection. The purified souls of the Israelites unify with the souls of other peoples to help liberate them from evil. When all the good has been separated from evil, both in individuals and in the whole of creation, then God's intended original harmony (*tikkum*) will be realized and the world with all its people will be perfected and redeemed.[69] To initiate this process, Luria prescribed practices of asceticism, self-mortification, fasting, and absolutions. These practices were not punishments for sin. Unlike those of Hindu Yoga (see chapter 6), they were not seen as, in themselves, purifying the body, nor did they gain for one merit with God. They were simply seen as aids to one's spiritual discipline. Luria insisted that the body was as pure as the soul. "The body was a sacred vessel comprehending the Divine spark, the soul, and, as such, was holy and had to be kept in health and the utmost purity."[70] But Luria takes what today could be called an "ecosystem approach," for the perfecting of the individual must not be seen as an end in itself but as playing a part in the greater goal of perfecting and restoring to original harmony the whole of creation.

Lawrence Fine has given a more detailed analysis of Luria's view of human nature and its perfectibility.[71] Luria's account of human nature is summarized by his disciple Hayyim Vital as follows: "Man is created from matter and from form, [the latter] consisting of soul [*nefesh*], spirit [*ruah*], and super-soul [*neshamah*], the divine portion from above, as it is said: 'and [God] breathed into his nostrils the breath [*nishmat*] of life' [Gen. 2:7]. And his body is dark matter from the side of the shell [*qelippah*], luring and preventing man from [achieving] perfection of his soul. . . ."[72] The pure soul when it is immersed in the stain of sinful life is unable to perceive and realize perfection. Human failure to follow the commandments of Torah becomes a barrier separating the soul from the Creator. However, "the law of the Lord is perfect, restoring the soul" (Ps. 19:8). Here Luria employs the metaphor of a physician. When ill, the sick person abhors good things and loves things that aggravate his or her illness. So the doctor to restore health gives medicines (including gall) to return one's nature to what it originally was. Likewise, "the sick soul, to remove the sickness from her must receive the bitterness of medicine and 'return' from . . . the stains of sin [by way of] mortification and fasts, sackcloth, ashes and stripes, ritual immersions and purifications."[73] Luria's talk of "the stains of sin" must not be mistaken for the Christian conception of "original sin"—an ontological taint inscribed on every individual at birth (see chapter 4). Luria, rather, is saying that every person is susceptible to the temptations of an "evil inclination" (*yetser ha ra*). Unlike the Christian idea of original sin, the *yetser ha ra* is an impulse that can be controlled and cleansed. Luria's language is not simply moral in nature but is mainly couched in notions of pollution and purification. The polluted nature of the human body follows from mystic notions of "the breaking of the vessels" and "Adam's sin" (described above) concerning the tainted nature of the whole cosmos. As Fine puts it, "Such pollution frustrates the human ambition to gain access to the sacred . . . defined in general terms as contact with the soul's creator and comprehension of the concealed mysteries of the world."[74] Only rigorous adherence to the Torah's commandments and ascetic practices, as prescribed by Luria, "the physician of the soul," is potent enough to cleanse the soul of the stain that clings to it. For Luria, the goal of such spiritual discipline is not simply the purification and perfecting of the individual but also the redemption of the divine realm and the reestablishing of the original divine harmony (*tiqqun*) of the cosmos as a whole.[75]

In his diagnosis of the spiritual state of any human soul Luria also made use of the letters of the Hebrew alphabet. For the kabbalists, God's revelation throughout creation can be described not only in terms of the ten sefirot but also as the ever-unfolding word of God— the Torah comprises "a vast network of 'names,' each of which signifies a particular concentration of divine power or energy. . . . Nowhere is this divine/linguistic construction of all creation more evident than in the case of human beings themselves."[76] The twenty-two Hebrew letters are said to be present in each of three primary aspects of the human soul—in ascending order, nephesh, ruach, and neshamah. The letters found in each soul include: those in the nephesh are small, those of the ruach are of medium size, and those of the neshamah are large. "These three dimensions of the soul clothe one another, as it were, with the body's skin constituting the outer covering of all. The skin is tantamount to the husk or shell of materiality, the *qelippah*, which surrounds all the lights of holiness in the world. The lights, or letters of the various parts of the soul, on the other hand, are manifestations of divinity itself, inasmuch as the constituent elements of the soul are identical with God."[77] If a person is sinful, the lights/letters of the soul are covered and concealed by the skin. "But when one perfects oneself by practicing the commandments and studying the Torah, that person gradually purifies the various parts of the soul, thus enabling the power and light of the letters within each part to come to the surface."[78] The letters reveal themselves to one like Luria who has a skilled eye and is able to see the divine part of human nature—namely, the soul itself. The letters that are seen are "a faintly material expression of something that is essentially immaterial. In the case of one who has sufficiently mended all three grades of soul, the entire alphabet belonging to *each* grade of soul at one time or another appears on the skin, most especially on the forehead."[79] A person who performs all the commandments regularly and has purified all sin will manifest all the letters upon the forehead. Such a person is considered to be perfected.

According to Luria, the degree of soul purification reached can be determined by the letters that appear. For example, if a person has only perfected the nephesh level of soul, the letters on the forehead will be small. At the higher levels of purification, the spirit (*ruach*) and supersoul (*neshamah*), the letters appear to be larger and clearer. These letters of the Hebrew alphabet are also held to have a sefirotic correspondence such that it is possible to identify different letters with each of the ten sefirot. In this way a skilled master such as Luria can determine the sefirotic root of a person's soul.[80] By using the combination of the letters and their corresponding sefirot, Luria could observe on the forehead of a disciple his or her particular kind of sin and then prescribe the practice needed for purification. Fine describes the process as follows. Every evening Luria would gaze upon the faces of his disciples. He would see a scriptural verse shining upon the forehead. The visualized verse was one that pertained to the particular student's soul and its spiritual condition. Luria would explain the meaning of the verse for the student, who would then be instructed to meditate upon the meaning and to recite the verse before going to sleep. This would help to purify the soul and enable it to ascend to the upper realm during sleep and gain full knowledge of the verse's meaning. "In this way, the individual's soul would increase in purity and ascend to still higher levels in the divine realm . . ."[81] until perfection was realized.

Such a method of spiritual diagnosis, prescription, and practice using the letters and verses of Torah bears marked similarities to the "Yoga of the Word" spiritual discipline for perfection, the Vak-Yoga tradition developed by the Hindu Grammarians (see chapters 6 and 7). Although the emphasis in Luria's approach seems to be on the spiritual state of the soul, the full participation of the body is always assumed—in good biblical style both body and soul are seen to form a whole. For example, Luria's belief "that spiritual life-giving forces were to be found in the blood reflects a general premodern notion that the arteries were channels through which life-giving vital spirits flowed throughout the body."[82] Thus, Luria made good use of feeling the pulse with the assumption that the human soul is manifesting itself through such bodily signs. The divine portion that enlivens each person is present within their body. Although open to injury or disease, especially when the commandments are not followed, proper diagnosis of one's spiritual condition, as practiced by Luria, presents the possibility that one may be restored to health. Through acts of penitence including the reciting of Torah letters and verses, a cure can be effected and defilements purged away. Luria was regarded as having both the diagnostic skills and the spiritual knowledge to bring about the soul's purification and ultimate perfection.[83] But this also had a cosmic dimension. The basic principle is that any human transgression "has disrupted or violated the natural course of development within the structure of divine being . . . human transgression causes the lights within divinity to flow in improper and unintended ways."[84] However, contemplative concentration and penitential actions not only purify the individual but also repair the cosmic processes so that divine harmony is reestablished. Both individual and cosmic perfection are part of the same process. Luria's overall goal was to perfect his individual followers and through this community to bring about the redemption of the divine realm, and the cosmos as a whole.[85]

CONCLUSION

In this chapter we have briefly observed different approaches to our question regarding the perfectibility of human nature. Within Jewish thought there is no single answer. There is general agreement that humans are created in the image of God and have a role to play in the work of creation. Unlike the dualistic Greek view of human nature as composed of a separate soul weighed down by a materialistic body, the Hebrew view conceives of persons as a psychosomatic unity composed of many parts. In the Hebrew Bible, for example, the term *nephesh* (usually translated as "soul") is used to mean "breath" as the principle of life as well as to denote "human consciousness" fully identified with one's bodily organs. Another key term, *ruach* ("wind" or God's spirit), is God's inspirational or righteous energy through which God communicates to persons and particularly prophets. Because they are created in God's image, humans are seen to have been given both authority and responsibility. Israel's special role is laid out in the covenant established by God with Moses at Mount Sinai, and later reaffirmed by God speaking through the prophets. Israel's failure to live up to the covenant revealed other aspects of human nature—namely, its sinfulness that obstructs progress toward perfection. The psalmists also point out the frailty of humans—namely, that they are composed of dust and are subject to disease, diminution, and death. Sinfulness and frailty, taken together, work to prevent the actualization of the image of God within and call forth God's mercy, which makes progress toward a perfect covenant relationship possible. While the priests focused on the ceremonial holiness they deemed necessary, for the prophets perfection could only be realized through righteousness—ethical behavior along with ceremonial holiness as required by the Mosaic covenant. As defined by the prophets, ethical behavior required not just justice but also mercy, love of neighbor, and compassion for the poor. The goal to be achieved is called by the prophets "the day of the Lord" and symbolized as the rule of universal righteousness on earth.

While the prophets viewed righteousness as the path to perfection, for the rabbis or sages it was the observance of commandments and the study of Torah that was required. The rabbis adopted the biblical view of human nature and held that humans were created in the image of God with the purpose of knowing and following God's commandments as revealed in the Torah, both written and oral. The rabbis suggested that human nature is constituted by three parts; the father and mother provide the earthly parts of the body, while the soul is drawn from heaven. But unlike the Greek idea that the ultimate goal is the release of the soul from the body, the rabbinical idea is that human perfectibility is achieved by following the laws of the Torah and by the performance of good deeds. The rabbis fully embraced human freedom and responsibility for sin, and they lamented the conflict between good and evil in human life. The way forward is through observance of the commandments. This is not only seen as the path to perfection but also as an act of cocreation with God. To resist evil and to choose rightly, however, requires more than human effort; strength and help from God are needed in order to perfect and redeem oneself. Although the rabbis disagreed with each other over the role of the Messiah in all of this, Urbach maintains that when all views are taken into account, the dominant teaching remains that, as Rabbi Eliezer put it, "if they do not repent, they will not be redeemed."[86] For the rabbis, repentance and observance of the commandments was the key for progress toward perfection.

When we turn to the philosophers, however, it was knowledge of God rather than observance that occupied center stage. While the Jewish philosophers grounded themselves in biblical and rabbinic thought, they evidenced varying degrees of Greek influence in their understanding of human nature and the role of reason in the pursuit of perfection. For example, Philo, following Plato, located the biblical "image of God" not within one's corporeal body but rather within one's mind, and he defined it as human nature's ideal form. Following Greek thought Philo described the body as the prison of the soul. The ultimate goal was to free one's soul from the entrapping influences of the body. One does this by expelling all passion through the control of reason and through years of the faithful practice of God's commands—as did Moses, who offers an ideal to emulate. Knowledge needed for the final mystical state of perfection comes both through reason and through the commandments of Torah. Like Philo, Maimonides adopted a dualistic Greek view of human nature as having a soul separate from the body. However, Maimonides followed Aristotle more closely than Plato. To make progress toward perfection humans must overcome their finite material natures via metaphysical and scientific studies that give one an "acquired intellect." According to Maimonides it is the "acquired intellect" that enables one to transcend bodily desires and at death achieve immortality. Intellection is what characterizes both divinity and perfection. But God's intellect, as the Torah reveals, involves both knowledge ("theoretical perfection") and ethical action ("practical perfection"). Consequently, human perfection is understood as a perfection of the intellect together with ethical action—the latter made possible by God's divine "overflow" or "emanation," as observed in the prophets. So, even with the philosophers we see that some element of God's mercy or spirit (*ruach*) is required along with reason for the realization of perfection. In Maimonides thought this results in a balance between rational contemplation and the ethical activity required by the commandments of Torah. One will be freed from the pursuit of materialistic goals and sensuous desires so that all actions will be noble ones. But the perfected person's existence as a separate intellect will not be complete until the body drops off at death.

Finally we examined the thought of the kabbalists, the esoteric tradition of Judaism. Developing alongside Jewish philosophy during the medieval period, the kabbalistic tradition held that the unity of God's good creation, symbolized in the ten sefirot, has been broken apart by human sin. Perfection comes with the restoration of unity and harmony among the sefirot. Special attention was given to the thought of Isaac Luria, who taught that before creation, God, the Infinite (*en sof*) engaged in an act of self-limitation to make room for the universe. Into the darkness thus created, God shone divine light and vessels to receive the light. But some vessels were unable to withstand the inrush of divine light and broke apart. This caused a loss of harmony in the world above and chaos (a mixing of good and evil, light and darkness) in the world below. Perfection, for Luria, is the restoration of a state in which the breaking of vessels is completely mended and the originally intended harmony of the sefirot is realized. Human souls can help or hinder the restoration of harmony in the universe. All souls are created with varying mixtures of good and evil, and accordingly even superior souls have some evil. Although the Messiah will, in the end, come and restore harmony to all of creation, it is up to humans to take the lead in restoring this original harmony and perfection, and one possibility is to be reborn to help others who are weaker to get rid of their evil. When in all individuals and in the whole of creation good has been separated from evil, then God's intended original harmony (*tikkum*) will be realized. The cosmos with all its peoples will be perfected and redeemed. Unlike the Greek negative view of the body, Luria's view was that the body was as pure as the soul—it was a sacred vessel housing the divine spark, the soul. So Luria prescribed various ascetic practices to purify the body/soul complex of sin/evil and to aid in the perfecting and restoring to the whole of creation its intended harmony. In all of this, Luria sees the correspondence of the Hebrew letters and Torah verses with the state of both the individual body/soul and the divine sefirot to play a major role in mystically identifying the individual with God. This understanding enables Luria to function as a "spiritual physician" with his disciples; he diagnoses their particular sin and prescribes practices that purify one's body/soul until perfection is realized. Luria's ultimate goal, however, was not just the perfection of his individual followers. Through their perfection his larger purpose was the restoration of harmony to the divine realm and the cosmos as a whole.

With the possible exception of the kabbalists, Jewish thought sees human nature as limited by human sinfulness and frailty, and thus as unable to achieve perfection without God's help.

Chapter 4

The Perfectibility of Human Nature in Christian Thought

Like Jews, Christians understand perfectibility in terms of obedience to God—of being wholly turned toward God with all of one's being. That is the meaning of the key teaching of Jesus in this regard: "Be perfect, therefore, even as your heavenly Father is perfect" (Matt. 5:48). Response to this call has been understood by Christians as requiring not just moral perfection (e.g., the love of one's enemies) but also a religious perfection—the complete surrender of one's heart and will to faith in God through Jesus Christ. Response to God's call is a matter of faith. Because of the guilt and sin innate in human nature, most Christian thinkers judged that it was impossible for a human to attain moral perfection before death even with the aid of divine grace.[1] Thus, the Christian philosopher Immanuel Kant (1724–1804) argued that since we cannot achieve perfection or sinlessness in this life, we must postulate an afterlife in which infinite progress toward it will be possible.[2] Christian theologians dealt with this problem by emphasizing that the response to Christ's call to be perfect is a surrender of the heart and will in the obedience of faith. Faith involves the acceptance of God's grace that enables humans to love their enemies. It is God's love, made available through Christ, that is the essence of perfection, and it is this love that supernaturally perfects our less than perfect attempts to follow Christ's teachings. Within the church, as early as St. Ambrose (c. 340 CE), a distinction arose between the basic "precepts," according to which all Christians were required to live, and the "counsels of perfection," which only the few (e.g., monks and nuns of the religious orders) could follow. However, this distinction was completely rejected by the Protestant Reformers, such as Martin Luther.[3] For the modern Protestant theologian, Reinhold Niebuhr, it is the sin of pride that causes us to lack the faith and trust required to surrender ourselves to God. This pride, and the belief that we can perfect ourselves by our own efforts, is rooted in our human refusal to acknowledge our finite human nature. Humans are utterly dependent on God, and God's grace through Christ, for any progress toward perfection.[4]

In our survey of Christian thought we will begin with the biblical view of human nature and its perfectibility, then move on to Augustine, Aquinas, Luther, and Niebuhr.

THE BIBLICAL PERSPECTIVE

In the New Testament, human nature is described as having intelligence, emotions, free will, moral responsibility, and the possibility of eternal life.[5] The Gospels indicate that the views of Jesus regarding human nature are essentially those of the Hebrew Bible or Old Testament (see chapter 3). The concept of the physical body, expressed by either "body" or "flesh," represents the whole person or personality, with no sharp distinction between body and soul as in Greek thought. When Jesus says in Mark 14:38 "The spirit indeed is willing but the flesh is weak," it seems as if he is adopting a dualistic view of human nature. But this is not the case. Jesus fully adopts the Hebrew approach of thinking of the whole personality—mind, body, and spirit—as a psychosomatic unity.[6] Jesus frequently uses the terms "flesh" and "body" to represent the whole personality, as for example in Matthew 5:29 "that your whole body be thrown into hell." When Jesus uses the word "life" as in Mark 8:35, "Whoever would save his life will lose it," or the word "soul" as in Mark 14:34, "My soul is sorrowful," it is the Hebrew term *nephesh* (life or self including the body, its organs and blood) that is meant. In his teachings the most basic aspect of Jesus' view of human nature is his assumption of intelligence, free will, and emotions that require discipline. Human intelligence enables one to understand God's will, and human freedom gives one the opportunity to choose to follow it. These qualities of intelligence, freedom, and responsibility are seen in Jesus' sayings such as Matthew 5:28, "[E]very one who looks at a woman lustfully has already committee adultery with her in his heart." Here Jesus assumes that all moral actions are the responsibility of the self. "Heart" is used here by Jesus in the typical Hebrew sense that the heart is the seat of will and free choice, rather than the mind is, as in modern thought. Jesus knows that human nature is capable of good acts as well as bad, and so he says in Matthew 5:8 "Blessed are the pure in heart, for they shall see God." Humans have the ability to choose rightly because, as in the Hebrew Bible, they are understood to be created in the image of God. This responsibility is at the heart of Jesus' parables. For example, in the story of the prodigal son (Luke 15:11–32) the father, who represents God, allows his son the freedom to leave home, and the son returns only after he has freely decided that it is best for him to go back. The understanding of human nature that runs throughout Jesus' teachings is that of the Hebrew Bible or Old Testament. Although the idea of life after death is not found throughout most of the Hebrew Bible, it did appear in the final writers of the Old Testament such as in the book of Daniel. Jesus adopted this thinking. "There is hardly a word in his teaching which does not presuppose that the possibility of eternal life belongs to the nature of man."[7] As in the case with Hebrew thought, it is clear that Jesus had in mind a bodily resurrection and not, as in the Greek idea on afterlife, a disembodied soul.

Paul, like Jesus, adopts the basic Hebrew or Old Testament view of human nature.[8] Humans are created by God as a mind-body-spirit unity, and in the image of God. Further, all humans have God's natural law within as a kind of innate conscience written upon their hearts (Rom. 2:14–15). While God's requirements are made explicit to the Jews in the Torah, Gentiles have the natural law within, so no one has an excuse for disobeying God's requirements. In spite of this, there seems to be some inherent perversity in human nature that causes humans to sin. Paul introspectively searches within to identify what it is that causes himself to do this. While he is not a technical psychologist, Paul uses key words in conducting his analysis. He uses several words for "desire," which he frequently pairs with "flesh" to get "desires of the flesh." Here it is important to note that Paul is not separating the body from the soul or spirit and identifying one's evil desires with this separate body as Greek dualistic views of human nature do. Rather, Paul uses "desires of the flesh" in a poetic manner as a way of speaking of all desires—as if they are a sort of alien person residing within. In Galatians 5:16–21 Paul speaks of one's life (personality) as under the domination of either "flesh" or "Spirit." He says, "Walk by the Spirit and do not gratify desires of the flesh . . . for these are opposed to each other to prevent you from doing what you would." He goes on to identify the works of the flesh as including such things as immorality, impurity, idolatry, strife, jealousy, anger, selfishness, envy, and drunkenness, and concludes in verse 24, "Those who belong to Christ Jesus have crucified the flesh with its passions and desires." Paul's emphasis on desire in his analysis of human nature is reminiscent of the Buddhist approach, which we examine in chapter 8.

Paul also uses the term "body" in a similar poetic sense. In Romans 6:12, for example, he says, "Let not sin therefore reign in your mortal bodies, to make you obey their passions." Here "body" has much the meaning of "flesh" as described above. Indeed, Paul uses the terms "flesh," "body," and "sin" interchangeably to mean essentially the same thing—namely, living under the domination of desire in one's whole personality. In Romans 8:13, Paul says, "If you live according to the flesh you will die, but if by the Spirit you put to death the deeds of the body you will live." Here "flesh," "body," and "desires" are equated and put in opposition to living according to the dictates of the Spirit in one's body and mind. So in Romans 7:20 Paul says that when he is under the domination of desires of the flesh, "It is no longer I that do it, but sin which dwells within me." He states the dilemma of human nature as follows: "I delight in the law of God in my inmost self, but I see in my members another law at war with the law of my mind, making me captive to the law of sin that dwells in my members. Wretched man that I am! Who will save me from this body of death? Thanks be to God through Jesus Christ our Lord!" (Rom. 7:22–25). Paul states clearly that although he wants to do the good that he finds within, without the grace of God he has received through his Lord Jesus Christ he remains under the domination of the sinful desires of the flesh.[9] Although Paul does not use the technical term "will" in the above analysis of the human condition it is clearly implied. With his reason a man understands the law of God either through revealed Torah, if a Jew, or through his innate conscience, if a Gentile. But his ability to obey is obstructed by the desires of the flesh. In between is a conscious "I" that has free will at its disposal. But the ability to choose to obey is constantly obstructed by desire. This leads Paul to conclude in Romans 7:25, "So then, I of myself serve the law of God with my mind, but with my flesh I serve the law of sin." Only by bringing his will into harmony with the will of God can Paul find freedom from sin and experience salvation. But does this allow for the perfection demanded by Jesus when he said "Be perfect, therefore, even as your heavenly Father is perfect" (Matt. 5:48)?

In Matthew's gospel this demand of Jesus follows his restatement of the Old Testament commandments as requiring inner purity and radical obedience to the spirit of the law over and above the letter of the law. Jesus summarizes the major commandments as: (1) to love God with all your heart, soul, and mind; and (2) to love your neighbor as yourself (Matt. 22:37–39). These two commandments may also be taken as the essence of Jesus's requirement for perfection. Jesus further described perfection in his dialogue with the rich young man who wanted to know what he had to do to obtain eternal life (Matt. 19:16-21). Telling Jesus that he kept the commandments, the young man asked Jesus what more he must do. Jesus replied: "If you would be perfect, go and sell what you own and give to the poor, and you will have treasure in heaven." For Jesus the essence of perfection seems to be to live in accordance with the radical demands of the principle of love.

Biblical scholars, however, try to make the requirement seem less impossible for human realization. In Jesus's saying "be perfect," the Greek word translated as "perfect" is *teleios*. *Teleios*, they point out, means "full-grown, mature, having reached the appointed end (*telos*) of its development."[10] Although the perfection of God is absolute, such complete perfection cannot be required of humans. God's perfection provides a standard or ideal to which humans must aspire in their character and action.[11] In this sense, perfection is an ideal to be progressively realized—it represents a way of living that is always less than absolute perfection, which belongs only to God (Luke 18:19). For humans, perfect love is both a possibility and an obligation toward which progress can only be made with the help of God's grace. Without grace, people find themselves in the situation Paul described in Romans 7:19: "I do not do the good I want, but the evil that I do not want." However, with God's grace given through Jesus Christ, says Paul, one is able like an Olympic athlete able to strive toward the goal of sharing in Christ's righteousness and becoming like him. "Not that I have already obtained this or am already perfect; but I press on . . . toward the goal" (Phil. 3:12, 3:14). Unlike the Greek view of perfection as a static, finished state (which has parallels in the Hindu view; see chapter 7), the Christian perspective that Paul presents is one of entering ever more fully into a dynamic, living relationship with God. Perfection is to be understood in qualitative rather than quantitative terms. In this sense, perfection is not beyond human reach but is "very near you . . . so that you can do it" (Deut. 30:14) by being imitators of God as seen in Christ (Eph. 5:1). "Since perfection is qualitative, a way rather than a state, a man can be progressively transformed. . . . A foretaste of the resurrected life is possible here and now."[12] To be perfect, according to Paul, Christians must strive to be complete, fully realizing their intended purpose, maturing, and bearing the proper kind of "fruit" or action. Indeed, says one scholar, most translations use "mature" to convey the Christian sense of the Greek term *teleios*.[13]

Paul's thinking on the perfectibility of human nature comes to a climax in Romans chapters 8 and 12. In Romans 8 Paul says that those who are in Christ are no longer dominated by the desires of the flesh, for the Spirit of God rules in them. "If the Spirit of him who raised Jesus from the dead dwells in you, he . . . will give life to your mortal bodies also. . . . So then . . . we are debtors, not to the flesh, for if you live according to the flesh you will die; but if by the Spirit you put to death the deeds of the body, you will live" (Romans 8:11–13). That this is part of an ongoing renewal, not only of humans but also all of creation, is made clear in Romans 8:18–27. Paul evokes a childbirth image to represent our struggle toward renewing and perfecting both ourselves and nature. Just as the whole of creation is struggling to free itself from its bondage to decay, so "we ourselves, who have the first fruits of the Spirit, groan inwardly while we wait for adoption, the redemption of our bodies" (Rom. 8:23). It is the hope given by the Spirit in this foretaste of the future that enables one to press on toward the final goal of living fully in Christ (Rom. 8:24ff). What that final goal of nature perfection entails is spelled out by Paul in Romans 12:1–2: "[P]resent your bodies [selves] as a living sacrifice, holy and acceptable to God, which is your spiritual worship. Do not be conformed to this world, but be transformed by the renewing of your minds, so that you may discern what is the will of God—what is good and acceptable and perfect." Implied in this passage is Paul's idea that what is "perfect" is an ongoing process, one in which the Christian must, with the help of the Holy Spirit, continue to grow and mature toward the end goal of being heirs and cocreators with God in the renewal of the world. What is clear throughout the New Testament is that perfection is a process that engages humans as a result of God's initiative—it is not a purely human achievement. As Paul puts it, "God's love has been poured into our hearts by the Holy Spirit that has been given to us" (Rom. 5:5). The perfection of humans, although it requires their voluntary cooperation, is seen as "the crowning handiwork of God."[14] As we shall see, postbiblical theologians, such as Augustine and Aquinas, continue to give priority to God's love by which all human virtues are seen to be supernaturally perfected.

AUGUSTINE

Augustine (396–430 CE) was the first Christian theologian to focus on human nature and its perfectibility. According to Margaret Miles, Augustine began by noticing himself—he came to understand the human condition by analyzing his own experience.[15] The first thing he noticed was that things are not as they should be. People seek after happiness but instead encounter overwhelming pain. As a newly elected bishop in the community of Hippo, North Africa, Augustine wrote a journal, *The Confessions*, in order to understand his own experience.[16] In it he focuses on the anxiety he feels in his habitual grasping at every object that crosses his path, out of fear that something will be missed—this he calls concupiscence. He sees the paradigm of concupiscence in the infant's anxious grasping for milk or whatever it desires. As the child grows, these anxieties of infancy give way to the anxieties of childhood, adolescence, and adulthood. Thus, this compulsive anxious grasping, this concupiscence, "pervades and organizes human life, from the first moment of the infant in which be grasps breath, to the adult's pursuit of sex, power and possessions."[17] Rather than bringing happiness, zest, and motivation to life, this compulsive grasping after things brings only anxiety and unhappiness. Augustine understood concupiscence as a sickness arising from an ancient fall that radically debilitated human nature—his notion of original sin. Things sought after through this habitual behavior (sex, possessions, power, fame) never satisfy but only lead to a redoubled effort to get more. Augustine summarizes his enslavement to this habit pattern as follows: "From a disordered will came concupiscence, and serving concupiscence became a habit, and the unrestrained habit became a necessity. These were the links—so I call them a chain—holding me in hard slavery."[18]

In Augustine's description of human life as organized by the compulsive pursuit of objects, what are the roles of the body and the soul? Augustine interpreted his own experience of human life as anxious suffering and unhappiness to be evidence that human life and the human race as a whole is in a state of punishment. He found the experiences of concupiscence and death to offer clear evidence of this "state of punishment." Death and its separation of the soul from the body was seen by Augustine as a "harsh and unnatural experience" and evidence that humans were being punished.[19] Miles notes that, like concupiscence, death's most obvious effect appears in relation to the human body. But Augustine did not think that the body caused these evils; rather, they result from the soul's insubordination to its creator. Rather than being responsible for concupiscence and death, the body is a helpless victim of the soul's selfish pursuit of objects. "Unlike earlier Christian authors and classical thinkers who understood the body as insignificant, merely the 'lowest' of a series of stacked components that compose the human being, Augustine recognized the permanent integrity of the human body as . . . a cornerstone of human nature."[20] He rejected the Greek idea of the body as the soul's prison and argued instead that the Christian doctrines of creation, the incarnation of Christ, and the resurrection of the body all give the body a high metaphysical status as an integral, good, and permanent part of human nature. Thus, we find in Augustine a significant reshaping of the Neoplatonic views of human nature that dominated many writers before him.[21] This revaluing of the body to be more in line with biblical thought had significant implications for Augustine's view of human nature.

Originally, Augustine was strongly influenced by the Greek thought of Plotinus, who flourished in third-century Rome. Plotinus's view of human nature shows no sign of influence from Christian biblical sources—he saw himself simply as a follower of Plato. In humans Plotinus distinguishes two different souls: the "upper" or true soul, and the embodied lower soul. Sin and suffering belong only to the embodied soul, which, to achieve spiritual progress and perfection, must free itself from the body. Only as the embodied soul frees itself from being imprisoned by the body can one, by the process of intellectual contemplation, discover one's true nature as the "upper" or divine soul. Thus, for Plotinus, the individual finds perfection by "cutting away" whatever ties it to the body.[22] Although Augustine's view of human nature retains Plotinus's hierarchy with the soul at the top and the body at the bottom, he rejects the idea that the body is the prison house of the soul. Rather than putting the blame on the body for human sinfulness, Augustine sees the habit pattern of selfish desiring or concupiscence as coming from the embodied soul's self-absorption with its own powers. According to Miles, "Concupiscence, in Augustine's description, is an agenda perpetrated on the body rather than instigated by the body. It includes all the debilitating forms of anxious grasping—whether it pursues the objects of power, possessions or sex."[23] The cause for such sinful behavior is a failure of the soul to serve God the way it is supposed to. The problem is with the flawed will of the "embodied soul," not with the body. Says Miles, "The resulting disorientation and disequilibrium pervade the whole human being and all his activities. What appear to be bodily desires, then, are in fact the soul's desires which use the body as a tool (*organon*) for the soul's agenda of self-promotion and deficit gratification."[24]

What is Augustine's proposal for rehabilitating the body from the negative view of Greek thought and instead seeing it as a good part of the way God created human beings? The source of sin is the human failure to obey God, and that Augustine locates in the embodied soul as a problem of the will. For Augustine a major example of the failure of the soul's will to serve God is seen in human sexuality. Speaking from his own experience, Augustine found that when he was involved in sexual relationships he felt unfree, driven, and compulsive. His conversion experience, however, allowed him to overcome this compulsiveness by adopting a pattern of chastity. While this was Augustine's way of resolving his own particular problem of compulsive sexual behavior, it has had a negative impact on many Christians since Augustine, who have taken his analysis of his own personality to be normative for them. Augustine's personal rejection of sexuality was unfortunate, for it seemed contradictory to his lifelong effort to construct a new theological view of human nature in which the body is affirmed. In Augustine's model of how human nature should function, the body is controlled by the soul, and the soul is controlled by subordinating its will to the will of God.[25] Because of the force of original sin—which Augustine saw in "the incremental, monumental weight of the habit of concupiscence, the result of an ancient and pervasive flaw in human nature"[26]—humans could not by their own efforts bring their souls to choose to serve God. For this, conversion is required. As Augustine reports in *The Confessions*, conversion occurs at God's initiative as an act of God's grace. Nor was Augustine's conversion the result of a choice made by his rational mind. Rather, conversion resulted from a change of his will, made possible by God's grace. The point of Augustine's description of his own conversion is that change is possible in one's behavior and the way one's human nature is actualized in daily experience. What is required is not the rational contemplation counseled by Greek thought, but by a biblical change of will in obedience to God.

How does Augustine's view of human nature play out in terms of perfectibility? Unlike in the Greek view where the body as a prison house of the soul must be shed, in Augustine's view the body participates in the perfection and completion of human nature. Augustine describes this as the resurrection of the body in the last book of *The City of God*.[27] As Miles notes, his vision as to what human nature is capable of is inclusive, sensual, and exuberant. "Human bodies, sexually differentiated, 'risen and glorious,' will be the 'ultimate fulfillment' of whole persons. But although there will be sexes in the resurrection, since sexes are not an 'imperfection,' *there will not be sex.*"[28] As there is to be no sex in the resurrected state, Augustine concludes that our present sexual activity cannot be understood as a foretaste of perfection but rather a result of the present "state of punishment" of humankind.[29] It is also clear that for Augustine perfection is postponed to another time and place. Although through conversion, made possible by God's grace, we can progress toward it, full human actualization is to take place beyond human life and this sensible world. In Augustine's vision of resurrection perfection, there is equality among all human beings and all injustice disappears. There is also equality among all aspects of human nature, all aspects of body and soul. The embodied soul will no longer be subverted by a disobedient will, and, says Augustine, "how much more beautiful will the body be there . . . where there will be unending eternity, and beautiful truth, and the utmost happiness."[30] Although Augustine's vision of human perfection is enticing, it has not led Christians to attack problems of injustice and inequality in this world, or to work toward experiencing the beauty and goodness of sexuality in the present. Rather, it has provided an excuse, in the Christian West, for postponing the full actualization and perfection of human nature until the afterlife.

In summary, Augustine held that due to original sin, humans had fallen from their original good and loving nature as created by God. "Departing from the love of God above him, man has followed the love of self and become subject to what is below him."[31] Humans have fallen by an act of their own will, which Augustine attributes to the desires of the "embodied soul" rather than to the body itself. This "fall," however, cannot be reversed by a similar exercise of human will. That can only happen by a gracious descent of God's love of the sort Augustine experienced in his own conversion. Only then can progress be made toward the perfection spoken of in the New Testament. But full perfection will not be realized until the resurrection of the body occurs in the afterlife. Augustine was opposed in his own lifetime by Pelagius, who argued that Jesus would not have commanded humans to become perfect if they were incapable of doing so—humans have the freedom of will to do what is right when they see it and Jesus has given them that example. Pelagius rejects Augustine's notion of original sin as inherent in human nature. For Pelagius sin is simply a bad habit and, like any habit, can be broken by a deliberate exercise of one's own free will. Thus, humans by their own efforts can perfect themselves. After some debate, the Council of Carthage (418 CE) accepted in their essentials the teachings of Augustine as opposed to those of Pelagius. This decision was given further blessing by the Council of Orange (529 CE).[32] Although the debate between Augustine and the commonsense approach of Pelagius has continued to simmer within Christian thought, there is no doubt that Augustine's position has dominated. Augustine's continuing influence in the thought of Aquinas and Reinhold Niebuhr will be seen as we examine their understanding of human nature and its perfectibility.

THOMAS AQUINAS

Born in Italy, Thomas Aquinas (1224–74) spent most of his life teaching at the University of Paris. Especially in the modern period, the writings of Aquinas have had a major influence upon the Roman Catholic Church. Aquinas's writings on human nature form a small part of his *Summa Theologiae*.[33] His viewpoint was strongly influenced by Aristotle, Augustine, and by the Bible, along with the psychological treatises of Islamic and Jewish scholars.[34] Aquinas's method was to work one's way in "from the external action to the internal capacity that explains the action, and eventually to the nature of the soul itself. We have no direct access to the soul, not even our own soul."[35] But he begins by asking, What is a human being's ultimate end? Aquinas, following Aristotle, argues that the end or goal for humans is happiness, which is the reward of virtuous activities and which ultimately consists in a vision of the divine essence.[36] Of all Christian theologians, Aquinas is most dominated by the thought of the ultimate perfection of humankind. In his view, human nature contains an implicit promise of the realization of this goal, but it is a goal that cannot be reached without the aid of revelation.[37] Let us begin by examining Aquinas's view of human nature and then move on to his understanding of perfection.

In its use by Aquinas, "soul" means something quite different than what we usually mean by it today. "Soul" is the English translation of the Latin *anima*, which Aquinas, like Aristotle, uses in a wide sense.[38] Soul is the first principle of life in all living things. Like Aristotle's *psyche*, Aquinas's anima is the first principle or component factor of plants, animals, and humans and makes them living things. A plant is capable of nourishing itself and of reproduction—it is the plant's "vegetative soul" that makes these activities possible. Animals, like plants, are capable of nourishing themselves and of reproduction, but also of sensation; thus, we attribute to animals "sensitive souls" and not just the "vegetative souls" of plants. Humans are capable of all of the activities common to plants and animals (nourishing themselves, reproduction, and sensation) but also of thinking and choosing freely, which plants and animals cannot do. Therefore we attribute to humans a higher level of soul, a "rational soul." In Aquinas's view we accordingly find a hierarchy of souls or vital principles. This does not mean that animals and humans have more than one soul—for example, a vegetative soul in addition to their sensitive and rational souls. Rather, it means that a human being with one rational soul can not only exercise all the vital activities of plants and animals, but also the higher activities related to the possession of a rational mind. For Aquinas, the "soul" is related to the body as form is to matter. The human soul is the form of the human body, which means that "the soul is what makes the body a human body and that soul and body together are one substance. The human being is not composed of two substances, soul and body; it is one substance, in which two component factors can be distinguished. When we feel, it is the whole man who feels, neither the soul alone nor the body alone."[39] Similarly when we understand something, that is an activity we could not do without a "rational soul," but it is the whole person's body-mind unity that understands. Indeed, for Aquinas, the unity of the body and soul is so complete that he suggests a good sense of touch requires a clear mind, and a good understanding of the good disposition of the body plays a part. Aquinas would take his understanding of the unity of body and soul or mind to be in agreement with the modern view that the person is a psychosomatic unity. He consequently rejected views of human nature in which the soul is united to the body as a punishment for sin, or in which the soul would be better off if it had no body at all. The human ability to sense things, for example, requires a soul that is united with a body. Indeed, for Aquinas, it is necessary for the soul to be united with a body for the perfection of its nature.[40]

But Aquinas also held that in spite of its clear unity with the body, the human soul is also separable from the body—as, for example, at death. Evidence for this belief comes from the observed fact that while many activities, such as sensing, require a body, others, such as the abstract ability to pursue logic or mathematics, or the experience of self-consciousness or free choice, are signs of a mind that can transcend the material aspects of the body. Thus, "if some of the activities or operations of the human soul transcend the power of matter [e.g., sense organs], then the soul itself, which manifests its character in these activities [e.g., logic and mathematics], must itself transcend matter."[41] By this line of analysis, Aquinas is not attempting to prove that there is a soul in humans. That he takes to be self-evident from the fact that humans are living beings—of whom the soul is the vital principle for life, just as it is for animals or plants. But the ability of the soul to transcend death is not self-evident and must be "discovered." This humans do through their experience of activities like mathematics, self-consciousness, or free choice that transcend the power of matter and indicate that the soul itself is not material and does not therefore depend on the body for its existence. Yet at the same time the soul is naturally the form of the human body, and it is the human unity of body and soul that gains knowledge via sense experience. But this does not mean that the soul's higher activities, such as self-reflection, are impossible apart from the body. Indeed, when the soul is separated from the body after death, the soul cannot know things via sense perception, but it can know itself and spiritual objects. Such an existence of the soul apart from the body, although possible, is not its natural state (remember that the soul is the form of the body). It is better for the soul to be united to the body, as this is its natural form. Hence, after death it would be unnatural for the soul to remain without a body, and this leads Aquinas to suggest that the resurrection of the body is to be expected.[42] Copleston comments about Aquinas, "He admits . . . the soul is naturally the form of the body that in its state of separation between death and resurrection it is not in its natural condition and that it is not strictly a human person, since the word 'person' signifies the whole complete substance, the unity of body and soul."[43] Although the soul is immortal and survives death, it is not whole until it is joined by the resurrected body. Human nature, for Aquinas, even in the afterlife requires both body and soul to be complete. But the ability of the soul to survive death, says Aquinas, points to both its spirituality and its incorruptibility.[44]

While a key activity of the soul is its "intellection" or "rational appetite," a complete human person also requires the "sensitive appetite" for things like food and sex. Both of these appetites—the intellectual and the sensual—are seen as good. A key quality of the intellectual or rational appetite is its activity of choosing, which is called "will." The motivation behind and in all choice is seen by Aquinas to be love of the good. "The first movement of the will and of any appetitive power is love . . . and this inclination of the will towards the good is natural and necessary . . . and is not subject to free choice."[45] While different persons may desire different things, whatever they seek is thought of as a good that will bring happiness and fulfill some need of human nature. "Happiness" (*beatitudo*), for Aquinas, includes more than what we usually mean by the word today—for him it includes a sense of blessedness or beatitude. More than just the psychological condition of feeling happy, *beatitudo* connotes the actualization of human nature's potentials, thus making a person satisfied or happy. As Copleston puts it, Aquinas's beatitudo "means fundamentally the activity of enjoying the possession of that which perfects a man's potentialities, though it can also mean the state of satisfaction or happiness which accompanies this activity."[46] With this understanding of Aquinas's view of human nature in mind, let us now consider his thought regarding its perfectibility.

Although Aquinas's view of human nature is much influenced by Aristotle, he adopts a very Christian approach to human perfection. For Aquinas, the perfection of the Christian life consists chiefly in love—love for God and for one's neighbor. All our appetites, sensual and rational, work toward the end goal of human nature, which is its return to God. As Flew puts it, the rational will has an inherent tendency toward this end—"finally resting in the will of God, the silencing of itself, when the end shall have been obtained."[47] This is the perfection of Aquinas' beatitudo or ultimate human happiness and blessedness, and is the actualization of human nature's potentials. But how completely can humans silence themselves in their surrender to God's will? How completely can they become like God? Aquinas allows that although a man can achieve a perfection that is in some analogical sense like God's perfection, "he cannot be perfect *as* God is perfect."[48] Jesus did not say "Be perfect even as I am perfect" but be perfect as God your heavenly Father is perfect (Matt. 5:48). Perfection cannot be achieved by imitating Jesus. Humans, because of the Fall, cannot become sinless like God. In regard to the Pelagian-Augustinian controversy, Aquinas was strongly influenced by Augustine, but he develops his own position. It is summarized by Passmore as follows.[49] Before the Fall humans could so far perfect themselves as to be able, without special grace, to perform the works of justice and fortitude, and thus fulfill all the commandments of the law. But Christianity requires that humans not just fulfill the law but do so out of the deeper motive of charity or the "love of God." Aquinas maintains that even before the Fall humans needed God's special grace to fulfill the commandments in the spirit of charity. Since the Fall, humans need an additional kind of grace, "healing grace," to fulfill the law even in an external sense. Aquinas points to Paul, who in Romans 7:25, as one already healed by grace, says, "With my mind I myself serve the law of God, but with the flesh, the law of sin." For Aquinas this means that grace can repair the rational mind so that none of the sins arising from reason will be committed, and these are the mortal sins, which involve a deliberate turning away from God. But the appetite of sensuality has been so corrupted by the Fall that even with the aid of God's grace humans cannot avoid all venial sin. Thus, they can never live a wholly sinless life and achieve the perfection of sinlessness.

For Aquinas, however, perfection involves more than just sinlessness. It also involves "being 'like God' in that special way in which man can be 'like God,' i.e., by contemplating him."[50] Here Aquinas is clearly influenced by Aristotle's idea that ultimate human perfection is reached by contemplating the highest object of contemplation, which Aquinas finds in Matthew 5:18 "Blessed are the poor in heart, for they shall see God." Rather than taking the love of God as the highest goal, Aquinas adopts a more typically Greek approach of seeing perfection as the contemplation that results in a vision of God. It is through such a vision that we become most like God. Because the soul's reason is the highest part of human nature, it is by knowing God through rational contemplation rather than loving God by an act of the will (lower in human nature) that the highest perfection is realized. But, like sinlessness, the vision of God, says Aquinas, can only be had in eternity. The kind of knowledge of God humans can achieve in this life falls short of seeing God clearly. Here we can only see God imperfectly, as "through a glass darkly." No matter how hard a person tries or how much grace God grants one, the most one can achieve in this life is what Aquinas calls "evangelical perfection," which consists of being free of mortal sin and loving God above all else. Absolute perfection, which requires the clear vision of God, can only be realized in the afterlife.[51]

The effect of Aquinas's teaching on perfection was to decrease the emphasis on grace and increase the role of free will. It led Aquinas to postulate a hierarchy of perfection with afterdeath contemplation by the soul at the top, and the activities of love lower down. It is through the soul, not through eyes, that one will "see God." In his "Concerning Perfection" Aquinas lists a hierarchy of perfection with bishops first, the religious orders second, parish priests and archdeacons third, and ordinary laypersons at the bottom.[52] Flew admits that Aquinas's teaching on perfection favors the clergy and religious orders, but says that otherwise it is quite comprehensive. He summarizes Aquinas' four theses on perfection as follows.[53]

1. *The contemplative is superior to the active life.* It is not that Aquinas disparages the active life; indeed, it is through it that the required moral virtues are expressed. By such actions we show God's love to our neighbor, as Jesus required. Without God's love manifested in the active life we cannot achieve perfection. Aquinas, himself a teacher, gives highest place to the activities of preaching and teaching, but judges all such activities as a necessary preparation for contemplation. Further, since love is also the motivating force behind contemplation of God, the result is the ultimate perfection in which God is both seen (as divine truth) and loved.

2. *Christian perfection consists in love.* Although love is the motive of the contemplative life, Aquinas is careful not to confuse love with the contemplation of truth. While the locus of the contemplation of truth is in the intellect, the locus of love is in the will, the source of the moral virtues—the love of God and the love of neighbor. But the contemplative life requires a rest from external actions, which also rejuvenates one to reenter active engagement in worldly life. Here the function of love embodied in moral actions is to curb the impetuosity of the passions so that they are virtuous and will not distract the soul from its focus on truth (God) by being caught up in the objects of this world. It is in this sense that love serves to unite us with God and predispose us to the ultimate perfection—contemplation of divine truth.

3. *God must be loved for his own sake.* The study of perfection leads Aquinas to distinguish between perfect and imperfect love. In perfect love, God or one's neighbor in loved for his own sake. In imperfect love, a person loves something not for its own sake but for what he or she can get out of it to satisfy his or her own desires. The true love of God (*caritas*) is perfect love, which is given to God for God's own sake. But no matter how pure such a love may be, it can never reach full perfection, because God is infinite while human nature is finite and limited. Thus, human love leads us to hope for God and the full perfection of eternal happiness in the life to come.

4. *Full perfection is in the life beyond the grave.* For Aquinas the full perfection of the soul's beatific vision of God is pointed to by the words of Paul in 1 Corinthians 13:12, "For now we see as in a mirror dimly, but then we will see face to face." Although the soul will be capable of seeing God in the life to come, the soul will not be able to see all that God sees, for God is infinitely greater than we are. For the saints, however, the ultimate happiness and perfection will come after the Day of Judgment and the resurrection of the body. "After the resurrection, all in the body that hampers the full perfection of the soul will be removed . . . the happiness of the saints will be greater after the Judgement than before because their happiness will be not only in the soul but also in the body."[54]

We may summarize Aquinas's understanding of perfection as follows. At the human level in this life, perfection requires "first, the removal from man's affections of everything that is contrary to the love of God, such as mortal sin, and secondly, the removal of whatever hinders the mind's affections from turning wholly to God."[55] The actions of love toward God and one's neighbor are seen as a necessary prerequisite for the higher perfection of the next life—namely, the direct vision of God, achieved through the soul's contemplation, and made all the more complete by the union of the resurrected body with the soul. In his approach Aquinas offers a unique blending of Aristotle's Greek thought, the Hebrew perspective found the New Testament, and the theology of Augustine. His influence has been and continues to be strong, especially within Roman Catholic theology and philosophy. But his thought is at many points attacked by the Protestant reformers, especially by Martin Luther.

MARTIN LUTHER

While Aquinas places monks close to bishops in his hierarchy of perfection, Martin Luther (1483–1546) became a Protestant Reformer by rejecting the ideal of perfection he had been striving toward as a monk. As a monk, says Luther, "I thought that I was utterly cast away, if at any time I felt the concupiscence of the flesh."[56] As a monk he had struggled to perfect himself by overcoming the desires of the flesh. With a great sense of relief Luther abandoned this struggle toward perfection and admitted that, as a man, he would always be subject to frailties of the flesh. Thus, he concluded that no person could hope to be made perfect by his or her own efforts. In examining his own experience, Luther, like Paul, found himself to be a sinner no matter how hard be tried to do the good.

True freedom in Christ, for Luther, came not in trying to perfect oneself through the overcoming of sin, but rather in admitting one's sinfulness, repenting, and having faith in God. Unlike Augustine, it does not appall Luther that his human nature is still subject to the desires of the flesh. For Luther such sin is the result of human egoism, which prevents humans from wholly submitting themselves to God's will. Consequently, no one can hope to achieve perfection. The biblical command to "love God" for Luther came to mean "Have complete faith in God."[57]

Luther's view of human nature is influenced by the New Testament (especially Paul) and Augustine with regard to original sin. With Augustine Luther taught that the source of all sin is original sin—the corrupt state resulting from the Fall. It is a state of spiritual death from which humans cannot escape or in any way contribute toward their salvation.[58] Luther's thought on human nature is outlined in two writings: his treatise entitled "The Freedom of a Christian" and his "Freedom of the Will." In "The Freedom of a Christian" Luther says that humans have a twofold nature, a spiritual and a bodily one. Basing himself on Paul (2 Cor. 4:16), Luther writes, "According to the spiritual nature, which man refers to as the soul, he is called a spiritual, inner, or new man. According to the bodily nature, which men refer to as flesh, he is called a carnal, or old man."[59] Nothing the body does (e.g., what it eats or drinks) has any influence in producing Christian righteousness or freedom. Nor do the things the soul can do (e.g., acts of contemplation) help. One thing only is needed for both the body and soul to experience Christian freedom—namely, the word of God in Jesus Christ: "I am the resurrection and the life, he who believes in me, though he die, yet shall he live" (John 11:25). Without the word of God, the soul can do nothing. But with God's gospel through Christ, the soul is fed, made righteous, and set free—provided it believes the preaching. Luther concludes, "[T]he soul needs only the Word of God for its life and righteousness, so it is justified by faith alone and not any works. . . ."[60] The lack of faith (unbelief of the heart) makes a person guilty and a servant of sin. Works, even good works, cannot save the person's body and soul from sin. Only by faith in God through the word of Christ can the whole man, the psychosomatic union of body and soul, be saved. Faith alone and the word of God must rule in one's human nature. Luther describes this as faith, which unites "the soul with Christ as a bride is united with her bridegroom. . . . By this mystery . . . Christ and the soul become one flesh" (Eph. 5:31–32).[61] Then one is free from all sin, secure against death, and endowed with eternal righteousness. In one's freedom, one follows the example of Jesus, and with the help of the Holy Spirit makes oneself servant of all and does all kinds of good works (Phil. 2:6–7). Living within Christ's Spirit one disciplines one's outer or bodily nature so that it will conform to the Spirit and not revolt against faith, as it is the nature of the body to do. Then one may joyfully serve God in love, and act always only out of love, and without thought of gain. But in striving to do this, says Luther, one encounters a "contrary will in his own flesh which strives to serve the world and seeks its own advantage. This the spirit of faith cannot tolerate, but with joyful zeal it attempts to put the body under control and hold it in check."[62] Thus, one is led to do many good works to keep the body in subjection to God, but these works are done out of spontaneous love for God. In this sense one will work and obey God as Adam and Eve did in paradise before the Fall. Through faith the believer has been restored to paradise and created anew to act toward one's neighbor in love. Faith in Christ does not free us from works but from false opinions concerning works—namely, that through good works one may be saved. Yet human nature and natural reason lead us to think that through works and the law righteousness may be obtained. Only by God's grace through Christ can one avoid falling into this way of thinking and finally experience the freedom of the Christian life.[63] Throughout this analysis, Luther adopts the biblical view of human nature, especially as understood by Paul. Body, mind, and soul are a unity that in its natural state lives according to one's selfish desires (called by Paul the "flesh" or "body"). But when "in Christ," this same body, mind, and soul unity lives in obedience to the Holy Spirit. Humans, however, cannot believe in Christ or come to him by their reason or strength. "It is the role of the Holy Spirit alone to bring man to Christ and Christ to man, to call, enlighten and regenerate. If man is saved, it is entirely by the work of the Holy Spirit . . . if he is lost it is entirely due to his own resistance to the offers of divine grace."[64]

What role does the will play in human nature and its perfectibility? Once again Luther's thought is influenced by both Paul and Augustine. But he differs from Augustine in his understanding of the relationship between humans and God. While humankind is active in its behavior toward the world, it is passive in its relationship with God.[65] In line with this emphasis, Luther went beyond Augustine and denied that human will, even with the aid of God's grace, can choose the good. Luther rejects the idea that human free will could choose to surrender to God's grace. Luther does not see this as a limitation; rather, accepts it with a great sense of relief. In his "Bondage of the Will" Luther says "that, for myself even if it could be, I should not want 'free-will' to be given me, nor anything to be left in my own hands to enable me to endeavour after salvation."[66] No matter how much he did, he would still be feeling that he might have done more. Even if I lived and worked to eternity, says Luther, my conscience would never be sure I had done enough to satisfy God, and achieve perfection. The only way to overcome the idea that one ought to be perfect was to completely reject the idea that any action of free will, even when combined with God's grace, would make it possible for humans to perfect themselves. In rejecting that human nature possesses any such free will, Luther suggests that it is a term applicable only to God. Human claims to free will are just another manifestation of the mistaken attempt by humans to think of themselves as godlike.[67] In his very negative assessment of free will, Luther is joined by his fellow Reformer John Calvin. In Calvin's view whatever is in human nature from the understanding to the will, from the soul to the flesh, is completely corrupted by concupiscence. Since the Fall, human corruption is not just a lack of innocence but a forceful drive toward sin. Says Calvin, "[O]ur will is not only destitute and idle of good, but so fruitful and fertile of sin that it cannot be idle."[68] For both Luther and Calvin, it is only by virtue of some miserably deformed image of God persisting in human nature that humans can employ reason and will in their earthly activities. Luther does allow that a Christian, in following his or her vocation and serving his or her fellow humans, can and should achieve a kind of technical expertness or perfection. But when it comes to God and spiritual questions, human reason is "blind as a mole" (Calvin) and human will is "the devil's whore" (Luther).[69] For Luther, the most positive thing about humans in relation to God is that while their will is powerless, there is something in human nature (a relic of God's image) that opens humans to the possibility of being granted God's grace.

While human nature cannot perfect itself, Luther did believe that through faith a person could be made holy. In "The Freedom of a Christian," Luther says that when through faith God's word is united with the soul, the soul glows as if it is on fire with God's love. In this condition the soul shows itself ready to do God's whole will. The grace of faith then unites the soul with Christ so that, to use biblical language, they are made one flesh. Then holiness realized in Christ can be manifested in the soul in two ways. First, the Christian, says Luther, attains mastery over affliction and hostility, but not freedom from sin. Second, he or she is given the status of being a member of the priesthood of all believers, which makes him or her worthy to appear before God, to pray for others, and to teach others the things of God. Flew comments that here Luther is "trembling on the verge of the New Testament teaching on perfection."[70] In this world, however, even with God's grace, one can do no more than make progress toward perfection. For

Luther and Calvin final perfection can occur only in the afterlife.[71] Modern Protestant theologians have tended to reaffirm the views of Luther and Calvin on human nature and perfectibility.

REINHOLD NIEBUHR

About human perfectibility, Reinhold Niebuhr (1892–1971) wrote, "The ethical demands made by Jesus are incapable of fulfillment in the present existence of man . . . their final fulfillment is possible only when God transmutes the present chaos of this world into its final unity."[72] In his *Moral Man and Immoral Society* Niebuhr stressed the egoism, pride, and hypocrisy of people and nations—the fruit of human insecurity and anxiety resulting from human finiteness, as the source of "original sin." Writing in twentieth-century America, Niebuhr attacks various Pelagian views that had become popular along with the ideas of evolution and science— namely, that although humankind is sinful by nature, humans are progressing toward perfection. Niebuhr, together with Karl Barth, rejects the idea that humans can somehow make progress toward perfection by their own efforts. Indeed, for Niebuhr, ideas of this sort are the very essence of sinfulness—of the refusal to acknowledge human finiteness and limitation. Nevertheless, Niebuhr remained optimistic about human beings and their destiny. With influence from Augustine, Niebuhr says that humans still have a relic of their original righteousness or image of God within them, and that this relic gives a point of contact with God. On this point, Niebuhr also follows the thinking of Martin Luther.

For Niebuhr a correct understanding of human nature is all-important. In his Gifford Lectures, entitled *The Nature and Destiny of Man*,[73] Niebuhr attempts to reconcile the major teachings of Protestant theology with the findings of modern science and the historical criticism of the Bible. In his preface, Niebuhr rejects Greek thought, in which human nature was viewed as a body-soul dualism with reason as its essence, and instead accepts the biblical-Hebraic understanding of the self as a unity of body, mind, and spirit that is both subject to the natural necessities of human existence and free from them. This unity of the self, he says, can only be expressed in poetic, religious, and metaphorical language. Niebuhr claims that he offers a "realistic" rather than "idealistic" interpretation of human nature[74] that takes seriously human possibilities for both "majesty" and "tragedy." As he puts it, "The fact that man can transcend himself in infinite regression and cannot find the end of life except in God is the mark of his creativity and uniqueness; closely related to this capacity is his inclination to transmute his partial and finite self and his partial and finite values into the infinite good. Therein lies his sin."[75] Wolf summarizes Niebuhr's view of human nature as follows.[76] Following Augustine, Niebuhr sees the dilemmas of human creativity and destructiveness as rooted in problems of the will rather than in reason. The problem lies in the proud unwillingness of humans to accept their finiteness and dependence upon God. Thus, modern secular movements such as naturalism, idealism, and romanticism are less realistic than Christianity in their emphasis upon the infinite possibilities of the human spirit. They exhibit the sin of humanity in falling prey to its own hubris, of being unwilling to accept its own finiteness. The source of Niebuhr's critique of modernity in this regard is his approach from Christian scripture. He understands revelation as twofold: the individual's personal experience of God, and the biblical record of the Hebrew prophets that prepares the way for Christ, who finally reveals the essentials of human nature. The inclusion of the revelation of God in human experience along with scriptural revelation is essential for Niebuhr. In the New Testament Christ is seen to be a twofold revealer. First, he reveals the character of God in historical action in the world. Second, he reveals that humans are created in love and for love (the perfection of Adam before the Fall). As the "Second Adam" Christ shows "that all men contradict their essential natures and that only the revelation of Christ which is the solution to the human dilemma fully reveals the depth of human self-contradiction. Otherwise the feeling of normality which we give to long-established . . . forms of sinfulness would blind us to the true dimensions of the problem."[77]

Niebuhr experienced his own human nature as sinful, a sinfulness that finds its chief expression in pride—pride of power, of learning, and of goodness. This pride in humankind's refusal to accept its finiteness is rooted in the human capacity for self-transcendence. By this Niebuhr means the capacity of the self to transcend not only its natural bodily processes but also its own reason, and to stand, as it were, above the world. Herein lies the radical freedom of human nature, which is the source of both human creative power and human destructiveness. According to Niebuhr, the self in its radical freedom does not find its norm in either nature or reason. Neither is able to control the self's freedom or guarantee its virtue. Reason does not secure the virtue of the self, as Kant suggested, for the self can make use of logic for its own ends. Nor is evil in the self simply the result of confusion of the natural passions before they are ordered by the mind, as Aristotle contends. There is, therefore, no form (e.g., the soul), structure, or Logos in nature to govern the freedom of the self. The self is therefore free to defy God, and does so. This radical freedom of human nature is the source of both its dignity and its misery.[78] For Niebuhr the position of humankind is highly ambiguous. Humans are finite, yet they are free. As Harland puts it, "Although he is a frail, limited creature, subject to every natural and historical contingency, he is free to reject the position of relatedness with God in and for which he was created."[79] In this ambiguous situation, humans sense their own insecurity and seek to overcome it. But in attempting to gain security for oneself, a person must trample on other life, on the environment, and on one's relationship with God and one's fellow humans. As Niebuhr puts it, "Therefore all human life is involved in the sin of seeking security at the expense of other life."[80] This ambiguity of the human position provides the occasion for, but is not the cause of, sin. Sin is caused by anxiety resulting from the insecurity of human life. Niebuhr explains as follows: "[M]an, being both free and bound, both limited and limitless, is anxious. Anxiety is the inevitable concomitant of the paradox of freedom and finiteness in which man is involved. Anxiety is the internal precondition of sin. It is the inevitable spiritual state of man, standing in the paradoxical situation of freedom and finiteness."[81] Here Niebuhr acknowledges his debt to Kierkegaard, who maintained that the psychological condition that precedes sin is anxiety.[82] For Niebuhr anxiety is the precondition of sin, but it is not itself sin. Following from this analysis comes Niebuhr's description of original sin. Original sin lies not in the inheritance of a trait, not in concupiscence (as Augustine maintained), "but in man's refusal to accept his ontological status[;] sin is man's unwillingness to accept his finiteness."[83] From this it follows that humans cannot hope to overcome their sinfulness by the exercise of their own freedom, since independence and freedom are the very source of their sinfulness. "Only by complete trust in God's grace, only by surrender to God's love, has the soul any prospect of escaping finitude and, with it, sin. As for the belief that man can perfect himself by his own efforts, this is of the very essence of sinfulness, of man's refusal to 'acknowledge his finiteness.' "[84]

Niebuhr's optimism regarding human destiny stems from his New Testament understanding of God's grace. Niebuhr says, "Grace represents on the one hand mercy and forgiveness of God by which He completes what man cannot complete and overcomes the sinful elements in all of man's achievements. Grace is the power of God over man. Grace is on the other hand the power of God in man; it represents an accession, which man does not have of himself, enabling him to become what he truly ought to be."[85] Regarding human destiny in the resurrection and world to come, Niebuhr follows New Testament thought closely. In the Christian belief in the resurrection of the body,

Niebuhr finds five fundamental facts.[86] First, the resurrection faith of Christians places human destiny in the hands of God. Only God can complete what remains incomplete and redeem what is distorted by sin. This is the hope Paul speaks about in Romans 8. Second, this faith assumes a unity of human nature and guards against attempts (influenced by Greek thought) to dissect humans into mortal and immortal parts, into a sinful body and a spiritual soul. It is the whole person—the unity of body, soul, and spirit—that is destined for fulfillment in the resurrection. This is Paul's vision of the transfigured "spiritual body." Third, the Christian idea of the resurrection affirms that the human self in its final freedom transcends the conditions of time and history, which ultimately have meaning and fulfillment in eternity. Fourth, the Gospel belief in the resurrection of the body "both guards the dignity of the self which transcends death and recognizes the misery of the self, which faces the problem of sin, as well as the fact of death."[87] Fifth, the resurrection hope is not just for the salvation of the individual self but for all humans—the promised fulfillment will be for the *whole* self and for *all* persons who have lived through the years. The climax of God's drama of creation and history, when seen from the vantage point of faith and hope, affirms both the misery and grandeur of human nature.

Niebuhr's analysis of human nature and it perfectibility attempted a synthesis of both Reformation and Renaissance thought. He also did much to encourage the revival of Luther and Calvin with their emphasis on sin and grace. During the first half of the twentieth century, Niebuhr's view of human nature exerted an enormous influence on American political thought, both inside and outside the Christian church.[88]

CONCLUSION

In this chapter we have seen that New Testament thought adopted the Hebrew Bible's understanding of human nature as a psychosomatic unity of body, mind, and spirit. This is evident in the Christian adoption of the Jewish teaching of the resurrection of the body. In this view human nature is described as having intelligence, emotions, free will, moral responsibility, and the possibility of eternal life. Human intelligence enables one to understand God's will, and human freedom gives one the opportunity to follow it. Jesus describes the goal for Christians in terms of perfection when he says in Matthew 5:48 "Be ye perfect even as your heavenly Father is perfect." Paul, like Jesus, says humans are created by God as a mind-body-spirit unity and in the image of God.

In spite of this, there seems to be some inherent perversity within human nature that causes people to sin. As Paul puts it in Romans 7:19, "I do not do the good I want, but the evil that I do not want." Salvation is made possible by God's grace given through Jesus Christ, which enables Paul to strive on toward the goal of perfection.

Although a great number of theologians offer interpretations of New Testament teaching on human nature and its perfectibility, we chose to survey the thinking of Augustine, Aquinas, Luther, and Reinhold Niebuhr. Augustine combined some elements of Greek thought with the biblical view in his understanding of human nature. He introduced the idea of "original sin"—namely, that by an act of their own will, humans had fallen from their original good and loving nature as created by God. This fall cannot be reversed by a similar exercise of human will but only by an experience of God's grace such as Augustine experienced in his own conversion. Only then, said Augustine, can progress be made toward perfection, but full perfection will not be realized until the resurrection of the body occurs in the afterlife. Aquinas offers a unique blending of Aristotle's Greek thought, the Hebrew perspective of the New Testament, and the theology of Augustine. Aquinas agreed theologically with Augustine but held out more hope for human perfectibility. Although absolute perfection belongs to God alone and cannot be possessed by humans, a lower perfection, "evangelical perfection," is not only possible but incumbent upon them. This involves removing all mortal sin and cultivating the love of God and one's neighbor. The teaching of Aquinas had the effect of reducing the emphasis on grace and increasing the emphasis on free will. Although humans must cultivate sinlessness, even with the help of God's grace they can never live a wholly perfect and sinless life in this world. Furthermore, Aquinas follows Aristotle in maintaining that perfection requires not only sinlessness but also the contemplation of God until a vision of God is achieved. For Aquinas, it is by knowing God through rational contemplation, rather than by loving God through an act of the will (which is lower in human nature), that the highest perfection is realized. But, like sinlessness, this highest seeing of God clearly can only occur in the afterlife. In this life, however, Aquinas does propose a hierarchy of perfection with bishops at the top, religious orders and parish priests in the middle, and laypersons at the bottom.

Luther rejects Aquinas's "hierarchy of perfection" and his emphasis on free will that he, Luther, had been taught as a monk. Like Paul, Luther found himself a sinner no matter how hard he tried to do the good. Freedom came, not from trying to perfect oneself through the overcoming of sin, but rather by admitting one's sinfulness, repenting, and having faith in God. Such faith is made possible by God's grace through Christ—namely, the Holy Spirit—to which humans must surrender. Sin, for Luther, is human pride or egoism that prevents humans from wholly submitting to God's will. Consequently, no one can hope to achieve perfection in this life. For Luther, the biblical command to "love God" came to mean "have complete faith in God." Such faith does not free us from good works toward our neighbors, but from false opinions regarding works—namely, that through good works one may be perfected and saved. While human nature cannot perfect itself, it can be made holy when God's word is united with the soul and it glows, as if on fire, with God's love. Such holiness, says Luther, is manifested in two ways: by overcoming hostility (but not sin), and by being given the status of a member of the priesthood of all believers, which enables one to appear before God to pray for and to teach others. But perfection can only occur in the afterlife. Niebuhr agrees with much of Luther's teaching, but is strongly influenced by Kierkegaard in identifying the existential anxiety resulting from the refusal to accept the finiteness of human nature as the root cause of sin. Only by surrender to God's grace is there hope of escaping the anxiety of finitude and, with it, sin. The idea that humankind can perfect itself by its own efforts through science, technology, or progress is the essence of sinfulness and the refusal to acknowledge human finiteness. Nevertheless, Niebuhr remains optimistic about human destiny, which is to be realized in the resurrection and the world to come.

Chapter 5

The Perfectibility of Human Nature in Islamic Thought

Like Jews and Christians, Muslims view human nature as a unity of body, mind, and spirit. They also believe in the resurrection of the body after death. Although the Qur'an presents humans as inclined to err, they can also recognize the good by reflection, reason, or instinct. Innate human responses to good and evil reveal a human nature that is not fatally flawed and can be rightly guided. Unlike in Christianity, in Islam there is no notion of original sin. In the Qur'an's view of human capabilities, there is nothing to suggest humans cannot act ethically; thus, there is no need for supernatural grace—although ideas of God's help and even predestination do develop in later theology. However, Qur'anic teaching for the most part assumes that ethical and virtuous action is possible. Indeed, "In its description of human nature, the Qur'an maintains an artful tension between the possibility of human perfection and the reality of human moral deficiency."[1] The possibility of realizing human perfection is especially emphasized in mystical Islam—in Sufi teaching and practice.

The Qur'an suggests, according to Muslim interpretation, that Muhammad was the last in a line of prophets (including Abraham, Moses, and Jesus) that Allah or God sent to warn his people of impending doom. The clear sense of the teaching of the Qur'an is that obedience and submission to Allah is required of humans, and that Allah is merciful. Allah's mercy is presented in the form of guidance (*huda*). Qur'an is *huda* in that for those who obey, it brings them out of darkness and into light, out of polytheism and into worship of the one God, out of lawlessness and into loving obedience that, at the Day of Judgment, will land one in heaven rather than hell. This Qur'anic guidance leads to *falah* (success) in this world and the next. Falah, as the goal to be achieved by all humans, depends on human effort as well as God's

81

mercy in following the Qur'an's teachings. As Fazlur Rahman puts it, for Islam there in only success (*falah*) or failure in the task of building an ethical order in the world by submitting oneself to the Qur'an. Success can be achieved in this world as well as the next, but it all depends on submission and obedience.[2] M. A. Quasem makes the dependence on huda or guidance from the Qur'an quite clear: "Scripture is guidance for mankind and what this guidance aims at is his salvation, whether in this world or the world to come."[3] Guidance is also provided by the *shari'a* or Muslim law, which is based on the Qur'an and the example of Muhammad. Observance of this law, which covers such things as ritual practice, marriage relationships, inheritance, diet, and commerce, is a prerequisite for pursuing the path of perfection. In addition to this very outward dimension, Islam has two important internal dimensions, "intellectuality" and "spirituality." "The first deals mainly with the conceptual understanding of the human situation and the second with the practical means whereby a full flowering of human potentialities can be achieved."[4] It is in the intellectual and spiritual traditions of Islam that we find clear descriptions of human perfection along with the guidelines for reaching it. For most Muslims progress toward perfection can be made in this life, but it can only be fully realized in the next. With this overview of the Islamic approach, let us begin our study of human nature and its perfectibility by examining the human condition as it is presented in the Qur'an. Then we go on to the teachings of al-Ash' ari, al-Ghazali, and Ibn 'Arabi.

THE QUR'AN AND HUMAN NATURE

According to the Qur'an, God created humans out of dust and clay by blowing into them his divine spirit, thus making humans capable of being God's viceroy (*khalifa*) on earth (Qur'an 2:30). Having created Adam and breathed his spirit (*ruh*) into him, God granted Adam (and his progeny) the faculty of knowledge, conceptual thinking, a conscience, free choice, and the ability to progress toward human perfection. As a mixture of clay and God's breath or Spirit, human nature represents a mixture of darkness and light, ignorance and knowledge, activity and passivity. All the divine attributes are present in human nature, but they are obscured. Between the divine Spirit and the body there are many admixtures and permutations where the divine light is reflected brightly, dimly, or not at all. This mixture of spirit and body is a microcosm of the human person that is given guidance by the Qur'an. In it each person has his or her own unique capacity to respond to God's guidance (Qur'an 2:286). The later schools that interpret the Qur'an often refer to a person's actualized capacity in terms of the degree to which a person acts as a mirror for the attributes of God.[5]

The freedom of choice that has been given to humans sets them apart from all of nature (earth, plants, animals, etc.). While nature has no choice but to behave in accordance with God's laws, humans have been given the ability to freely choose between belief and disbelief, good and evil, right and wrong. "Having been given the choice, humanity, the Qur'an asserts, has in principle accepted the *amanah*, the trust or responsibility, to struggle in order to establish a just and moral social order on earth."[6] This is humankind's role and responsibility as the viceroy of Allah on earth. While the heavens, earth, and mountains, along with the rest of nature, are involuntarily Muslim (meaning obedient to God and acting in accordance with his will), the challenge and opportunity given to humans is to voluntarily become Muslim. In so doing they would, by free choice, realize their human potential as moral agents and progress toward perfection. "But this lofty objective cannot be realized," says 'Abd al-Rahim, "without a real and arduous struggle (*jihad* in classic Islamic terminology) to curb one's evil impulses and inclination on the one hand, while scaling the ladder of moral and spiritual refinement to the highest possible point of human perfection on the other."[7]

Nowhere does the Qur'an teach that human nature (*fitra*) is basically flawed and must be regenerated. In this Islam is quite different from the Christian concept of original sin, according to which all humans are inherently tarnished by Adam's disobedience to God in the Garden of Eden and thus need regeneration to be saved (see chapter 4). Although the Qur'an acknowledges that Adam did indeed sin, his sin was not passed down to all humankind. Like Adam, individual humans have the capacity to sin, but it is not predetermined. The view of human nature presented in the Qur'an has a more positive tone. Humans are not cast out of the Garden of Eden as a punishment for their sinfulness, but rather are exiled so that they can use their free will to choose to work with God in creating a moral and beautiful world. As Nomanul Haq puts it, God created Adam to work on earth as a viceregent (*khalifa*)—someone to work with God at the historical level of earthly existence. "The human exit from the Garden, then, was . . . akin to natural birth—a baby coming out of a mother's womb, a bird breaking out of an egg, or a bud sprouting forth from a branch. Indeed, like nature, Adam had to evolve, morally, spiritually, intellectually—just as a baby grows into adulthood, and a seed grows into a lofty tree."[8] Thus, the human condition in Islam does not involve the recovery from a Fall so as to regain some original state of glory, but rather entails the fulfilling of a set of obligations given by God in the Qur'an.

A. Ezzati translates the Arabic term *fitra* as "primordial human nature."[9] Fitra has no simple English counterpart. It occurs in Qur'an 30:29 with the sense of "a way of being created."[10] Denny describes fitra as humankind's primordial state that is sound and sinless. It is the God-given, innate, sound human constitution.[11] All infants are born with a sinless (*'isma*) nature as established in their fitra.[12] Ezzati adds that along with fitra human nature contains reason (*al-'aql*) as the guiding mechanism that enables humans to distinguish what is good and what is evil—an innate sense of conscience. The term *fitra* also denotes common sense (*'urf*) and undiluted, sound rational judgment (*al-'aql al-salim*) as properties of primordial human nature. "*Fitra* thus covers a large area of intellection, intuition and reasoning."[13] It provides the means for humans to know the truth and establishes that desire in them. *Fitra* is a term used in the Qur'an that was not in common use by Arabs before the advent of Islam.

In the Qur'an animals are created with instinct (*ghariza*); it is their natural way of knowing without being aware of it. Primordial human nature (*fitra*) enables humans to have double knowledge: knowing and knowing that they know. It is this extra quality of self-awareness in knowing that separates humans from the rest of nature and endows them with special ethical and spiritual qualities. Ezzati notes that in the Qur'an the term *tabi'a* (to create a disposition, state, or condition) is used by synonymously with fitra. Thus, fitra literally means the natural constitution with which a child is created before he or she was born. This, Ezzati says, is the meaning of fitra in Qur'an 30:29, which reads "So set thy face truly to the religion being upright. The primordial nature (*fitrah*) in which Allah has made mankind. No change [there is] in the work [wrought] by Allah."[14] Muhammad's hadith or saying on the verse is "Every child is born in a state of *fitra*"—that is, "on God's plan" or according to "Allah's kind or way of creating."[15] Then the child's parents could make him or her a Jew or a Christian or a Muslim. Thus, the definition of fitra is "an inborn natural disposition which cannot change, and which exists at birth in all human beings."[16] Ezzati comments that in modern Western thought the nearest idea to the Qur'anic concept of fitra is Immanuel Kant's suggestion that every human is born with an innate sense of "ought" or consciousness of a moral law within.[17] Ezzati also notes the sharp contrast between the Christian concept of human nature and that of the Qur'an. "According to Christianity Adam's disobedience plunged the entire human race into ruin and fallen man could not of himself do good, please God or gain salvation. The Christian is thus born in sin and in an impure state and cannot redeem himself by his inner resources. . . . By contrast, Islam recognizes both the innate goodness of human nature, and the innate potential of man to earn his own salvation. . . ."[18] In the Islamic view, sin is the result of the human misuse of free choice. "Everything is good in its original shape and form, until man decides voluntarily to misuse it."[19] Allah's role is to enrich the soul (*nafs*) of the person who is devoted to him and makes good choices.[20] Let us recall here that, like the Hebrew Bible, the Qur'an understands human nature as a unity of body, mind, and soul or spirit. In the Qur'an there is no trace of the dualistic Greek view of an evil body and divine soul, with the soul being set free from the "prison house" of the body at death. Instead Islam, like Judaism and Christianity, embraces the idea of the resurrection of the body.

In addition to being created with reason and free choice being created good in its original shape and form, human nature is seen by Ezzati as having three major properties. First, included in human nature are certain innate principles that form the basis of human knowledge, such as the invalidity of circular argument, infinite causal regression, and contradiction in argument leading to the being and nonbeing of the same thing. These basic cognitive principles are not learned but are a priori in human thought at birth. Second, human nature contains inherent normative ethical and moral properties, such as the sanctity of justice and truth. Third, psychological properties such as love for children, love of the arts, the love of knowledge, and the love of perfection are all considered to be included in human nature at birth. These natural and divinely given properties are considered to be universally present in all infants at birth. In infancy they are present as potential properties, and they fully manifest themselves when individuals become rationally mature. The Qur'an states that it is a reminder (*dhikr*) to people that they have these capacities within and it is the duty of God's prophets not only to remind humans of their potentialities present in their fitra, but also to urge their actualization. Fitra or primordial human nature, with its richness of inherent properties, is seen by the Qur'an to be a blessing given by Allah to humankind.[21] Ezzati notes that virtually all Muslim sects and schools of thought have accepted the authority of fitra and see it as the source of both knowledge and ethical values. However, humans with their rationality and free will (also, according to Ezzati, parts of fitra) can choose against their inherent ethical natures and thus interfere with the actualization and perfectibility of their fitra properties (described above). But this interference does not change the reality of a person's primordial nature should the person have a change of heart sparked by hearing the revelation of the Qur'an. The voice of Allah speaking in the Qur'an calls people back to their true primordial nature. The ethical dimension of human nature implies that humans are naturally inclined to do good and to avoid evil, and to search for perfection, happiness, and salvation (*sa'ada*). Thus, "moral excellence and perfection is a characteristic of human nature because man is innately inclined to virtue."[22] But humans can choose to follow "that part of man (*ghariza*) that also has animal desires and needs, which if met in the right manner may help man's desire for perfection, but which otherwise leads to evil. This is termed 'the soul which incites to evil' (*al-nafs al-ammarto be al-su'*). At the same time the Qur'an also refers to the 'upbraiding soul' (*al-nafs al-lawwama*), that is[,] the soul whose conscience is awakened, and thus blames or upbraids itself for its own transgressions and deviation from its divine natural course."[23] The role of the Qur'an in all this is to be a "warner" or "awakener," recalling a person to his or her true nature (*fitra*). The Qur'an also refers to the "soul at peace" (*al-nafs al-mutma'inna*)—a soul in the primordial nature is manifested in a state of perfection.

That such perfection of human nature is possible for human beings is suggested by the idea that Muhammad, an otherwise ordinary human, manifested the perfection of his fitra. As Schimmel points out, this idea grew strong among pious Muslims as early as 150 years after Muhammad's death in 632 CE. Two centuries later, the Sufis praised Muhammad as the "Perfect Man."[24] We will say more about this later in this chapter. The notion of the "Perfect Man" also appears in Ismaili sources, which describe the imam as "the man of God" or "Perfect Man." When one manifests the perfect human form, that is at the same time "the image of the divine form" of which each prophet and imam is the earthly exemplification. Their human natures are so perfectly manifested that it is Allah's voice and Spirit (*ruh*) that acts through them.[25] Consequently, they are thought to be well suited to being leaders of their community. For Muslims in general it is claimed that one looks toward the Prophet Muhammad as the most beautiful example of perfected humanity.[26] The Qur'an itself says of Muhammad, "[Y]ou are, indeed, of great moral character" (68:4) The Qur'an and *sunna* (the example in word or custom given in Muhammad's life) represent God's guidance for the full actualization of human perfection on every level, from the outer level of action and social concerns to the more inward levels of knowledge, morality, love, spirituality, and every human virtue. The purpose of the Islamic community with its social order as established by the Qur'an is to provide a stable framework within which human perfection can be achieved.[27]

Having examined human nature and its perfectibility in the Qur'an, let us now turn to a survey of the philosophers and theologians of Islam to see how they developed these ideas beginning with al-Ash'ari. But first, a note about Islamic philosophy. *Hikma* is a technical term used in Islamic philosophy for philosophical principles and in the legal rulings of Islamic law or Shari'a. Hikma carries a notion of restraining, as in the rein used to control and restrain animals or in the sense of a ship's anchor that prevents the ship drifting. In philosophy, hikma is defined as putting a thing in its proper place through the disciplines concerning knowledge, science, the science of religious law, and the truth concerning divine essence.[28] The philosopher Avicenna describes hikma as the perfection of the human soul by speculation about truth.[29] For Islamic philosophers such speculation begins with the teachings of the Qur'an and makes use of reason and intuition as they are found in human nature.

AL-ASH'ARI

Al-Ash'ari (873–935) who lived in Basra and Baghdad, developed his thinking against the background of the Mu'tazilite ideas. They suggested that before making humans the gift of his revelation in the Qur'an, God had already given the gift of reason in primordial human nature. Since both gifts came from God, there should be nothing in right reason that would contradict revelation.[30] With regard to the Qur'anic notion of fitra or primordial human nature and its inherent ability to distinguish right and wrong, good and evil, the Mu'tazilites accept these ideas and their implication that humans have free will, the freedom to choose between right and wrong. They dominated Islamic thinking for about one hundred years (850–950). Al-Ash'ari, however, while still claiming to accept fitra, rejects the idea that humans freely choose between good and evil, and instead suggests that good and evil are predetermined by God.[31] The idea that a person is damned or saved by the actions of God's will harkens back to passages such as Qur'an 7:177, "He whom God guideth, and they whom He misleadeth shall be lost," or Qur'an 6:125, "And who God shall be pleased to guide, that man's breast will be open to Islam; but who he shall please to mislead, straight and narrow will he make his breast." Muhammad, in the Qur'an and the hadith, at times emphasized God's total control, and at other times presented humans as having free choice and responsibility for their actions. Al-Ash'ari is most influenced by the former and sees fitra or primordial human nature as limited in terms of its free will.

Al-Ash'ari argued that in the final analysis it is God who acts and determines who ends up in paradise or in hell.[32] His reasoning runs as follows. Since God alone is the creator, all must ultimately be attributed to him. As he is the Lord he can do what he likes with his creation. God is above everything and at the same time is the cause of everything, including who ends up in heaven or hell. Regarding the problem of how then it would matter what humans do or do not do, al-Ash'ari developed a theory that humans "acquire" the acts that God creates. "God does not will absolutely. He wills something to be the act or acquisition of the human being. Man is connected with his acts in the sense that he has given them the character by which they merit recompense."[33] In this way al-Ash'ari tried to create some room for human responsibility and action within the choices God had already made. Al-Ash'ari's approach picked out those passages of the Qur'an that emphasized God's total control over creation and pushed that thinking to its logical conclusion—humans are little more than pawns in God's hands, with no real free choice or responsibility for their actions. Al-Ash'ari tries to temper this result with his theory of the acquisition of God's action by humans. Because al-Ash'ari's theory had a strong basis in the Qur'an, it was accepted and is reflected in the creeds of orthodox Islam. For example, the Creed of al-Nasafi (c. 1050 CE) states, "Allah is the Creator of all actions of his creatures, whether of Unbelief or of Belief, of obedience or disobedience."[34] And al-Taftazani, a commentator on this creed, spells out the implications of this doctrine clearly: "So if the creature proposes a good action, Allah creates the power to do good, and if he proposes an evil action, Allah creates the power to do evil, and thus loses the power to do good."[35] Thus, it would seem that it is God's choices and not those of humans that determine if they are to be delivered to paradise and if the potential for good inherent in their human nature is to be actualized. If perfection occurs, it would seem to be more the result of God's action rather than of human effort. The Ash'arite school, founded in the middle of the tenth century by the disciples of al-Ash'ari, had a dominating influence on Sunni Islam that lasted until the nineteenth century.[36] Miller says that it is still present in the thinking of orthodox Islam today. Most orthodox mullahs, he suggests, would generally agree with the interpretations of al-Ash'ari, and it forms a background to the thinking of many ordinary Muslims as they consider salvation and conclude: "I cannot say I am saved, I can only say, I am saved if God wills."[37] Following al-Ash'ari, the next major thinker on these issues in Islamic philosophy is al-Ghazali, and it is to his thought we now turn.

AL-GHAZALI

Al-Ghazali (1058–1111) was a theologian, philosopher, jurist, and mystic who taught in Baghdad. He knew Greek philosophy, especially the logic of Aristotle, and in his own writing he defended Islam against Neoplatonist philosophers such as Avicenna (Ibn Sina). His great work, *The Revival of the Religious Sciences* (in four volumes) made Sufism or Islamic mysticism an acceptable part of orthodox Islam.[38] The first two books of this work describe the minimum intellectual knowledge needed, not for worldly advancement, but for the attainment of perfection in the world to come. He also describes the prescriptions of the shari'a or Muslim law in detail and tries to show how they help to perfect human nature and realize final salvation. In so doing he sought to reform the Sufi attitude of his day of indifference to this world in favor of a focus on the world to come. Instead, Ghazali taught that careful observance of religious law and ritual in this life ("knowledge of action") and "knowledge of revelation" together constitute "knowledge of the world to come." As created by God, human nature is to be perfected by these two forms of knowledge, which lead to the realization of everlasting joy in the presence of God. If a person does not seek to perfect himself through the realization of this true, eternal knowledge for which he was created, "he degrades himself to the level of the beasts. But if he pursues it with all his might, he can exalt himself to the ranks of the angels. This 'knowledge' brings man to the true love of God, which is the source of the love of one's fellow-men and of all the other human virtues, and thereby gives him a slight foretaste in this world of the joy everlasting in store for him in the next."[39] However, humans usually go astray in their search of perfection. The divine element of their fitra or primordial human natures is as dangerous as their animal desires. "Thus, instead of seeking their perfection in true 'knowledge,' men try to find it in worldly power, wealth, scholarship and all the other primrose paths to the soul's destruction."[40] In attempting to guide humans back onto the right way to reach true knowledge, he emphasizes the need for both the "knowledge of action" (observing the shari'a) and the "knowledge of revelation." The particular function of observing the commandments in the "knowledge of action" is to help humans master their passions.

Before examining his views on the necessity of observing the requirements of shari'a in the practice of perfection, let us briefly summarize al-Ghazali's comments on the makeup of human nature.

Al-Ghazali's view of human nature is part and parcel of his understanding of creation—namely, "There is not in possibility anything more wonderful than what is." In this world God has created the best of all possible worlds. This is nowhere more effectively shown than in the way God has created us as humans. The human body itself with its limbs and organs displays what al-Ghazali calls, "the perfect rightness of the actual."[41] Humans, however, in their ordinary lives remain stubbornly unaware of this. Although humans are the most amazing of animals, says al-Ghazali, they are not amazed at themselves. In an attempt to awaken their missing sense of amazement, al-Ghazali gives a detailed description of the human body. Using the medical texts of his day he details the number and structure of the bones, the intricacy and elegance of the nerves and muscles, the complex orchestration of the tiny muscles that move our eyelids—all of which manifest hidden depths of divine wisdom. Thus, there is a perfection in every aspect of our bodies—nothing could have been different or arranged better than it actually is.[42] Anticipating our current fascination with genetics and human genome, al-Ghazali reminds his readers that all of this grew from a drop of semen within the womb: "Turn now to the drop of semen and consider its state at first and what it becomes. Reflect that if *jinn* and men had joined together to create for the drop of semen, hearing or sight or intellect or power or knowledge or spirit, or to create in it bones, veins, nerves, skin or hair—would they have been able to do that? Assuredly not! Even if they wished to know its real nature, and how it took shape after God created it, they would be incapable of that."[43] Human nature, as created by God, is perfectly right just as it is, and is a wonder of divine wisdom. In this passage al-Ghazali seems to evoke the Qur'anic concept of fitra (described above) as a way of being created that is sound, sinless, and possesses spirit and free will. In the Qur'an Allah creates humans out of dust and clay plus a drop of semen into which he breathes his spirit (*ruh*). As al-Ghazali speaks of the intricacies of the body together with the capacities for intellect, power, knowledge, and spirit, he seems to be referencing the holistic Qur'anic view of human nature rather than the dualistic Greek idea of a divine soul imprisoned within a separate and sinful body.[44] When it comes to life after death, al-Ghazali is clear that there will be a resurrection of the body together with an immortal soul, so that bodily pains and pleasures are able to be experienced. Such a constitution of human nature, says al-Ghazali, refutes the claims of philosophers that the bodily pains and pleasures that the Qur'an describes as being felt in the afterlife are impossible.[45]

    When it comes to the goal of human nature's highest possible experience of God, al-Ghazali refers to it as the confession of God's unity (*tawhid*) or sometimes as "extinction in unity." For al-Ghazali this confession of unity meant that God was the Sole Being, the Sole Agent, and the Sole Light in the universe. This Being could not be known through the human mind's rational discourse or speculation, as the philosophers claimed. "Rather, He could be known through His self-unveiling (*kashf*) in the wake of an arduous and personal process of constant observation (*mushahadah*); that is, through the effulgence of the divine light."[46] The Qur'an describes God as "the Light of the heavens and the earth," the "Light of Lights" from which all humans derive their light and their being. However, at the highest level of mystical awareness, one's human nature with its own image of God or divine light appears as nothing in relation to God. As al-Ghazali puts it, "[E]verything[,] considered in itself, is pure nothing; but considered from the standpoint of the being which it receives from the First Reality, it appears as existing, not in itself, but rather in relation to the Face of its Maker."[47] Thus, in the mystical experience of its highest perfection, human nature is seen to be nothing in itself, but to exist in its relation of unity with God, from whom it receives its inner light. It is in this sense that al-Ghazali sees humans as occupying a preeminent position in the universe, for they are created in the image and likeness of God. The cognitive powers manifested by human nature are called by al-Ghazali "spiritual." They begin with sense experience and the imagination and "then culminate in reason, with its two subdivisions, the intuitive and the deductive, called by him reflective. Above these powers, corresponding roughly to the philosophers' teaching, the prophets, says al-Ghazali, attribute to humans a higher power, the 'prophetic spirit,' which enables them to partake of knowledge of the 'unseen' (*al-ghayb*). . . ."[48] The highest human cognitions are God-given. Al-Ghazali says there is "a light which God Almighty casts in the heart, and this light is the key to all modes of cognition."[49] Human perfection thus depends more on the inspiration or revelation received from God than on the carefully constructed arguments or proofs of philosophy. At the highest level of mystical experience, the mystic is so totally absorbed by the object of his or her contemplation that the mystic is no longer aware of himself or herself. Al-Ghazali calls such experience "extinction in unity."[50]

Unlike many Sufis before him, however, al-Ghazali was quite clear that the achievement of such mystical experiences required the disciplining of human nature's animal desires, and for this the observances of the shari'a are indispensable. For al-Ghazali, observance of the shari'a is a basic requirement for the full development and perfection of the capacities inherent in a person's primordial original nature. It helps to prevent a person from being sidetracked from seeking perfection by attempting to find it in worldly power, pleasure, and possessions. This seems to have been a major part of al-Ghazali's own struggle toward the perfection of his human nature. Montgomery Watt observes that already by the age of thirty-three al-Ghazali had been appointed professor at the university by the Turkish sultan of Baghdad. For four years he lectured to an audience of over three hundred students. He was one of the most prominent men in Baghdad and held one of the most distinguished positions in the academic world of his day. But then he experienced a psychological and spiritual crisis. "He came to feel that the one thing that mattered was avoidance of Hell and attainment of Paradise, and he saw that his present way of life was too worldly to have any hope of eternal reward."[51] He resigned his teaching position and became a wandering ascetic for a period of eleven years before returning to teaching. During this period he composed his great work, *The Revival of the Religious Sciences*, which requires religious observance and ritual along with philosophical reflection. In "The Beginning of Guidance," the introduction to that work, says Watt, al-Ghazali sets out the religious practices and conduct in social relationships as one side of the ideal to be followed in this life.[52] As al-Ghazali puts it, "You will never arrive at fulfilling the commands of God, my dear student, unless you watch over your heart and your members every single moment from morning to night."[53] He then details requirements in waking, doing ablutions, washing, entering the mosque, preparation for other acts of worship, and so forth, and the avoidance of sins such as lying, backbiting, self-justification, cursing, fornication, pride, and such.[54] Having applied all of this to himself in his own spiritual journey, al-Ghazali ends up his life as a religiously devout scholar rather than a worldly teacher of philosophy and theology. For him, as his great work, *The Revival of the Religious Sciences*, makes clear, the perfecting of human nature must give primacy to practice along with the rigorous conceptual study of philosophy and theology.[55]

In *The Revival of the Religious Sciences*, the holistic approach to human nature is highlighted in the way that al-Ghazali speaks of the heart (rather than the mind) as the locus of perception of the true nature of objects. This function of the heart is often compared to the way in which a mirror reflects the objects around it.[56] There are many things that can obstruct the mirror's reflection of its surroundings or the heart's perception of truth. Scholars often strive to attain knowledge of divine truth through their senses and minds, instead of receiving it through the entrance to their hearts. Ascetics, however, seek divine truth by constantly rubbing and polishing the mirror of their heart through careful practice of the religious commandments. For al-

Ghazali it is via the latter practice that human nature is perfected to its highest level enabling it to receive what he calls "prophetic revelation."[57] In his own life al-Ghazali found that this goal could not be achieved by scholarly study alone. It is by observance of the ritual commandments of the Qur'an as detailed in religious law that "blotches of greed and lust" are polished away from the mirror of the heart by divinely ordained good deeds. Thus, a person must become well acquainted with the states of one's heart, with one's good and evil attributes, before one can carry out the commandments in the right way and progress toward perfection. Every commandment is to be carried out with single-minded devotion, purity of thought, and absolute sincerity. "Single-minded devotion is, as it were, the breath of life of the commandments, without which they become meaningless notions of the body instead of divinely ordained good deeds."[58] Even with such purity of devotion in the doing of religious actions one will be left with mingled feelings of hope and fear—fear that one's deed may be found wanting by God, and hope that by God's grace it may be deemed acceptable. Al-Ghazali likens this activity to the farmer's preparation of the soil for sowing with seed. Only when the heart has been purified and its mirror polished by the "knowledge of action" will the more intellectual approach of knowledge and contemplation bring forth knowledge of the world to come (*'ilm al-akhira*). Al-Ghazali rejects the assumption, popular in philosophical circles, "that intellectual cognition is itself sufficient to ensure the perfection of the soul and its everlasting bliss."[59] Only with the help of the commandments and God's grace can one master one's passions and attain the knowledge and love in which lies true happiness in this world and the next.

When it comes to the question of the role of free will in human nature and its perfectibility, al-Ghazali applauds the Ash'arite school of thought for steering a middle course and teaching that actions are from God in one sense and from humans in another.[60] The extreme free will position of the Mu'tazilites he rejects, because it tends to make God seem powerless. As we noted above, al-Ghazali affirms the perfect rightness of the world as it actually is—as God has created it. What room does this leave for human free will? For al-Ghazali, this is the best possible world because it contains imperfection as well as perfection. In the world around us we see grades of perfection. The more perfect shows the goal to be achieved as contrasted with the less perfect. In creating us, God gave humans intellects and power of understanding so that they could perceive this, and freedom of choice so that they could choose the good. The prophets show us the perfect and how to achieve it. Then it is up to humans to use this help provided by God, to use their free will to move up the continuum from the imperfect toward the perfect. And this continuum extends between this life and the next. Anyone who does not know this has not yet "glimpsed the transcendent world with the vision of the heart (*bi-basar qalbihi*), nor crossed the limits to what is lowest in his own nature, i.e., he has not realized that these extremes co-exist within his own nature as well."[61] All of this, says al-Ghazali, subsists within God, exists through his power, and continues through his knowledge and wisdom. Thus, conditions like happiness and sadness, and belief and disbelief, along with created distinctions such as male and female, earth and sky, all subsist, not in themselves, but only in God as part of his "best of all possible worlds." When humans use their free will to follow the teachings of the prophets, to practice the observances of religious law, and to meditate on the truths of philosophy, one progresses toward perfection—not because any of this has intrinsic excellence in itself, but only because that is the way God in his wisdom created things to be. As Ormsby concludes, the assertion that things, as they are, are optimal because of the dictates of divine wisdom provides al-Ghazali with a strong and useful argument regarding human free will, the problem of evil, and God's omnipotence.[62] Al-Ghazali's thinking on free will and theodicy (the problem of understanding God's love and justice in the face of the world's evils) is compatible with and a logical outgrowth of the thinking of al-Ash'ari before him.[63]

IBN 'ARABI

Ibn 'Arabi was born in 1165 in Spain but lived most of his life in Damascus; he died there in 1240. He is called the "Great Master" of Sufi mysticism.[64] In the view of Seyyed Hossein Nasr, the outpouring of Divine Love that we find in Ibn 'Arabi's concept of human nature and its perfectibility cannot be attributed to Neoplatonism or any other source than the dimension of love present in the Qur'an and in the inner life of Islam.[65] However, he does betray some Neoplatonic influence when he describes the soul as separate from the body.[66] Ibn 'Arabi's conception of human nature has the notion of perfection inherent within it, as seen in his view of primordial creation: "Creation existed originally in the divine mind as a series of exemplars, which [Ibn 'Arabi] calls 'fixed entities' (*a'yan thabitah*) . . . God produces the whole creation by stint of his own command (*amr*), as repeatedly mentioned in the Qur'an."[67] The motive for God's decision to bring creation into existence is love and his desire to be known. According to Ibn 'Arabi, the highest manifestation of the divine is to be found in original human nature, associated with Adam, and he calls this original human nature the Adamic Logos or the Perfect Man (*al-insan al-kamil*). Having been created in God's image, the Perfect Man is the visible manifestation of the divine and "is the paragon of creation . . . which embodies all the perfections of the universe, as well as those of the divine Being Himself."[68] This is what is meant when the Qur'an says that humans are to be God's vice-regent in the world. Humans may be distinguished from all the rest of creation in that only in humans are God's attributes fully reflected, enabling them to completely know God. "The angels, as pure spiritual entities, are able to know Him only as a spiritual Being, whereas humans are able to know Him both as a spiritual Being, which is the Reality, on the one hand, and as the visible manifestation of this Reality, which is the creation, on the other."[69] And for Ibn 'Arabi, Muhammad assumes the role of the Perfect Man—the medium through which God is known and manifested. Thus, Muhammad is to be venerated. Schimmel comments that for Ibn 'Arabi, "Muhammad is the prototype of the universe as well as of man, since he is like a mirror in which each sees the other. . . . The Muhammadan reality, *haqiqa muhammadiyya*, bears in itself the divine word that reveals itself in its particulars in the different prophets and messengers until it reaches, once more, its fullness in the Prophet of Islam."[70] The Perfect Man is he who has realized all the possibilities inherent in the original human nature, and thus is the model for everyone to emulate.

The relationship between God, as creator, and his creatures is seen by Ibn 'Arabi as one of mutual yearning and longing. This is so even in the creation of Adam or humankind as an act of speaking born out of God's loneliness. As part of the process of breathing in and out, God reveals himself by speaking the divine names—the Logos forms of humans as they exist in mystery—and then by manifesting the concrete forms of these names as earthly persons. As Corbin puts it philosophically: "[T]hese Names exist from all eternity within the divine Essence, and are this very Essence, because the Attributes which they designate, although they are not identical with the divine Essence as such, are nevertheless not different from it."[71] Schimmel, more poetically, suggests: "Creation is 'the effusion of Being upon the heavenly archetypes' [or names]; it is as if glass pieces of a mirror were hit by light so that their iridescence becomes visible through this coloring. Or creation may be compared to articulation—did not the Koran speak of the *nafas*, the 'breath' of the Lord, which is infused into Adam . . . to create a new being?"[72] It is as if God held his breath until he could no longer do so, and the world appeared in name and form. It is as if the world is breathed out and created, or breathed in and taken back to its divine origin. So also in the two parts of the profession of faith "*la illah* points to the emanation of 'things other than He,' and *illa Allah* indicates their return to Him, to the everlasting unity."[73] Thus, this living and breathing creation is constantly withdrawing and re-creating itself through the eternal names that exist with God's essence. Schimmel finds the most fascinating part of Ibn 'Arabi's theory to be the correlation between the names and the named ones. The names, she suggests, may be compared to forms or archetypes through which God's creative energy is channeled to produce human beings. Or, to return to the mirror metaphor, "God becomes the mirror in which the spiritual man contemplates his own reality and man in turn becomes the mirror in which God contemplates His Names and Qualities."[74] This theory also implies that a certain form of faith is designated for each person within his or her primordial human nature. Thus, a believer can only have the particular religion. The Muslim will manifest his or her religion differently from a Christian or Jew. In this context, notes Schimmel, Ibn 'Arabi's poetry is often misunderstood to point toward a mystical ideal of religious tolerance and indifference toward exterior forms and rituals. The poet says, "My heart is capable of every form, a cloister of the monk, a temple for idols, a pasture for gazelles, the votary's Kaaba, the tables of the Thora, the Koran. Love is the creed I hold: wherever turn His camels, love is still my creed and faith."[75] But this verse, often quoted in support of religious tolerance, says Schimmel, is really a statement about Ibn 'Arabi's high mystical perfection. "The form of God is for him no longer the form of this or that faith exclusive of all others, but his own eternal form which he encounters at the end of his *tawaf* (circumambulation—as in pilgrimage going around the ka'ba). It is highest self-praise, acknowledgement of an illumination that is far beyond the 'illumination of names,' but not tolerance preached to the rank and file."[76]

The *Encyclopaedia of Islam* describes Ibn 'Arabi's conception of the path for the perfecting of human nature as a series of three journeys.[77] First, humans journey from God and are born into this world, where they are the furthest removed from God. Second, the human traveler, with the help of a guide, journeys to God (*al-safar ila' illah*). Third, one's spiritual journey continues within God. While the first two journeys have an end, the third has no end. The traveler on the third journey performs those precepts of Islamic law or shari'a that are *fard* (a duty). Although one is externally living in society, internally one is dwelling with God. Most people are capable of no more than the first journey, due to the limited capacities of their natures. Only the specially endowed few may advance to the vision of God, but even this depends on certain conditions—some fulfilled by the traveler, others provided by the guide (*shaykh*). Even Muhammad had a guide in the form of the angel Gabriel. "The *shaykhs* perform the function which the prophets had performed in their day, except that they do not bring a new *shari'a*."[78] On one's spiritual journey, says Ibn 'Arabi, the "traveler" must observe the following practices: (1) silence; (2) withdrawal from society; (3) hunger; and (4) wakefulness. If one engages in these practices with sincere intention, there will be awakened in one's heart a love that grows to be a passion that is quite distinct from selfish desire. It is this passion which particularly brings a person to perfection with God. "When the heart is thoroughly purified, the veil (*hidjab*) of those 'other' things which hide God (*ma siwa' Allah*) is drawn aside, all things, past, present, and future, are known; God grants the manifestation (*tadjalli*) of Himself; and finally union with Him (*wasl*) is achieved."[79] All of this complements Ibn 'Arabi's conception of the "Perfect Man," created in God's image, as embodying all the perfection of the universe as well as that of God himself, and thus qualifies as, the Qur'an suggests, to be the vice-regent (*khalifa*) of God in the world.[80] Thus, as noted above, humans may be thought of as more complete than the angels. As spiritual beings, angels can know God only as a spiritual being. Humans, however, are able to know God both as a spiritual being and in his visible manifestation as the created universe. Humans are thus the only beings in whom the divine attributes are fully reflected and are thus capable of knowing God fully. Like al-Ghazali, Ibn 'Arabi sees this highest state of perfection as the human soul's direct experience of God.[81] Not all travelers of the journey toward the third stage will reach this final state of perfection. Although Ibn 'Arabi seems to focus on the third stage, of withdrawal and ascetic contemplation, he does see the shari'a and its commandments as a key prerequisite of the first two stages in the perfecting of one's nature. In this way he is somewhat like al-Ghazali before him. With regard to the ultimate mystical vision of God, Ibn 'Arabi's inclusion of both God's spiritual being and his visible manifestation in creation is richer and more inclusive than that of other Sufi mystics (such as al-Bistani and al-Hallaj), who focus only on the former.[82]

CONCLUSION

We have seen that Muslims view human nature as a unity of body, mind, and spirit. In its accounts of creation and resurrection the Qur'an never suggests that the soul (*nafs*) joins or enters the body. "Rather, in the Qur'an, it is the entire person in all of his or her physical, emotional and spiritual capacities that is created, dies and will be resurrected on judgement day."[83] Within Islam there is no notion of original sin; rather, the Qur'anic concept of fitra argues for a human nature that, in its primordial state, is sound, sinless, and capable of progressing toward perfection in this life and the next. To achieve this goal God's guidance is given in the Qur'an and in the shari'a. Human effort is required to actualize human nature's inherent capacities by following the guidance offered in scripture and law. According to a modern Muslim view based in rationalism (that of A. Ezzati), although humans are innately inclined to do good and avoid evil, they also possess rationality, free choice, and animal desires. Sin occurs when a person uses free choice to go against the guidance given by God and follow his or her base desires. (This modern Muslim reading of the Qur'an, which differs from that of al-Ashari, emphasizes the diversity of views within Islam.) But the possibility of actualizing the inherent goodness in human nature by making the right choices in following God's guidance is always present and is exemplified by Muhammad, who is seen as the "Perfect Man."

In surveying the views of Islamic thinkers on human nature and its perfectibility we examined the thought of al-Ash'ari, al-Ghazali, and Ibn 'Arabi. Al-Ash'ari focused his analysis on the tension present in the Qur'an's teaching of God's omnipotence and omniscience in relation to human free will. Although he argued that God's powers were absolute, he attempted to present a middle position between complete human free will and divine predestination through his theory of the acquisition of God's actions by humans by using their human choice to follow God's teachings in the Qur'an. Perfection in this approach seems to be more the result of God's action than it is of human effort. Al-Ghazali opposed the dominant Neoplatonic Muslim thinking of his day, which downplayed the actions and responsibilities of this world in favor of the contemplation of the perfections of the world to come. Instead, al-Ghazali, through the existential crisis of his own life, found that the careful observance of religious law and ritual together with intellectual knowledge and contemplation is the way to perfect human nature for this world and the next. For al-Ghazali such perfection is both fully embodied and a mystical experience of unity with God ("extinction with unity"). This realization requires the use of human free will to give obedience in following the commandments of the Qur'an and shari'a so as to discipline human nature's animal desires. This results in a polishing of the mirror of the heart so that God's creation as "the best of all possible worlds" is clearly reflected and meditated upon until human nature is perfected to its highest level. Regarding free will, al-Ghazali reformulates al-Ash'ari's line of thinking as follows: when humans use their free will to follow the teachings of the Qur'an and the observances of shari'a, and to meditate on the truths of philosophy, then they progress toward perfection—not because any of this has excellence in itself, but only because this is the way God in his wisdom has created things.

With Ibn 'Arabi we encounter a Sufi mystic who sees the perfecting of human nature to be made possible by the outpouring of divine love present in the Qur'an. God's motive in bringing forth the created universe is love and a desire to be known. This is present in seed form in the original human nature given to Adam, and is called the "Perfect Man." Created in God's image, the Perfect Man is the paradigm of creation and embodies all the perfection of the universe as well as those of God himself. Muhammad is such a Perfect Man—the one who has realized all the possibilities inherent in our original human nature and thus is the model for each of us to follow. Ibn 'Arabi's mystic vision is of God creating and sustaining the universe by his breathing in and out. Every created being has a name and form. When God breathes out, the names of creation are filled with life and, like mirrors, reflect the divine light. When God breathes in, the whole of creation is taken back into its divine origin. To reach this vision of God one must perfect one's human nature through a series of journeys: from God when we are born into this world, toward God with the help of a guide, and finally within God—the journey which has no end. In this last journey, although one is externally performing shari'a and living in society, internally one is dwelling with God. Only the specially endowed few have a human nature with the capacity to advance to this vision of God. Even for those few, such a vision will not be realized until a love is awakened within the heart that grows into a passion—and it is this passion that brings one to experience perfection in the vision of God. Of all created beings only humans have this high possibility of sharing with God the direct experience of all creation and of God himself. It is this intimate knowledge in the state of human perfection that qualifies humans to be God's *khalifa* or vice-regents on earth, and gives to them the responsibilities that go with that state of perfection.

In the Islamic view of human nature and its perfectibility, we find a spiritually rich and inspiring vision that is open to all to follow. As William Chittick notes, it encouraged a never-ending search for knowledge and spiritual growth aimed at fully developing the human personality, especially in its moral and spiritual dimensions. "The most gifted students were led by their innate desire for learning and a system that emphasized praxis as much as theory to a personal quest for *tawhid*, or the right relationship between themselves and God on the deepest levels of awareness and existence."[84] Chittick laments that too often today the idea of human perfection is oriented toward social and political objectives—"objectives inspired by those dominant currents in the modern world which see material gain as the highest good."[85]

Part II

The Perfectibility of Human Nature in Eastern Thought (arising in India)

Chapter 6

The Perfectibility of Human Nature in Indian Philosophy and Yoga Psychology

In part 1 we have seen that Western philosophy, psychology, and religion generally see human nature to be limited in various ways and not perfectible in this life. Judaism, Christianity, and Islam, to the degree that they see perfectibility as realizable, tend to see it as something to be achieved in the afterlife—and then only with the help of God's grace. By contrast, Indian philosophy and religion (Hinduism, Jainism, and Buddhism—all religions born in India) understand the perfecting of our human natures as the purpose for which each of us has been created, and as a goal to be realized while we are alive on earth. If we do not succeed in this life, then we will simply be reborn over and over again until we do. This is a quite different way of conceiving of human nature and its potential for perfection, and it is couched in the basic presuppositions of the Indian worldview: ideas of creation as beginningless, of karma, of rebirth and release from rebirth (*moksa* or nirvana). We will examine these ideas first and then go on to the approach of Indian philosophy and Yoga psychology to the question of human nature and its perfectibility.

THE INDIAN WORLDVIEW

Four basic ideas of the Indian worldview are *anadi, karma, samsara* and *moksa. Anadi* is the notion that the universe is beginningless—everything has been going on beginninglessly. This includes the sacred sounds of the mantras or scriptures which are held to be uncreated and eternal. Of course, these are cycles of creation, with each cycle going through the stages of sprouting, growing, maturing, and dying, but leaving behind a seed form out of which the next cycle may arise. The image is an agricultural one of a seed sprouting, maturing, blossoming, withering, and dying but dropping off a seed out of which the cycle may arise again. The difficult aspect to grasp, from the Western perspective, is that there is no first cycle. These cycles of the universe have been going on beginninglessly. And at the start of each cycle, say the orthodox Hindus, the sacred mantras of the Veda are spoken as an important part of the creating process itself as well as a revelation of divine truth.

Karma is a word that is now fairly common in the West, but often little understood. There are many definitions of karma in the Indian tradition, some making karma appear quite deterministic. One of the clearest descriptions, however, is found in the Yoga Sutras of Patanjali.[1] This concept is widely influential and has the added advantage of making room for free will. It runs as follows. Every time you do an action or think a thought, a memory trace or karmic seed is laid down in the storehouse of your unconscious. There it sits waiting for circumstances conducive to its sprouting forth as an impulse, instinct, or predisposition to do the same action or think the same thought again. Notice that the karmic impulse from the unconscious does not *cause* anything; it is not mechanistic in nature. Rather it simply *predisposes* you to do an action or think a thought. Room is left for the function of free will. Through the use of your free will you decide either to go along with the karmic impulse, in which case it is reinforced and strengthened, or to say no and negate it, in which case its strength diminishes until it is finally removed from the unconscious. Karmas can be either good or bad. Good actions and thoughts lay down good karmic traces in the unconscious for the predisposing of future good karmic impulses. Evil actions and thoughts do the reverse. Scripture and tradition taken together distinguish between good and evil.

Let us take an example: the chanting of a mantra or verse of scripture. Speaking or thinking a mantra is an action that lays down a karmic trace in the unconscious. Chanting a mantra over and over reinforces that karmic trace (*samskara*) until a deep root or habit pattern (*vasana*) is established. Correctly chanting a good mantra, such as OM or a verse of Vedic scripture, reinforces good karma and removes negative karmas or impulses by preventing their blossoming or maturing, so that they wither away, leaving no trace behind. In this way, mantra chanting can be seen to be a powerful psychological tool for purifying and transforming consciousness.

According to karma theory, then, all the impulses you are experiencing at this moment are resulting from actions and thoughts done in this life. But what if you experience an impulse, either good or evil, that seems completely out of character with the way you have lived since birth? That karmic impulse is arising from an action or thought you did in a previous life—which introduces the third basic idea, namely, samsara or rebirth. Your unconscious contains not only all the karmic traces from actions and thoughts done in this life, but also in the life before this and so on backward infinitely, since there is no absolute beginning. In reality, then, your unconscious is like a huge granary full of karmic seeds or memory traces that are constantly sprouting up, as conducive situations arise, impelling you toward good or evil actions or thoughts. No wonder we constantly feel ourselves being pulled and pushed by our karmic desires. But the ability to choose freely always allows us to take control over these impulses, and mantra chanting gives us a powerful psychological and spiritual tool to use in directing this process.

Samsara provides us with the idea of a ladder of rebirth. At the bottom are the animals, in the middle the humans, and at the top the gods.

gods, no free choice
humans, free choice
animals, no free choice

Assume that you are a human being. If in this life you use your free choice to act on the good karmic impulses and negate the evil ones, then at the end of this life you will have increased the number of good karmas, and decreased the number of evil karmas in your unconscious. At death (where the karmas function like coins in a banker's balance) the increase in good karmas will automatically cause you to be reborn further up the ladder. If you repeat the same procedure of acting on the good and negating the evil over many lifetimes, you will gradually spiral toward the top of the ladder and be reborn in the realm of the gods. Unlike humans, gods have no free choice, no power to act. All you can do is enjoy the honor of being a god—of sitting in the mayor's chair for a day, as it were—until the merit built up from your good choices over countless lives is used up and you are reborn a human at the top of the human scale with the prospect of continued birth, death, and rebirth to look forward to. But what if in this life you used your free choice to go the opposite way—to act on the evil karmic impulses and to negate the good? Then at death you would have increased the number of bad karmas, reduced the number of good karmas, and automatically been reborn a step lower down the ladder. And if this negative pattern was repeated through many lifetimes, you would spiral down and eventually be reborn as an animal. Animals are simply human beings in a different karmic form (which logically explains the Indian practice of vegetarianism—to eat an animal is to engage in cannibalism). Unlike humans, animals have no free choice. Their fate is to endure the sufferings that their instincts cause them. When they have suffered sufficiently to expiate or purge the bad karma they built up through many lifetimes of making evil choices, they are then reborn as human beings with free choice and a chance to move up the ladder again through the process of birth, death, and rebirth.

In Indian thought the thing that causes one to be reborn is the karma within one's own consciousness. The chanting of mantras is one of the most powerful practices for the purging of karmas, and when the last karma is removed, release from rebirth—perfection, is realized. Although conceptualized differently by different philosophical schools, release may generally be thought of as the removal of karmas that make us appear to be separate from the Divine. When the last veiling or obstructing karma is removed, the fact that one is, and has always been, nothing but Divine is revealed. That is release—the direct realization of one's own oneness with the Divine and perfection.

When one thinks of this process as having been going on beginninglessly and sees the prospect of being born, growing old, dying, and being reborn apparently endlessly, the question comes to mind, "How can I get release (*moksa*)?" Hinduism gives one answer (see chapter 7); Buddhism gives a different answer (see chapter 8).

The above four basic concepts of the Indian worldview are found revealed in Indian scripture, the oldest of which is the Veda, dating from about 1500 BCE. The teachings of the various schools of Indian philosophy take their rise either by saying yes to the Vedas (in which case they are considered to be orthodox or Hindu schools), or by saying no to the Vedas (in which case they are considered to be heterodox schools, such as the Jain or Buddhist). For both groups of philosophical schools, the Vedas function foundationally in either a positive or negative fashion. Thus, before considering the schools and their views of human nature and how it is to be released or perfected, let us first get acquainted with the Vedas and the way they function to remove karma.

The concept of mantra as powerful sacred sound is associated with one of India's ancient scriptures, the Rig Veda.[2] India shares with the rest of the world a fascination with what Rudolf Otto has called numinous sounds,[3] sounds that go beyond the rational and the ethical to evoke a direct, face-to-face contact with the holy. Otto conceived of the numinous with a typically Western emphasis on the experience of the distance, the separation, between human beings and God. For Hindus in the context of the Rig Veda the cosmos is peopled by gods sometimes thought of in personal ways. For example, prayers or mantras are spoken to gods such as Varuna to maintain relationships with them so that they will act for the devotee. However, the Rig Veda also saw mantras as the means by which the power of truth and order that is at the very center of the Vedic universe could be evoked. That truth, however, is not thought of as a personal God like Yahweh or Allah, but as the impersonal *rta* or divine order of reality. In his classic article, "The Indian *Mantra*," Gonda points out that mantras are not thought of as products of discursive thought, human wisdom, or poetic fantasy, "but as flash-lights of the eternal truth, seen by those eminent men who have come into supersensuous contact with the Unseen."[4] Sri Aurobindo puts it even more vividly: "The language of the Veda is itself a *sruti*, a rhythm not composed by the intellect but heard, a divine Word that came vibrating out of the Infinite to the inner audience of the man who had previously made himself fit for the impersonal knowledge."[5] The Vedic seers supersensuously "heard" these divine mantras not as personal but as divinely rooted words, and spoke them in the Hindu scripture or Veda as an aid to those less spiritually advanced. By concentrating one's mind upon such a mantra, the devotee invokes the power and truth inherent in the seers' divine intuition and so purifies his or her consciousness. It is this understanding that is behind the long-standing Indian practice of the repeated chanting of mantras as a means for removing karmic ignorance or impurity from one's personality and progressing toward perfection. The more difficulties to be overcome, the more repetitions are needed. The deeper is one's separation from the Eternal Absolute, the more one must invoke the mantra. Contrary to what our modern minds quickly tend to assume, the Hindu chanting a mantra in morning and evening worship is not simply engaging in an empty superstition. From the Indian perspective such chanted words have power to confirm and increase truth and order (*rta*) within one's character and in the wider universe. Chanting a Vedic mantra has a spiritually therapeutic effect upon the devotee and a cosmic significance as well. Hindus maintain that the holiness of the mantra or divine word is intrinsic, and that one participates in it not by discursive understanding but by hearing and reciting it.[6] Vedic mantras can be single words, sentences, or complete verses.

During the period of the Rig Veda (1500–1000 BCE) the notion of mantra comes to focus more on the language of ritual and less on the poetic insight born of the face-to-face contemplation of *rta* or divine order. A new view of ritual speech arises. The creatively eloquent insight of the Vedic seer is transformed into a known formula that will function effectively in a ritual context.[7] For the poets of the Rig Veda, mantras have power, and the source of that power is the rta that stands at the very center of the universe. The power encapsulated in a mantra is released when it is spoken. As Hacker put it, mantras when spoken are capable of bringing about a reality not only at the psychological level but even in the material order of things.[8] Therefore, the speaker of the mantra must realize that he or she is handling power; power that can be used for good or for ill. In Hebrew thought as well, the notion that spoken words have power is present (see Exod. 20:7). Speaking the mantra can have a purifying effect upon the speaker and the universe, or, if spoken in malice or ignorance, the power unleashed can be harmful to the individual and to the universe. In this sense mantra as sacred word can bless or curse. It is powerful for purifying human nature.

Such holy power should not be treated lightly, and so supervision of the ritual chanting of mantras was a responsibility given to the priests of India. Indeed, mantras are thought to be so highly charged that unless properly handled by a priest or by a person under the close supervision of a priest, the mantra can fall back upon and burn its speaker. The Vedic mantra is like a high voltage channel that puts its speaker in direct connection with the power-source of the universe. And that power source is rta, the transcendent truth of the cosmic and human orders. It is the power of that truth that is released when the mantra is spoken and then repeated over and over.

Chanting the mantra fills one's consciousness with the power of truth and fosters the dominance of truth over chaos in the surrounding universe. Through the truth power of the mantra one attunes oneself to the rta of the universe. One is placed in the midst of revelation of ultimate truth. For the Rig Veda, revelation is not a matter of God intervening in the affairs of the world; rather, it is the insight that naturally arises through the chanting of the mantras truly formulated by the ancient *rsis* or seers (perfectly purified persons). The rsis themselves directly experienced the ultimate truth, meditated upon it in their hearts, and carefully expressed it in well-formed mantras. "*Mantras* formulated in the heart are true not just because they capture the truth of some cosmological occurrence but because they themselves have participated, and continue to participate, in the same cosmological events."[9] Mantras not only articulate truth, they are the truth. They have participated in the primordial revelation of truth by the Vedic rsis, and through their repetition they become the means by which the cosmic truth and order is manifest and preserved.

The devotee sitting on the banks of the Ganges at dawn and chanting the Agni mantra aids in the daily retrieval of the sun out of darkness and reestablishes the light of truth at the center of his or her consciousness for the coming day. Agni is the god of fire, light, and truth. As dawn becomes visible to humans on earth, the contemplation of Agni links the worshiper to the mystery of the recurrence of the sun each morning, to the light and truth at the center of the cosmos.

Agni, then, is the vital energy at the mysterious center of the cosmos. It is from Agni that all insight, all revelation, comes. Humans would not be able to think, imagine, speak, or sing without the words bestowed by Agni. It is these words, as a gift of grace from Agni, that the inspired poets or rsis can turn into mantras with power for ritual use.[10]

The development of the priestly class in the later periods of the Rig Vedic and the Brahmanas (1000–800 BCE) focuses on the question of how to use this power that the mantra possesses for good. The answer reached is clear: to make the mantra work, one must pronounce it. As the Rig Veda puts it,

> If these *mantras* of ours remain unspoken they will bring
> no joy, even on the most distant day.[11]

Pronouncing the mantra correctly in its proper ritual context releases its power. For this to happen, the supervision of a priest is seen as essential. Under the guidance of a priest, the Vedic mantra is an instrument with the power to produce results both personal and cosmic. Mantras spoken in ritual activity actually do something. Thus, even from their earliest conception in the Rig Veda, mantras are classical examples of what are now called "speech acts."[12] However, whereas modern thought emphasizes the performative nature of the speech act at the expense of its communication function, the Vedic seers are emphatic that while the spoken mantra can purify one's nature; the basis for that power is located in its revelation of truth (*rta, satya*). Although mantras from later Indian tradition can be of a nonsensical nature, in the period of the Rig Veda it seems clear that a mantra must reveal meaning.[13] Indeed, the original sense of mantra as a vehicle for reflection and revelation is made operative by the late seers and priests. "*Mantra* is the tool, the mechanism, for yoking the reflective powers of the seer into the machinery of ritual."[14]

As the use of mantra goes through later developments, one or the other of these two aspects receives elaboration. On the one hand, the mantra becomes a key to meditation, to the establishment and maintenance of divine accessibility. On the other, mantra chanting becomes merely an instrumental power to achieve worldly ends (e.g., getting sons) with little attention paid to the aspect of divine revelation or the perfecting of one's inner nature. Indeed, there are many people who treat mantra in this quasi-magical fashion. Even in these cases, however, we must remember that for many of the faithful of India—Hindu, Jain, and Buddhist—being a householder and a parent are simply stages in the inestimably long journey to a fully spiritual existence. Therefore, seeking in a quite vulgar way the material blessings associated with these stages is part of that ultimate journey. As the seer is transformed from a poet-saint who meditates and makes his life an empty channel to the Divine to a priest who knows how to make the ritual effective, the performative function of mantras is given more emphasis. Consequently, there is a stress on proper pronunciation in the correct ritual context for the desired result to be achieved. These are indeed the issues that become central in the Brahmanas—the prose ritual commentaries that are added to the earlier collections of Vedic hymns. But the other aspect of mantra, its revelation function, is not lost. Indeed, the Vedic poet's wish that the mantra be both powerful and have an inspired meaning is nicely expressed: "May we pronounce that *mantra* well that was fashioned for him from the heart; he will understand it to be sure (*Rgveda* 2.35.2ab)."[15]

With the Upanishads (800–500 BCE)—a second level of prose commentaries on the Vedic hymns—the pendulum swings away from the emphasis on ritual and back to mantra as the means to revealed knowledge. Instead of the ritual priest it is the guru or teacher in the context of student-teacher dialogue who skillfully uses the mantras. The result desired now, however, is not material wealth or sons but ultimate perfection or release (*moksa*) from the beginningless and seemingly endless cycle of birth-death-rebirth (*karma-samsara*). When enough of the obscuring karma or ignorance has been removed by the dialogues with the guru and individual meditation, the teacher's speaking of mantras such as *tat tvam asi* (that thou art) evokes a flash of insight revealing the unity of the individual devotee with the cosmic reality, now called Brahman. When at the right moment the guru speaks "tat tvam asi" to the student, an awakening so powerful as to remove all remaining karma dawns upon the mind and grows into an insight so brilliant and all-embracing that the unity of all things in Brahman is directly realized. This, for the Hindu, is the moment of perfection, of final release that, in the Upanishads, is effected only by mantra-induced knowledge. Later philosophical traditions such as the Yoga, Mimamsa, Grammarian, and Vedanta schools give further development to the initial insight of the Vedas. The Buddhists develop their position as a reaction against Vedic teaching (see chapter 8).

Some medieval yoga traditions take the *nada* or sound vibrations themselves to be the basis for meditational techniques aimed at the realization of *moksa* (release). The Gorakhnath (or Nath) tradition specialized in the use of sacred sound as a yoga in itself.[16] Thus, the original mantra experience of the Vedic seers, mantra as a means to realize the truth of ultimate reality, is given systematic elaboration.

Such purifying uses of mantras as a means to realize perfection in this life are, however, very much in the minority in India. Within Hinduism most mantras are employed for ritual purposes to seek immediate benefit or to purify and nurture an individual's journey toward ultimate reality, which will continue over many lifetimes. Whether employed in worship (*puja*) or in the ritual acts of daily Hindu life, mantra use is mainly for the achieving of benefits in this life or the next, and not for moksa. In all such cases the ritual action is either accompanied by mantras or consists simply of their utterance. In the structure of virtually all the *samskara*s or sacraments that accompany a new stage in life for the individual, mantra is central. Characteristically, these mantras evoke the benefits of life progeny, prosperity, and longevity—for they initiate and speak of the journey to liberation, the ultimate goal of moksa. Before moving on to a detailed consideration of some Indian philosophical schools and their view of the perfectibility of human nature, there is one other idea to be introduced that is basic to Indian thought—namely, the notion of the four stages of life: student, householder, forest dweller, and holy wanderer. These four *asrama*s, as they are called, provide a framework for the religious, psychological, and social needs of the individual from childhood to old age. Each stage, ideally a twenty-five-year span, has its appropriate commitments and disciplines. Each span properly lived out will serve the human community through ethical fidelity and nurture the soul along the path leading to ultimate liberation or perfection.

The first stage is a period of celibacy and learning, and the nurturing of physical development, mental and spiritual health, and strength and endurance. It is the *brahmacarya asrama*, the student life, hinged, as its title suggests, on mastering the basic religious rituals and texts (which are to be learned by heart). There is no sexual activity at this stage, as all one's energy is directed to study.

The second stage, the *grhastha asrama*, sees the individual take up all the duties, responsibilities, and opportunities of a householder, including getting a job, marrying, having children, and fulfilling community responsibilities. *Artha* (the pursuit of wealth), *kama* (the pursuit of legitimate desires), and *dharma* (the doing of religious and moral duties) are all appropriate goals for the householder stage of life.

When the primary responsibility of raising children has been properly discharged, the householder is freed from immediate needs and interests of his family. When hair turns gray, skin wrinkles, and grandchildren arrive, he may retire into the forest with his wife. This is the *vanaprastha asrama*. There they devote themselves to spiritual study and discipline under the guidance of a guru. While husband and wife may remain together, their relationship is purely platonic—sexual activity is considered appropriate only to the householder stage.

The final stage of life, characterized by complete surrender, is the life of the recluse or holy wanderer. This is the *mahaprasthana asrama*. This period of life is devoted—with the support of the community—to the practice of meditation until one's human nature is purified of karma and moksa is realized. No longer is there special attachment to husband, wife, or children. It is not that affection for these is lessened or lost, but that all others are raised to that same level in one's love. All women are seen as one's mother, wife, or sister; all men as one's father, husband, or brother. As a holy wanderer (*sannyasin*) one is completely freed from restrictions of family, caste, and village loyalties, and instead is universally committed to love, teach, and help whomever one meets on life's path. In short, one has become a guru. As with the forest dweller, there is no sexual activity at this stage. It is at this stage of life that the goal of final release from rebirth is sought.

THE PERFECTING OF HUMAN NATURE IN SOME HINDU PHILOSOPHICAL SCHOOLS

The way in which mantras reveal the meaning and power of rta and purify and perfect human nature is analyzed by various schools of Indian philosophy. Two principal schools, the Mimamsa and the Grammarians, made the most significant contributions. Both of these schools follow the Brahmanical tradition stemming from the Veda that takes language and mantras as of divine origin (*daivi vak*), as Spirit descending and embodying itself in the vibrations of words. The well-known Rig Veda verse 4.58.3 expresses this truth in poetic form. It symbolizes speech as the bellowing bull of abundant fecundity, as the Great God descending into the world of mortals. Patanjali, the great Grammarian scholar, asks "Who is this Great God?" and answers "Speech itself" (*mahan devah sabdah*).[17] To this view of mantra the Mimamsa, Sankhya-Yoga, and Grammarian schools of Hindu philosophy are loyal.

In opposition to this high evaluation of mantra, there are the Indian schools, like Jainism and Buddhism, that reject the Veda as an authoritative source of revelation. Although the Jains and the Buddhists adopted a naturalistic view of language—namely, that it is but an arbitrary and conventional tool—the chanting of mantras continued to play an important role in Buddhist spiritual practice (see chapter 8). But first let us examine the Hindu philosophical understandings of mantra arising from the Vedas.

Hindu thought sees a direct relationship between ritual action and mantras. Indeed, it has been suggested that in India language is not something with which you *name* something; it is something with which you *do* something.[18] Each spoken mantra corresponds to one ritual act. In post-Vedic India activities such as bringing the goddess Kali into a stone image, bathing to wash away sins, sowing seeds in the fields, guarding the sown seeds, driving away evil spirits, and meditating to achieve release all had to be accompanied by the chanting of mantras in order to achieve success in purifying one's nature.[19] In some situations the ritual act itself was later modified or even abandoned, yet the action of mantra recitation was retained.[20] Within the ritual action, it is the uttered mantra that has central importance for perfection or moksa.

THE MIMAMSA THEORY OF MANTRA AS ETERNAL WORD (SABDA) AND ITS PURIFYING FUNCTION

The task of providing a theoretical explanation for the power of spoken mantras was taken up by the Mimamsa school of philosophy.[21] The Mimamsa (founded by Jamini c. 600 BCE) proposed a theory of *sabda* that suggests that the sound produced in pronouncing a word is not the result of human choice or construction; rather, every sabda or word has an eternal meaning. Each sabda is the sound-representative of some aspect of the eternal cosmic order. The mantras of the Vedas, therefore, are not words coined by humans. They are the sounds or vibrations of the eternal principles of the cosmic order itself. It is for this reason that the rsis or speakers of the Vedas are called "seers" or "hearers" of the mantras and not the authors of the mantras. Thus, the Hindu claim that the Vedas were not composed by human beings. They are not like other human literature. The Vedas, as the collection of the mantras, are not about everyday things. Rather, they give us negative and positive commands concerning ethical action in daily life that represent the eternal principles of rta for ourselves and the universe around us. Even when the cosmic process ceases to be, between cycles of the universe, the mantras, as eternal truths, remain present in their seed state, ready to sound forth afresh as the eternal Veda in the next cycle of creation. Thus, the mantras are said by the Mimamsakas to be authorless and eternal. Another important aspect of this view is that these mantras are not written but passed on orally. The Vedic mantras are, accordingly, the eternal sounds of the ethical truth of the universe and ourselves. Words other than the Vedic mantras were regarded as human-made; their meanings were seen as established by human convention and were incapable of giving us ethical guidance. Only the meaning content of the Vedic mantras can teach us the required continuous ethical action and enjoyment of its fruits that are the end goal of life.

For the Mimamsa the ultimate reality is nothing other than the eternal words of the Vedas. They did not accept the existence of a single supreme creator god, who might have composed the Veda. According to the Mimamsa, gods named in the Vedas have no existence apart from the mantras that speak their names. The power of the gods, then, is nothing other than the power of the mantras that name them.[22] This concept of sabda as divine, eternal, and authorless is given further development in the Grammarian notion of *sabdabrahman*. Patanjali's Yoga Sutras seem to take over the Mimamsa view with little change and then identify it with the mind of Isvara,[23] the master yogi. Let us examine each of these in turn.

THE GRAMMARIAN SCHOOL'S APPROACH
TO PERFECTING HUMAN NATURE

We have seen that for the Mimamsa School mantra is sabda, the eternal authorless words of the Veda. The Grammarians adopt all of this but add to it the notion of Brahman, God as unitary pure consciousness. Consequently the Grammarians offer a theory of mantra as a manifestation of *sabdabrahman* or divine word-consciousness.[24] Although unitary in nature, this divine word-consciousness manifests itself in the diversity of words that make up speech. The mantra OM is identified as the root mantra out of which all other mantras arise.[25] This sacred syllable is held to have flashed forth into the heart of Brahman while absorbed in deep meditation, and to have given birth to the Vedas, which contain all knowledge. OM and the Vedic mantras are described as being at once a means of knowledge and a way of moksa.[26] Fundamental to all of this is the notion that language and consciousness are inextricably intertwined. Indeed, the great Grammarian philosopher Bhartrhari (c. 500 CE) puts it this way: "There is no cognition in the world in which the word does not figure. All knowledge is, as it were, intertwined with the word."[27] Bhartrhari goes on to make clear that the word meaning, as the essence of consciousness, urges all beings toward purposeful activity. If the word were absent everything would be insentient, like a piece of wood. Thus, Bhartrhari describes the Absolute or Divine as sabdabrahman.[28]

When everything is merged into sabdabrahman, as in a high moment of mystical experience, no speaking takes place, and no meaning is available through mantras. But, when the Divine is awakened and meanings are manifested through words, then the knowledge and power that are intertwined with consciousness can clearly be perceived and known. Because consciousness is of the nature of word meaning, the consciousness of any sentient being cannot go beyond or lack word meaning.[29] When no meaning is understood, it is not due to a lack of word meaning in consciousness but rather to ignorance or absentmindedness obscuring the meaning inherently present.[30] For Bhartrhari and the Grammarians, words, meanings, and consciousness are eternally connected and, therefore, necessarily synonymous. If this eternal identity were to disappear, knowledge, communion, and the means to perfectibility would all cease to exist.[31] T. R. V. Murti concisely sums up the Grammarian position when he says it is not that we have a thought and then look for a word with which to express it "or that we have a lonely word that we seek to connect with a thought. Word and thought develop together, or rather they are expressions of one deep spiritual impulse to know and to communicate."[32]

Some Indian theories of mantra take the view that mantras are meaningless. From the Grammarian perspective a meaningless mantra would imply a piece of consciousness without a word meaning attached. According to Bhartrhari, that is impossible. It is possible, however, for a person to be obstructed by his or her own karmic ignorance and so not understand the meaning of a mantra—even though the word or words of the mantra are inherently meaningful. Let us take the word "love" as an example. This word can be used in two ways: in one way it seems to be meaningless; in the other it overflows with meaning. When a young man and woman develop a deep, respectful, and trusting relationship, they may say "I love you" and call each other "my love." In so saying they express a fullness of meaning that no other word could better convey. Now imagine a couple in a divorce court, and the one says to the other, "Well, my love, let us separate." In the first case the word is a mantra evoking deep meaning. In the second case "my love" is a figure of speech that is no longer life-giving. It had the potential to become a mantra but failed due to the couple's obscuring karma.

The reason for the speaking of mantras is also traced to the nature of word-consciousness by Bhartrhari. He states that word-consciousness itself contains an inner energy (*kratu*) that seeks to burst forth into expression.[33] For example, the rsis see the Veda as a unitary truth but, for the purpose of manifesting that truth to others, they allow the word's inner energy to assume the form of the various mantras. On an everyday level, this inner energy or *kratu* is experienced when, at the moment of having an insight or idea, we feel ourselves impelled to express it, to share it with others by putting it into words. Indeed, the whole activity of scholarship and teaching is dependent upon this characteristic of consciousness.

Bhartrhari offers a detailed analysis of how the uttered sounds of the mantra reveal meaning. He describes three stages in the speaking and hearing of mantras on the analogy of a painter.[34] Just as a painting is perceived as a whole over and above its different parts and colors, so our cognition of the mantra is of a meaning-whole over and above the sequence of uttered sounds. *Sphota* (that from which meaning bursts or shines forth) is Bhartrhari's technical term designating mantra as a gestalt or meaning-whole that can be perceived by the mind as an immediate supersensuous intuition. Let us return to the example of the rsi. At the first moment of its revelation, the rsi is completely caught up into this unitary idea, gestalt, or sphota. But when, under the expressive impulse (*kratu*), he starts to examine the idea (*sphota*) with an eye to its communication, he has withdrawn himself from the first intimate unity with the idea or inspiration itself and now experiences it in a twofold fashion. On the one hand, there is the objective meaning, which he is seeking to communicate, and on the other are the words and phrases he will utter. For Bhartrhari these two aspects of word sound and word meaning, differentiated in the mind and yet integrated like two sides of the same coin, constitute the sphota. Bhartrhari emphasizes the meaning-bearing or revelatory function of this two-sided gestalt, the sphota, which he maintains is eternal and inherent in consciousness.[35]

For the person hearing a mantra the process functions in reverse. Each repetition of the mantra removes karmic ignorance and brings further illumination. After sufficient repetitions (depending on the darkness of the person's karma) the sphota of the mantra stands clearly perceived—it is perhaps something like "the lightbulb coming on" we find in cartoons. As Bhartrhari puts it: "The sounds, while they manifest the word, leave impression-seeds progressively clearer and conducive to the clear perception of the word."[36]

The logic of Bhartrhari's philosophy is that the whole is prior to the parts. This results in an ascending hierarchy of mantra levels. Individual words are subsumed by the sentence or poetic phrase, the phrase by the Vedic poem, and so on until all speech is identified with Brahman. But Bhartrhari focuses upon the *vakya-sphota* or sentence meaning as the true form of meaning. Although he sometimes speaks about letter sounds or individual words as meaning-bearing units (*sphota*), it is clear that for Bhartrhari the true form of the sphota is the meaning-whole.[37] This has interesting implications for single-word mantras. Since the fundamental unit of meaning is a complete thought (*vakya-sphota*), single words must be single-word sentences with the missing words being understood. For example, when the young child says "Mama," it is clear that whole ideas are being expressed, such as, "I want Mama." Even when a word is used merely in the form of a substantive noun (e.g., "tree"), the verb "to be" is always understood, so that what is indicated is really a complete thought (e.g., "This is a tree").[38] In this fashion Bhartrhari suggests a way to understand single-word mantras as meaningful. A devotee chanting "Siva" may well be evoking the meaning "Come Siva" or "Siva possess me" with each repetition. Thus, such single-word mantras are far from being meaningless. They may invoke a world of meaning along with the power to purify one's human nature.

In Vedic ritual mantra is experienced on various levels, from the loud chanting of the priest to silently rehearsed knowledge of the most esoteric formulas.[39] Probably a good amount of the argument over the meaningfulness of *mantras* arises from a lack of awareness of the different levels of language. On one level there is the intuitive flashlike understanding of the meaning of the mantra as a whole. At this level the fullness of intuited meaning is experienced in the "seen" unity of sound and thought in sphota. This is the direct supersensuous perception of the truth of the mantra that occurs at the mystical level of language—when "mystical" is understood in its classical sense as a special kind of perception marked by greater clarity than ordinary sense perception.[40] Bhartrhari calls this level of mantra experience *pasyanti* (the seeing one)—the full meaning of the mantra, the reality it has evoked, stands revealed.[41] This is the rsi's direct "seeing" of truth, and the tantric devotee's visionary experience of the deity. Yet, for the uninitiated, for the one who has not yet had the experience, it is precisely this level of mantra that will appear to be nonexistent and meaningless. If, due to one's ignorance, the pasyanti level is obscured from "sight," then the uttering of the mantra will indeed seem to be an empty exercise.

Bhartrhari calls the level of the uttered words of the sentence *vaikhari*. At the vaikhari level every sound is inherently meaningful in that each sound attempts to reveal the sphota. Repetition of the uttered sounds of the mantra, especially if spoken clearly and correctly, will each time evoke afresh the sphota, until finally the obscuring ignorance (*karma*) is purged and the meaning-whole of the mantra is seen. Between these two levels of uttering (*vaikhari*) and supersensuous seeing (*pasyanti*) there is a middle level (*madhyama*) corresponding to the meaning-whole in its mental separation into meaning and a sequence of manifesting sounds, none of which have yet been uttered. For Bhartrhari the silent practice of mantra is accounted for by *madhyama*, and is, of course, real, meaningful, and able to purify consciousness.

When all three levels of language are taken into account, as they are by Bhartrhari, it would seem that all Vedic and other types of mantra practice can be analyzed and shown to be meaningful and powerful for perfecting human nature. In cases where the karmic ignorance of the speaker or the hearer obstructs the evocative power of the mantra, it may indeed be experienced as meaningless and powerless. But even then the mantra is still inherently meaningful, because it prepares the way for the sphota to be finally understood. Also, there is the fact that the cultured person, not afflicted by ignorance, hears and understands the meaning even though the person uttering the mantra does not.[42] The argument, of course, is circular, and if it were merely a theoretical argument, then Bhartrhari's explanation would have no power and would have been discarded long ago. However, Bhartrhari appeals not just to argument but also to empirical evidence—the direct perception of the meaning-whole (*sphota*) of the mantra and its power to purge karma. As long as such direct perception is reflected in the experience of people, Bhartrhari's explanation of the meaningfulness and powerfulness of mantras remains viable.

In the Indian experience the repeated chanting of mantras is an instrument for the perfecting of human nature.[43] The more difficulties (*karma*) there are to be overcome, the more repetitions are needed. Repeated use of correct mantras removes all impurities, purifies all knowledge, and leads to perfection or release. The psychological mechanism involved is described by Bhartrhari as a holding of the sphota in place by continued chanting. Just as from a distance, or in semidarkness, it takes repeated cognitions of an object before one sees it correctly, so also concentrated attention on the sphota by repeated chanting of the mantra results in the sphota finally being perceived in all its fullness.[44]

For Bhartrhari and the Grammarians, then, mantras are inherently meaningful, powerful in purging ignorance and revealing truth, and effective in bringing about the realization of moksa. Indeed Bhartrhari's theory helps our modern minds to understand how the chanting of mantras can be experienced as meaningful and powerful—in fact, "a Yoga of the Word" by which human nature may be perfected.[45]

THE SANKHYA-YOGA SCHOOLS AS FOUND IN
PATANJALI'S "YOGA SUTRAS"

India's traditional psychological understanding of human nature and its perfectibility is rooted in Kapila's Sankhya school (c. 500 BCE)[46] and Patanjali's Yoga school (c. 200–300 CE).[47] As we have seen, within Indian thought conceptions such as karma (memory traces from previous actions or thoughts) and samsara (rebirth) are taken as basic to all Jain, Buddhist and Hindu schools. There are also certain common conceptions about the psychological processes of human nature (e.g., the existence of cognitive traces or *samskaras*). Jadunath Sinha supports this contention in his finding that the psychological conception of yogic intuition (*pratibha*) is found in all schools with the exception of the Carvaka and the Mimamsa.[48] Mircea Eliade states that Yoga is one of the four basic motifs of all Indian thought and T. H. Stcherbatsky, the eminent Russian scholar of Buddhism, observes that Yogic trance (*samadhi*) and the Yogic courses for the training of the mind in the achievement of moksa or nirvana appear in virtually all Indian schools of thought.[49] Probably the most complete presentation of this traditional Indian psychology is to be found in the Yoga Sutras of Patanjali, and it is from this source that the following overview is presented.[50]

Yoga starts with an analysis of ordinary experience. This is characterized by a sense of restlessness caused by the distracting influences of our desires. Peace and purity of mind come only when the distractibility of our natures is controlled by the radical step of purging the passions. But if these troublesome passions are to be purged, they must be fully exposed to view. In this respect, Yoga predated Freud by several hundred years in the analysis of the unconscious. In the Yoga view, the sources of all our troubles are the karmic seeds (memory traces) of past actions or thoughts, heaped up in the unconscious or storehouse consciousness, as it is called in Yoga, and tainted by ignorance, materialistic, or sensuous desire, as well as the clinging to one's own ego. Thus, it is clear that traditional Yoga psychology gives ample recognition to the darker side of humans—the shadow consciousness.

At the ego-awareness level of consciousness, Yoga conceives of human cognition on various levels. There is the function of the mind in integrating and coordinating the input of sensory impressions and the resurgent memories of past thoughts and actions (*samskaras*). These may all be thought of as "learned" if we use behavioristic terminology. But then there is the higher function of the mind in making discriminative decisions as to whether or not to act on the impulses that are constantly flooding one's awareness. This discriminative capacity (*buddhi*) is not learned, but is an innate aspect of our psyche and has the capacity to reveal our true nature. This occurs when, by our discriminative choices, we negate and root out the polluting passions (*klista* karmas) from our unconscious until it is totally purified of their distracting restlessness—their "pulling" and "pushing" of us in one direction and then another. Once this is achieved by disciplined self-effort, the level of ego-consciousness is transcended, since the notion of ego, I or me, is also ultimately unreal. It is simply a by-product of one's selfish desiring. Once the latter is rooted out, the former by necessity also disappears, and the final level of human nature, pure or transcendent consciousness, is all that remains.

According to Yoga, transcendent consciousness is not immaterial, but is composed of high-quality, high-energy luminous material. Since all ego has been overcome, there is no duality, no subject-object awareness, but only immediate intuition. All experience is transcendent of individuality, although this is described differently by the various schools of Indian thought. The Hindus, for example, overcome the subject-object duality by resolving all objectivity into an absolute subject (i.e., Brahman). The Buddhists seem to go in the opposite direction and do away with all subjectivity, leaving only bare objective experience (i.e., nirvana, which may mean "all ego and desiring is blown out"). For our present purpose, the metaphysical speculation, although interesting, is not important. What is significant is that Yoga psychology finds the essence of human nature to be at the transcendent level of consciousness, where ego and unconscious desires have been excised. The various kinds of Yogic meditation are simply different practical disciplines or "therapies" for removing conscious and unconscious desires, along with the accompanying ego sense, from the psyche.

Let us stay with Patanjali's Yoga Sutras, although there are many other yogic schools of disciplined meditation from which one could choose (e.g., tantra, Hatha Yoga, Jainism, Taoism, and Zen). For Patanjali there are five prerequisite practices and three ultimate practices. The prerequisite practices include: (1) self-restraints (*yamas*: nonviolence, truthfulness, nonstealing, celibacy, and absence of avarice) to get rid of bad habits; (2) good habits (*niyamas*) to be instilled (washing of body and mind, contentment with whatever comes, equanimity in the face of life's trials, study and chanting of scriptures, meditation upon the Lord); (3) body postures (*asanas*) such as the lotus position to keep the body controlled and motionless during meditation; (4) controlled deepening of respiration (*pranayama*) to calm the mind; and (5) keeping senses (e.g., sight, hearing, and touch) from distracting one's mind (*pratyahara*) by focusing them on an object or point of meditation.

The ultimate practices are: (1) beginners spend brief periods of fixed concentration (*dharana*) upon an object (usually an image that represents an aspect of the divinity that appeals to one, such as Isvara, Siva, Krishna, or Kali); (2) as one becomes more expert, mediation (*dhyana*) upon the object is held for longer periods and the sense of subject-object separation begins to disappear from one's perception; (3) *samadhi* (concentration) occurs when continuous meditation upon the object loses all sense of subject-object separation—a state of direct intuition or becoming one with the object is achieved.

Through these yogic practices one has weakened the hold of the egocentric memories and desires (*karmas*) from the conscious and unconscious levels of one's psyche, and the discovery of the true self has begun. Four levels of samadhi, each more purified than the last, may be realized through repeated practice of yogic meditation. The final state (*nirvicara samadhi*) occurs when all obstructing ego desires have been purged from the psyche, which is now like a perfectly clear window to the aspect of the divine (e.g., Isvara, Siva, or, for a Westerner, perhaps Jesus) that has served as the object of meditation. According to the Yoga Sutras, any image will do. The divine image is only an instrument to aid in the direct experience of the transcendent—at which point the image is no longer needed.

Meditation of the sort prescribed by the Yoga Sutras is esoteric in nature, requires the supervision of a guru who has achieved perfection, and is a full-time occupation that, even in traditional India, was not possible for most people until the final stage of life—retirement from worldly affairs and withdrawal to a forest ashram. A major part of Patanjali's Yoga has much in common with the teaching of Bhartrhari, the Grammarian, when it comes to the use of mantra. In Patanjali's Yoga Sutras Isvara, like sabdabrahman, is described as an eternal unity of meaning and consciousness from which all speech, including the Vedic mantras, evolves.[51] Mantra, as the scriptural truth of the rsis, is taken to be the authoritative verbalization of Isvara's word-consciousness. All this is expressed in the sacred mantra, OM, which, when spoken, connotes Isvara and his omniscient consciousness. As was the case for Bhartrhari, it is the obscuring power of consciousness veiled by karmic ignorance that robs mantras of their inherent meaning and power.[52] And like Bhartrhari, Patanjali states that this ignorance can be removed through a constant repetition of appropriate Vedic mantras. Patanjali says that, as a result of constant chanting or study (*svadhyaya*) upon mantras (including seed or *bija* syllables like OM) the desired deity becomes visible.[53] Through the practice of fixed samadhi upon an object, in this case an uttered mantra, consciousness is purified of karmic obstructions and the deity "seen." Since for Patanjali OM is the mantra for Isvara, the devotee is advised that the *japa* or chanting of OM will result in the clear understanding of its meaning. Vyasa, a commentator on Patanjali, puts it in more psychological terms: "The yogi who has come to know well the relation between word and meaning must constantly repeat if [the mantra] and habituate the mind to the manifestation therein of its meaning. The constant repetition is to be of the *pranava* (OM) and the habitual mental manifestation is to be that of what it signifies, *Isvara*. The mind of the Yogi who constantly repeats the *pranava* and habituates the mind to the constant manifestation of the idea it carries, becomes one-pointed."[54]

What does it mean for the mind to become "one-pointed"? The "point" is the mantra that is being chanted. "One-pointed" means that the continual chanting of the mantra is keeping it front and center in one's mind to the exclusion of everything else that one might perceive or think. Through the chanting the devotee has become one with the mantra ("OM" in this case). It is as though one's whole world becomes only the mantra, and for the period of the chanting nothing else exists. It is like the experience we sometimes have when we find ourselves "caught up" in a piece of music to which we are listening—for the moment your hearing of the music fills the whole universe. Or it is like the experience of being in a moment of love or sexual intercourse with another person—for the moment everything else ceases to exist. You are "one-pointed." The yoga discipline described here involves becoming "one-pointed" or one with the mantra "OM" and what it signifies, Isvara.

The power of such mantra samadhi to induce a perfectly clear identity with the signified deity is given detailed psychological analysis in the commentary on Yoga Sutra 1.42. With continued mantra samadhi all traces of uttered sounds and conceptual meaning are purged until only the direct pure perception of Isvara remains. Patanjali's analysis supports Bhartrhari's claim that the repetition of mantra samadhi has the power to remove ignorance and reveal truth.[55] This conclusion confirms the Vedic mantra experience (previously discussed).

As an additional aspect of the practice of mantra concentration and chanting, Patanjali prescribes the yogic discipline of making Isvara the motive of all one's actions (*isvarapranidhanam*).[56] It is as though one is to become an "empty channel" through which Isvara (who is being held steady at the center of one's mind through the chanting or meditation upon OM) acts. In one's yoga practice one is attempting to emulate Isvara, the master Yogi, so what better way than to attempt to act in every situation as though he were acting through you? It is rather like the young hockey player who tries to keep Gretzky front and center in his mind so that as he goes down the ice all his moves will be those of the Great One. While chanting OM one "dedicates" all one's moves (as it were) to Isvara. The result of such complete self-surrender, says the Yoga text, is a vision of Isvara. One has made one's consciousness so pure and transparent, or sattvic, that only Isvara, the master Yogi, shines through. One's human nature has realized Isvara's perfection.

We have seen that in traditional Yoga psychology it is generally accepted that the chanting of a special scriptural word or phrase, chosen for one by one's guru, has power to remove the obstructing ego desires until the transcendent stands fully revealed. The Yoga of the Word assumes that the scriptural word and the divine are mutually intertwined—very much as stated in John 1:1, "In the beginning was the Word, and the Word was with God, and the Word was God." The word is therefore filled with divine power, and when meditated upon by repeated chanting is able to remove obstructions of consciousness. The guru chooses the scriptural word best suited to remove current karma in the mind of the devotee. The power of the chosen mantra to remove obstructions is enhanced by the intensity and duration of the chanting. Chanting may be either aloud or silent. As the first obstructions are removed, the guru prescribes a new mantra better suited to tackle the remaining, more subtle obstructions. The more obstacles in the mind to be overcome, the more repetitions are needed. When the chanting removes the final obstacles, the psyche is like a purified or cleaned window fully revealing the divine as a direct intuition to the devotee— a vision of the Lord is experienced, and samadhi, or union with the transcendent, is realized. With proper Yoga, words are experienced as having the power to remove ignorance (*avidya*), reveal Dharma, and realize moksa. It is this traditional Yoga that is behind the mantra chanting, common throughout traditional Hinduism and Buddhism, and today encountered in North America or Europe in the chanting of "Hare Krishna" and the teaching of meditation mantras by Transcendental Meditation.

CONCLUSION

Indian philosophy develops around 500 BCE, the same time period as the rise of Greek philosophy in the West. The basic schools of Indian philosophy form two groups in terms of their relationship to the already existing Hindu scriptures, the Vedas. The Hindu Astika or "Yes-saying" schools drew their basic ideas from the Vedas, organized them into systematic philosophical form, and added philosophical speculation. The

Nastika or "no-saying" schools of Jainism and Buddhism developed their thinking as a rejection of the main teachings of the Vedas—especially in regard to the makeup of human nature and how it is to be perfected. Both the Astika and Nastika philosophical schools, however, adopt a common worldview marked by the basic presuppositions of anadi or beginninglessness of creation, karma, samsara or rebirth, and release from rebirth as the result of having perfected oneself by purging the obscuring karma from one's nature. How to get release is the fundamental question for Indian philosophy, psychology, and religion. It receives different answers from the Astika and Nastika schools—from Hinduism, on the one side, and Buddhism, on the other. But all agree that the goal for all beings is to perfect or release themselves and that we will be reborn over and over again until that goal is realized—not in the afterlife, as is often suggested in Western thought, but here on earth. All of this is quite different than the thinking of Western philosophy, psychology, and religion that we examined in part I.

In this chapter we began by describing the basic ideas of the Indian worldview and the ancient Rig Veda from which they arose. We then sampled the philosophical thought of some Astika or orthodox schools of Indian philosophy—the Mimamsa and Grammarian schools and their focus on the use of Vedic language, and the Sankhya-Yoga or school of traditional psychology and the specific yogic practices developed for the perfection of human nature. This traditional Yoga psychology functions in common for all Indian philosophy and religion at the level of physical and mental practice, in spite of major disagreements at the level of metaphysical beliefs. We also observed a common approach to the understanding and use of mantra chanting as having particular power to purify and perfect human nature. With this introduction to the Indian way of understanding and perfecting human nature in mind, let us now turn to a detailed study of Hindu ideas (chapter 7), and Buddhist ideas (chapter 8).

Chapter 7

The Perfectibility of Human Nature in Hindu Thought

Hindu thought adopts the presuppositions of the Indian worldview outlined in the previous chapter—namely, the ideas that creation is beginningless, that our personalities are structured by the karma or memory traces of previous actions and thoughts, that we are reborn from past lives, and that this process of birth-death-rebirth will continue until release from rebirth is realized. For Hindus such a release or moksa and is understood as the perfection of human nature and the end-goal of the various spiritual disciplines or yogas provided by the tradition. What these yogas offer are ways of overcoming or purging the karmas that are obscuring the divine *atman*, which is the true self within. Once the last obscuring karma is removed then one realizes that one's true self is not one's body or mind but rather the divine atman (pure being, consciousness, and bliss) within. In that moment moksa or release from rebirth is realized, and for Hindus that is the goal of perfection that all must eventually achieve. As to the question of whether moksa is realized at the moment of death or during life, there are differing views. But the idea that perfection or moksa is realized while one is alive became popular in Hindu thought and was given the name *jivanmukti*, which means "embodied liberation." We will begin our study of Hindu thought by examining the ideas about human nature and its perfectibility found in the Hindu scriptures, the Vedas, and then go on to consider the interpretation given to the idea of jivanmukti by thinkers such as Sankara, Ramanuja, Patanjali, Ramana Maharshi, and Vivekananda.

HUMAN NATURE IN THE VEDAS

Ideas of human nature in the early Vedic hymns (c. 1500–1000 BCE) are embedded in mythic and ritualistic contexts. In the early Vedas humans are treated as more earthly and temporal beings than in the later Upanishads and subsequent Hindu thought. In the Vedic hymns persons are referred to by the terms *purusa* (person), *atman* (breath), and *jiva* (life).[1] In the Rig Veda (RV) the word *jiva* designates a living breathing being—as, for example, in "Rise, woman and go to the world of living beings (*jivas*)" (RV 10.2.2.8), while the term *atman* is used in a cremation prayer to Agni in which the self (*atman*) is seen to be different from the body: "Agni, consume him not entirely. . . . Let the eye repair to the sun, the breath (*atman*) to the wind" (RV 10.1.16.3). In addition to evoking "breath," atman can refer to the body (RV 10.8.7.8) and the "whole person" (RV 10.12.12.5–6). Atman is also used to imply "existence" or "life force" (RV 7.6.12.6) as well as to designate one's essential identity (RV 9.4.18.3). In the Brahmanas, the commentaries on the early Vedic hymns dated c. 1000–800 BCE) humans are described as animals, but they are the preeminent animals and rulers of all other animals in that they are able to perform rituals with power to influence the universe. This power comes from the association of humans with Brahman, the divine principle.[2] The Vedic approach offers a body-oriented view of human nature, as evidenced by its emphasis on the human as the agent of ritual and sacrificial acts. Yet there is a pervasive holism of body and consciousness in Vedic views. While the person is seen dualistically in Greek thought, in the vision of the Vedic rsis or seers the person is a unity of embodied consciousness that requires the codependent action of both body and consciousness in order to carry out the required ritual and sacrificial actions.[3]

The supremacy of humans over other animals is seen in the human intelligence and the ability to know the future, which leads to the desire for moksa or freedom from worldly limitations. In the Vedic view such freedom is achieved by ritual action informed by the knowledge of dharma or righteousness. The capacity to understand and act according to the requirements of dharma is what makes humans superior to animals and capable of achieving perfection. According to the Veda the highest potential of humans is not found in the exercise of their superior rational power to achieve dominion over the earth and its creatures. Indeed, in the Vedic view such dominion is undesirable. Rather, the goal of humans is to become liberated or released from this world, not to become master of it. The purpose of life is to use our human existence as a vehicle of transcendence to achieve the final goal of liberation or perfection.[4]

The Upanishads (c. 800–500 BCE) are a portion of the Vedas written in the form of philosophical dialogues between teachers and students. The Upanishads offer a variety of descriptions of human nature, but in most of them the person's fundamental nature, atman, is identified with the one Divine, Brahman. For example, in the *Chandogya Upanishad*, book 6, Svetsketu is taught that the one Divine longed to become many, diversified into the elements of fire, water, and earth, and entered these elements as atman. Thus atman is the ground or essence of all created things, just as clay is the basis of all clay objects. In chapter 2 of the *Taittiriya Upanishad* we find an analysis of human nature that has been widely adopted within Hindu thought.[5] It describes the true self, the atman, as enclosed within five sheaths or *kosas*. These are the physical sheath (*annamaya kosa*), the vitality or breath sheath (*pranamaya kosa*), the mind sheath (*manomaya kosa*), the intellect sheath (*vijnanamaya kosa*), and the bliss sheath (*anandamaya kosa*). The five sheaths or kosas are conceived as enveloping one another with the atman, their true Self, at the center. "The outermost sheath is the *body of food*, or the material body, which is filled successively with the sheath or body of *prana*, breath (life-force), then *mind, consciousness*, and at the center, *bliss*. The sheath of bliss is interpreted as either identical to, or containing[,] the innermost true Self, the *atman*."[6] The five-sheath model of human nature in the Upanishads is adopted by the Vedanta school of Hindu philosophy and by many postclassical schools of Yoga, but not by Patanjali's classical school, which adopts a dualistic view of human nature more typical of that found in the *Maitri Upanishad*. With something of the dualism of Greek thought, *Maitri Upanishad* 1.3 describes the body as an ill-smelling conglomerate of bone, skin, muscle, semen, blood, mucus, feces, urine, wind, bile, and phlegm, and afflicted with anger, desire, covetousness, delusion, and envy, which must be separated from the true Self.

With these views of human nature in mind, let us now sample some specific teachings on moksa or release from rebirth as found in the Upanishads. The concept of moksa is sometimes thought of as the ability to perfect oneself by choosing one's own actions. The *Chandogya Upanishad* tells of the learned Narada coming to Sanatkumara for instruction on the nature of Brahman. Sanatkumara asks Narada what he knows. Narada replies that he knows the four Vedas and the Puranas, along with many other things. He also knows that he lacks the all-important knowledge that will enable him to escape rebirth and realize release. Sanatkumara responds that Narada's problem is that he has learned merely the names of things. His knowledge is too shallow. While Narada's knowledge allows him to talk about many things, he is limited by the words he uses and does not know reality itself. "Is there more than name?" asks Narada. "Assuredly there is more than name," says Sanatkumara, who then proceeds to lead Narada step-by-step into the full realization of the Self as Brahman: "The Soul (*Atman*), indeed, is below. The Soul is above. The Soul is to the east. The Soul is to the south. The Soul is to the north. The Soul, indeed, is this whole world."[7] The one who fully understands this, says Sanatkumara, is self-ruled (*sva-raj*); the one who does not understand this is ruled by others (*anya-raj*). The former has perfection or moksa; the latter does not.

Narada's problem is that while he had much knowledge of the scriptural texts and could describe them in such detail that he could pass difficult examinations, this descriptive knowledge—knowledge of "name and form"—did not give him perfection or release from rebirth. Indeed, with much descriptive knowledge comes the danger of self-conceit or scholarly pride. We think we know a lot, but the darkness of our intellectual conceit leaves us worse off than the ignorance of those who trust in worldly works. As the *Isa Upanishad* puts it, "Into blinding darkness enter those who worship ignorance and those who delight in knowledge enter into still greater darkness, as it were."[8] Release cannot be obtained by the works, or material possessions, of the world, although they are essential for the householder stage. Only when one's householder duties to family and society have been fulfilled is it acceptable to move on to the spiritual life of the forest dweller. And even then one must study the scripture with the correct motivation—not just to know what the texts say, as Narada did, but to have the direct experience of that to which they point, as did the rsis. The *Isa Upanishad* distinguishes between knowledge by description and knowledge by acquaintance. I can describe my wife in terms of her age, height, weight, color, her family and educational history, and so on, but that is a very superficial knowledge when compared with the knowledge I have of her as lover, when the two of us become as one. That is knowledge by acquaintance or direct experience—knowledge that can never be captured in words. A Shakespearean love sonnet may evoke it but not define it. It is like that with the Upanishads. Their aim is to move one beyond descriptions of the essence of the world or of oneself to the direct experience of it—an experience that brings perfection or release from karmic ignorance and rebirth. So the *Mundaka Upanisad* states, "This self [*atman*] cannot be attained by instruction nor by intellectual power."[9] Rather, when one's thought is purified and karma is purged, then one's Self (*atman*) shines forth.[10] Then one has the direct realization of being one with Brahman and is not reborn.[11]

It is important to understand this teaching of the Upanishads about moksa in the context of the stages of life described in chapter 6. Hinduism is not a world-denying religion. Only when the responsibilities and joys of the student and householder stages have been fully enjoyed is one ready—if one has the deep desire—to move on to the final stages of seeking perfection or release from rebirth. One seeks to be freed from a worldly and sensuous life that has been tasted to the full and from the limitations of conceptual knowledge that leave one's deepest questions unanswered. There is also the matter of evil (*papa*) or sin (*papman*), which according to the *Chandogya Upanishad* is the final karma to be overcome before moksa is realized.[12] The Upanishads are not specific as to how sin and evil are to be shaken off, but there are many references to cleansing via "fire." As the *Maitri Upanishad* puts it, it is the fire of *tapas* or intense meditation in the face of austerities that rapidly "burns off" one's accumulated sinful karmas.[13] Such a process, says the *Brhad-Aranyaka Upanishad*, consumes all one's evil until one becomes "clean and pure, ageless and immortal."[14] The evils from which one must be liberated are the imperfections of one's own physical, intellectual, and moral nature. Morality is required but, for perfection or moksa, much more than mere morality is needed. What is required is nothing less than a comprehensive vision of the whole rather than of the part, and a spiritual discipline or pathway (*marga*) that makes the realization of all human potentialities possible.

The Upanishads offer a very optimistic view regarding the perfectibility of human nature. The goal of moksa is to become the perfect person that underneath the obscuring karma one already is. The goal of one's spiritual quest, which may extend over several lifetimes, is to find the atman, the true Self within. Then the beginningless cycle of birth-death-rebirth (*karma-samsara*) will be ended and release realized. The *Brhad-Aranyaka Upanishad* tells of this quest for the self by Janaka, the king of Videha.[15] In dialogue with the rsi Yajnavalkya, Janaka asks what the light is that will guide a person through the earthly journey. The light of the sun, replies Yajnavalkya. But what guides one when the sun sets? asks Janaka. The moon, replies the rsi, testing the seriousness of his pupil and then offering fire and speech as the next answers. But, responds Janaka, when the sun has set and the moon has set, and the first has gone out, and speech is hushed, what light does a person then have for guidance? The Self or soul (*atman*) is the person's ultimate light, says Yajnavalkya, for with it one sits, moves around, does one's work, and returns.[16] The rsi then leads Janaka into a deeper awareness of the Self by describing various psychological states in which it is experienced—first in dreams, then in deep dreamless sleep, and finally in death. But in none of these states is the Self freed from its obscuring veil of karma and so it continually returns to worldly life. Throughout this dialogue with his teacher Yajnavalkya, King Janaka offers the gift of a thousand cows for the answer that will set him free. Finally, Yajnavalkya describes the atman that is released from rebirth and again the king offers a thousand cows for that knowledge. The liberated Self or atman, says the rsi, is not this, it is not that (*neti, neti*); it is unseizable, it is indestructible, it does not attach itself, it is unbound, it is not injured, and one sees everything as the atman. The moment of discovery finally arrives for Janaka when he realizes that this liberating and perfecting knowledge is not something he can buy with gifts of cows or any other worldly wealth, but is an insight he must realize within himself. The "lightbulb" must go on within, as the cartoons depict it. The king must be ready to give himself up in order to realize his own release. His salvation rests in his own hands. It is nothing less than the realization that one's true inner Self, for which one has been searching through many lifetimes is none other than Brahman, the Divine itself. As the great summary sentence (*mahavakya*) of the Upanishads puts it, *Tat tvam asi* (That thou art). That Brahman, the essence of the cosmos, is your atman or inner Self. Brahman = Atman.[17] You, minus your karmic constructions of body/mind/ego, are nothing but Brahman. That, for the Upanishads, is the liberating knowledge, the "lightbulb" experience by which moksa is realized. The purpose of the philosophical dialogue between the rsi and the student leading up to the statement of the *mahavakya* by the rsi is to systematically remove the obstructions of karmic ignorance in the mind of the student, which are preventing him or her from directly perceiving the Divine. The systematic use of reasoning in removing ignorance so that the immediate unshakable experience of Brahman can arise, is characteristic of the Upanishadic approach to the Divine. It is called the path of knowledge or the *jnana marga*. Various exegetical tactics are adopted by the Upanishadic rsis in their use of reasoning. One tactic is to seek to identify the essence of the empirical world with its underlying unity (e.g., *Mundaka Upanishad* 1.1.3). Another tactic is to raise the ultimate questions that seek to reveal the reality underlying all change and suffering (e.g., *Chandogya Upanishad* 6.2.1ff.). Perhaps the most difficult of these methods for the student is the wisdom required for the admission that one's own intellectual prowess and system-building achievements do not attain for one the Truth (e.g., *Katha Upanishad* 2.23). The use of the intellect will help by removing the obstructions of wrong ideas, but in the end all pride, even such a meritorious achievement as knowledge of the Veda itself, must be overcome by spiritual and mental discipline so that the intuition of the Divine can occur (*Katha Upanishad* 6.10ff.). And in this direct vision, the Divine is found to be the overflowing of peace and bliss, or *ananda*, upon which all life depends (*Taittiriya Upanishad* 2.8–9).

Following the Upanishads, the next category of Hindu scripture is the epic poems, which offer different descriptions of human nature, and more variety in the paths one may follow to achieve perfection. In the Bhagavad Gita (c. 150 BCE) the setting is a battlefield where the warrior Arjuna is instructed by Lord Krishna. At first Arjuna is overwhelmed to find himself in a situation where his caste duty as a prince or warrior might require him to do battle with uncles and cousins lined up in the opposing army; he may even be forced to kill them. This he does not want to do. But then Lord Krishna, disguised as Arjuna's chariot driver, teaches him that the true Self is not the body that may be killed in battle. The true Self is eternal and does not die but is reborn in a series of new bodies. In each new birth it is as if the true Self puts on a new set of clothes. As Gita 2.20 and 2.22 put it, the true Self does not kill, nor can it be killed: "[U]nborn, eternal, everlasting is this [Self], primeval. It is not slain when the body is slain. . . . As a man casts off his worn-out clothes and takes on other new ones, so does the embodied [Self] cast off its worn-out bodies and enters other new ones."[18] Having established the immortality of the embodied Self, Lord Krishna goes on to teach that the Self does become linked with an individual psychological organism or, as Indian psychology puts it, a karmic nature that constantly dies and is reborn (Gita 2.26). In itself, the true Self is timeless and eternal, yet in its transmigration from body to body it is connected with a given personality created by the person's freely chosen karmic actions in previous births. Perfection or release from rebirth consists in the final freeing of the eternal true Self from the karmic personality to which it is bound. All traces of being a separate ego or of having material possessions must be ruthlessly purged away if the true Self is to be recognized for what it is—namely, a "minute part" of Brahman, the Divine. While involved in the process of birth, death, and rebirth, the Self is so closely identified with the karmic personality that one is fooled into thinking that the embodied human nature is the true Self (Gita 3.40). But, according to the Gita, one can achieve perfection and realize one's eternal true Self by a process of "integration" or intense yogic concentration and by complete detachment from the outside world. Sitting in a yoga pose with all of one's senses and thoughts focused on the Lord, one cuts the habit patterns of karmic attachment to sensory actions or material possessions and is freed to experience one's true Self as a state of pure Brahman (Gita 2.61–72). No longer is one seduced by the wandering mind with its karmic attachment to objects and desires, or by thoughts such as "I am this" or "this is mine." Freed from such thoughts and desires, one rests in the peace of the fixed, still state of Brahman, the Divine (Gita 2.71–72).

To realize oneness with Brahman does not mean going into some different state of being from what we are now; it means to enter into fully perfected human life of eternal freedom. The Bhagavad Gita refers to it as *brahman-nirvana*—a state of freedom to be experienced here and now, not some time after death. Whereas the Upanishads focus on the path (*marga*) of thought or knowledge for realizing release, the Gita takes a more inclusive approach and identifies the additional paths of action, devotion, and discipline, each of which will also get one to moksa. And whereas in orthodox Hindu society, the Upanishadic path of knowledge (*jnana marga*) was reserved for males of the upper three caste groups, the teaching of the Gita opened the way to salvation for all, regardless of caste or gender. The path of action (*karma marga*) requires that one do one's duty in society, whether that be as a homemaker, mother, nurse, carpenter, or garbage collector, with no thought for one's own fame, privilege, or financial reward, but simply as a dedication to the Lord. The intensity of that dedication will rapidly burn up one's obscuring karma, and when the last karma is removed by such dedicated service, moksa, oneness with Brahman is realized. As the Gita puts it, "[W]ork alone is your proper business, never the fruits it may produce."[19] All work, whatever one's job may be, is to be done in a spirit of sacrifice, never with any thought for personal gain. This is the path of karma for realizing perfection or release.

The path of devotion (*bhakti*), like the path of action, is described in the Gita as open to all regardless of sex or caste status in society. All that is required is the intense practice of daily devotion to the Lord in ritual service, songs of praise, or depth of prayer meditation. The intensity of this devotion together with the grace given by God will burn up one's obscuring karma and when the last karma is removed, release is realized. And this response is not left solely up to our human effort, as was the case in the Upanishads. In the Gita, Lord Krishna is seen as an incarnation of the Divine who comes to earth to help humans achieve their goal of perfection or release. God's grace is given to the dedicated devotee in the form of help from Lord Krishna. As the Gita puts it,

> But men intent on me
> renounce all actions to me
> and worship me, meditating
> with singular devotion.
> When they entrust reason to me,
> Arjuna, I soon arise
> to rescue them from the ocean
> of death and rebirth.

> Focus your mind on me,
> let your understanding enter me;
> then you will dwell
> in me without doubt.[20]

The path of devotion introduced in the Gita is the one most followed by the masses of Hindus. Some suggest that it is the favored method of realizing release in the teachings of the Gita.[21]

The final path described in the Gita is that of Yoga, or self-discipline. It is a practical psychological technique of meditation that enables one to burn off karma and realize perfection or release. Yoga technique allows one to achieve the goals that are set forth in Hindu philosophy and religion. As the Gita puts it, "This wisdom has been revealed to you in theory; listen now to how it should be practiced."[22] It is this practice, in modified form, that has become popular throughout the world today, including sitting in the lotus position, controlling one's breathing, and focusing one's senses for long periods of meditation. The classic statement of Yoga practice in Hinduism is found in Patanjali's Yoga Sutras, texts dated to about 200 CE.[23] The Gita differs from Patanjali's presentation in seeing the true Self within, the purusa, not as an independently existing entity but as a minute part of God. However, regardless of differences of theoretical understanding, the Gita agrees that disciplined yogic meditation is yet another pathway or method by which one may obtain release. We will examine this approach along with the other margas of knowledge, action, and devotion in the next section. Commentaries and contemporary examples from each of these paths to perfection will be examined as they have been developed beyond the Hindu scriptures.

HUMAN NATURE IN HINDU PHILOSOPHY AND RELIGION

A great variety of philosophical and religious schools have risen out of the scriptures of the Hindu tradition. They give further development to the ideas of human nature and the ways to release of knowledge (*jnana marga*), action (*karma marga*), devotion (*bhakti marga*), and self-discipline (*yoga marga*). These developments were often fostered by major thinkers who composed commentaries expounding the seed ideas of, for example, the Upanishads and the Bhagavad Gita. Sometimes a path (e.g., the *bhakti marga*) was elaborated by the inspired singing of poet-saints who attracted large followings. Master Yogis appeared pioneering spiritual disciplines of austerity that resulted in ashrams of devoted students. These and many other developments have continued to evolve in the living tradition of Hinduism right up to today. In what follows we will give a brief sampling of these developments following the four paths of Hindu scripture. Out survey will conclude with an examination of the Hindu idea of jivanmukti or perfection while living.

Jnana Marga

As we have seen above, the Upanishads are filled with teachings about ignorance and moksa. These teachings provided the basis for the use of knowledge as a pathway or means of reaching perfection or release from rebirth. But the Upanishads do not offer a consistent point of view. While they share common ideas, there are also many conflicts. The basis for a unified path of knowledge was provided by Badarayana, who lived in the third or fourth century CE. Known as the *vyasa* or arranger, Badarayana selected and organized the key teachings of the Upanishads into a series of summary sentences known as the *Brahma Sutra* or "the summary sentences about *Brahman*."[24] These sutras, or summary sentences, established the foundational basis for the jnana marga. But they did it in shorthand form, most probably for ease of memorization. It has remained for commentators to draw out the meaning of these sentences. This they have done, beginning with Sankara (788–820 CE) and continuing right up to the present day. But there is wide agreement that Sankara was the greatest. He was the founder of the Advaita Vedanta school that was directed chiefly against Buddhism— a movement that at the time was very widespread in India. He set for himself the goal of defeating Buddhism on two fronts, the practical and the theoretical. On the practical side, much of the Buddhist success came from the monastic movement that the Buddha had pioneered and universities that had been established throughout India. To counter this, Sankara introduced the practice of monasteries to a tradition that had previously known only family worship and, in the last two stages of life, isolated holy wanderers (*sannyasin*). Following the Buddhist example, Sankara established communities of Hindu monks and located them strategically in, as it were, the four corners of India (Himalayas, Mysore, Gujarat, and Orissa). These four *mathas*, as Sankara called them, offered key locations from which the spread of Buddhism was effectively challenged.

But this organizational response would not have been successful without a knowledge-content to teach. Sankara developed his view of human nature in the *Viveka-cudamani* (The Crest-Jewel of Discrimination), written in the eighth century CE. In it Sankara simplifies the

Upanishadic notion of the person as being composed of five sheaths or kosas (described above) into a description of the essential Self or atman as clothed with three bodies.[25] The gross body (*sthula sarira*) is the physical body that in ordinary life we erroneously think of as the Self. This mistake is partly the result of our preoccupation with experiences of pleasure and pain. The physical body is the medium through which the Self experiences our physical world in the waking state. The physical body, as a finite object, is born, grows, gets old, and finally dies. The Self or atman is different from the body just as the householder is different from the house in which he or she lives. The Self is the knower of the experiences that come to us through the body and its sense organs, and gives consciousness to the body that would otherwise be inert. This essential distinction between the Self and the body does not mean that the body is unimportant. "While the self is equally present in all things, the *Upanisads* teach that the human being is uniquely capable of distinguishing the self from the non-self and arriving at knowledge of its true nature."[26] The value of the birth of the Self in a human body is that it provides the opportunity for the perfecting of oneself and eventual release from rebirth or moksa.

In addition to the physical body, atman is also associated with the *suksma sarira* (subtle body). It is called the subtle body because it is composed of the same elements as the physical body but in subtle form. It also includes five vital forces, five sense organs, five organs of action, the mind, and the intellect. Although the sense organs and the organs of action in their gross forms are located in the physical body, they receive their powers of functioning from their counterparts in the subtle body. Without the subtle body, the physical body is unable to function. But when the physical body dies, the subtle body continues to exist and is reborn with a new physical body in the next life. The subtle body is the repository of the individual karmic traces that make up our unique tendencies or characteristics and thus carry our personality from one life to the next. Throughout this process the subtle body remains in close association with the atman until the process of perfection is complete and moksa occurs.

The third and final bodily enclosure of the Self is the *karana sarira*, the causal or karmic body. This body is especially evident in the state of deep sleep when our individual karma or personality traits enter into a state of suspended potential or seedlike condition from which they again manifest themselves when we dream or wake up. This causal body, although it is the causal source of our dreaming and waking states, is also referred to as a body of ignorance, because when we are in the state of deep sleep we are unconscious. It contains the samskaras or karmic memory traces of actions and thoughts in this and previous lives. Thus it also contains the possibilities for future action and thought that our karmic memory traces may manifest if allowed to by our free choice. Therefore, the causal body contains and carries from life to life the possibilities of how a person's particular human nature will unfold.

As Rambacan emphasizes, in this view of human nature it is important to remember "that the self is different from all three bodies. In relation to them the *atman* is knower and subject. It is unchanging awareness, while all three bodies are subject to fluctuation and change."[27] In this simplification of the Upanishadic views Sankara established a conception of human nature that continues to be widely used, not only within the Vedanta school of philosophy, but within Hinduism in general. With this view of human nature in mind, let us see how Sankara suggests that it may be perfected until moksa is realized.

Sankara developed this description of human nature in his commentary on Badarayana's summary sentences of the Upanishads,[28] along with other commentaries on the key Upanishadic texts themselves and the Bhagavad Gita. Sankara's Advaita Vedanta or nondual teaching of the way to perfection or release runs as follows. The Upanishads teach us that ultimately there is only one reality, namely Brahman. Everything else that seems to be something different from Brahman—you, me, the world around us—is composed of the karma that covers and obscures our true Self. Sankara calls this obscuring karma *maya*, which he defines as neither real nor unreal but mysterious. It has the reality of a snake that one takes to be real when it is only a mistakenly perceived rope. Just as when one sees the rope clearly the illusion of snake vanishes forever, so also when we have a clear perception of Brahman—the essence of each of us and the world around us—then the obscuring maya that has made us seem different from Brahman is seen to be ultimately unreal and disappears permanently. That is release, moksa. As to how one reaches this new awareness of one's true nature, Sankara begins by stating two requirements. First, one must have fulfilled the ritual and moral requirements (*dharma*) to one's family and society. Second, one must have a burning desire to obtain release. Sankara's method is meditation on the mahavakyas, or great sentences of the Upanishads, under the guidance of a guru, or teacher. Study of the Upanishads will gradually cancel out incorrect ideas of our true nature (e.g., that the real me is my body, my thought, etc.), as we saw above in the dialogue of King Janaka with his teacher Yajnavalkya. The student is moved step-by-step from thinking of reality as the world external to the body, to thinking of it as the senses and the mind, until finally it is shown to be nothing but the inner light of consciousness itself—atman/Brahman. Sankara's method is for the guru to patiently show the student the inadequacy of each incorrect perception of reality until the common kinds of ignorance about life, with which we all begin, are shown to be wrong—like the mistaking of rope for snake. This is like the *neti neti* (not that, not this) approach of the Upanishads. When, through negation of wrong answers, the student's mind is almost fully cleared of obscuring incorrect ideas or karmas, the teacher, judging the time is right, says to the student *tat tvam asi*—"that thou art"—or one of the other mahavakyas. Hearing these words produces the final inner flash of insight, like the lightbulb-coming-on experience of the cartoon, which simultaneously cancels out the last remaining karma, leaving only the steady and continuous experience of Brahman. With the last karma removed so too is the cause of rebirth. Moksa is realized.

Turning to a contemporary exemplar of Advaita and Sankara, Ramana Maharshi (1879–1950), we find a similar emphasis on the primacy of direct experience. In fact, Ramana had his own experience of self-realization without any role whatsoever being played by scripture. When he was seventeen Ramana was suddenly overcome by a feeling that he was going to die. Rather than look for a doctor, he decided that he had to solve the problem himself. "With a view of finding out what it was that was mortal, he lay down and made his body stiff like a corpse. Then he realized suddenly that there was death only for the body and not for the Self, the 'I' within, which is deathless."[29] As Balasubramanian notes, Ramana had not yet been exposed to the Upanishads or the teachings of Sankara. He did not go through the traditional jnana marga pattern of disciplined scriptural study, rational reflection thereon, and repeated meditation until what we have called the "lightbulb" experience of oneness with Brahman occurred. Rather, Ramana began at a very young age with the "lightbulb" experience and then went on to study the scriptural texts. As he puts it, "I had never heard of *Brahman, samsara,* and so forth. I did not know yet that there was an essence or impersonal Real underlying everything and that Isvara [the Lord] and I were both identical with it. Later . . . as I listened . . . to sacred books, I learnt all this and found that the books were analysing and naming what I had felt intuitively without analysis or name."[30]

For Ramana, the *anubhava* or Self-realization experience was primary; the scriptures were secondary. The role of sacred texts and philosophy is not to convey anything positive about reality or the divine but simply to negate the false, which in ordinary life passes for reality. Like the "not that, not this" (*neti, neti*) of the *Upanishads,*[31] the purpose of Ramana's descriptive negation of ordinary thought is designed to reveal the substratum that underlies all names and forms. As Ramana says, "It underlies all limitations, being itself limitless. It is not bound in any way. It underlies unrealities, being itself Real. It is that which is. . . . It transcends speech and is beyond description such as being or non-being."[32] The major obstacle blocking this discovery is the I, or ego, which takes itself to be necessary for realizing knowledge. Ramana's claim, consistent with the Upanishads, is that only when the ego and the "I-thought" are removed is the veil of karmic ignorance lifted and the Self able to shine of its own accord. This is Self-realization or moksa— a state in which "there is neither the mind nor the body; and in the absence of the mind and the body, there is no such thing as the world. "Such a one has attained liberation."[33] The Self is not known in the way that we know material objects—through our sense organs and our mind. Unlike worldly objects, the Self is self-luminous and reveals itself when the obscuring obstruction (i.e., the karmic ego) is removed. This is the purpose of Ramana's method of Self-inquiry. It calls for intense meditation in which the mind counters its obsession with the objects of the world and turns inward. Only a mind that is pure will turn inward, and this requires a diet of moderate amounts of pure vegetarian food and fully moral conduct. As Ramana puts it, "The mind turned outward results in thoughts and objects. Turned inward it becomes itself, the Self."[34] The method of Self-inquiry aims at the removal of the mind by discovering its divine source. Ramana does acknowledge that there are other methods for the removal of ego and the realization of release, one of which is the path of love and devotion (*bhakti*) to which we now turn.

BHAKTI MARGA

The focus in the path of *bhakti* or devotion is on the love and worship through which one purges the obscuring karma and loses oneself in communion with the Lord. It is therefore a theistic path as opposed to the monism of the jnana path. While the jnana marga approach led to the monastic ashrams of Sankara, the devotional approach led to theistic communities centered around manifestations of the divine in the form of gods such as Siva and Vishnu. Let us take as an example the Srivaisanava community of South India, which worships the Lord Vishnu and his consort, Sri, and considers the theologian Ramanuja (1017–1137 CE) as its founding interpreter of scripture.[35] In addition to the Vedas, the epic poems of the Bhagavad Gita and the Ramayana, and the Puranas, the Srivaisanavas include some sacred texts written in Tamil composed by poet-saints who lived between the seventh and tenth centuries CE, the *alvar*s, who were immersed in the love of Lord Vishnu.

The alvars' poems are filled with intense emotion and intellectual devotion, or bhakti, which includes the senses of belonging to, attachment, trust, homage, worship, faith and love. "The *bhakti* of the *alvars* was manifested in ecstatic and ritual surrender to the Lord, singing the glory and majesty of the divine name, a sustained meditation on the divine attributes and service to the deity and other devotees."[36] In their interpretations of the founder Ramanuja's vision of how to reach release, the Srivaisnava community split into two groups—the Vadagalais (the Northern "monkey" school) and the Tengalais (the Southern "cat" school). The distinction between the two schools is the degree of self-effort or God's grace required for one's surrender to the Lord and release from rebirth. Let us begin with Ramanuja's teaching and then examine the differences his followers introduced.

Ramanuja knew Sankara's teachings well and disagreed with them sharply. While Sankara may have helped revive Hinduism in the face of the Buddhist challenge, Ramanuja saved Hinduism from becoming a "philosophers-only religion" and opened it to engage in the everyday experience of emotion and sense in the worship of God. Like Sankara, Ramanuja accepted that a person's human nature and its karma were what bound him or her to a repeated cycle of birth, death and rebirth. But unlike Sankara, who saw moksa as complete loss of identity in the oneness of Brahman's pure consciousness, Ramanuja described perfection or release from rebirth as the human soul (*jiva*) serving the Lord Vishnu in an eternal state of communion and happiness. Like Sankara, Ramanuja established his position by writing an interpretation of Badarayana's summary sentences of the Upanishads along with commentaries on the Gita and Upanishads. But he also wrote on the alvars and gave more priority to the Gita than did Sankara. Ramanuja is the great systematizer of the bhakti marga. The prerequisites of the bhakti path include performance of all the rituals and actions required by virtue of one's caste and stage in life, along with a systematic knowledge of Sanskrit scripture. This means that, at the start of its development, the bhakti marga, like the jnana marga, was restricted to men of the upper three classes of Hindu society—because women and the fourth class or caste group, the Sudras, were prohibited from learning the Sanskrit Vedas.[37] But, as we shall see, Ramanuja, in his later writings, seems to have changed to a more open approach.

Following the Bhagavad Gita, Ramanuja says that bhakti is attained by intense love. Narayanan summarizes Ramanuja's commentary by saying, "The devotee always remembers the divine names and seeks to worship and serve the Lord with joy. This loving activity is combined with a meditation on the Lord, a meditation filled with love and a realization of the knowledge that one is the slave or the 'owned-one' (*sesa*) of the Lord."[38] Ramanuja's image of God combines the advaita or nondual idea of one divine reality, Brahman, with the idea of God as the compassionate father, mother, lover, and so on. The cosmos is God's body, of which we as individual souls (*jivas*) are parts, and the Lord is God's soul (e.g., Vishnu who incarnates as Lord Krishna). To obtain release we draw near to the Lord by our practice of devotion—the intensity of which burns up karmas that are keeping us apart from God. As the karmas are "burned-up" by our devotion, we are drawn ever nearer until we are released into the perfection of an eternal communion with the Lord—"communion" rather than "union," because our existence as a soul separate from the Lord but "one" within Brahman is retained. Just as the iron bar when placed in the blacksmith's fire eventually begins to glow and look indistinguishable from the flame, so also the devotee in intimate communion with the Lord gradually takes on the characteristics of the Lord's intense love until he or she appears as identical. Yet the soul (*jiva*) still retains its individuality.

For Ramanuja, the commitment of love, with which one turns from the world to the Lord, contains a strong sense of humility; one trusts in the Lord as both a merciful father and a powerful sovereign. "One surrenders oneself to him because he is both mighty and compassionate (*Gita* 9–34), and these two aspects precipitate the faith, the confidence, the trust of the human being in the saving power of God and accelerate one's complete surrender."[39] Surrender, or taking refuge in the Lord (*prapatti*), is the essence of the bhakti path. It is through self-surrender that karmic ignorance is removed and the clear grace (*prasada*) of the Lord is obtained. Ramanuja says, "[T]he Lord out of 'loving grace' gives the understanding with which they can join him. Out of compassion alone he dispels the *karma* which is antagonistic to the *bhakta's* wisdom; for those whose thoughts are centered around him, for those who consign all their acts to him and contemplate him with devotion and worship, he becomes the saviour and delivers them from the ocean of life and death."[40]

Narayanan notes that under the influence of the Tamil alvars or poet-saints and in his later hymns like the Hymn of Surrender (*saranagati gadya*)—an apparent conversation between the goddess Sri, Ramanuja, and the Lord—or the *Sriranga gadya*, Ramanuja undergoes a change. Not as a leading scholar of the day, but rather as one who has no qualifications to reach the Lord, Ramanuja surrenders himself at the Lord's feet with intense meditation on the Lord as his only refuge. Ramanuja's final devotion and surrender rest on a promise of grace offered out of consideration for one's lowliness rather than for one's status and accomplishments. Salvation is assured to those who surrender themselves in their own weakness and seek refuge with the Lord. This opening of the perfectibility of human nature beyond the traditional boundaries of men of the upper three castes, Narayanan suggests, was the last word Ramanuja shared with his disciples. As evidence Narayanan cites Kurattalvan, Ramanuja's scribe and friend, as saying: "Whatever one's caste, whoever the person, whatever his nature [the Lord] does not make a distinction if he has taken refuge at [His] feet. Such a person, the handsome Lord favours through his motherly affection."[41] Presumably this then opens the way to salvation for women and Sudras, along with upper-caste men who know the Sanskrit texts, so long as they confess themselves to be sinners, having no other refuge but the Lord's mercy. It is this important development that sows the seeds of division among Ramanuja's followers.

The Vadagalai, or Northern school, took *prapatti*, or surrender, as only one of several means to moksa, and only to be followed if one could not follow others. Some effort was required from the devotee rather than total reliance upon God's grace. It was thus popularly called the "monkey" school because the baby monkey must make some effort to cling to the mother, after which she does everything for the baby. This was seen as a metaphor of the relationship between the devotee and God for the Vadagalai school. Prapatti needed to be constantly practiced for the atonement of sins and the destruction of past karma. All persons could theoretically practice prapatti regardless of caste or sinfulness, but full moksa could not be achieved by one of lesser status than a Brahmin. This school traces its lineage back to Vedanta Desika (1268–1368).

The Tengalai, or Southern school, took prapatti as the only means to moksa and held that it was equally open to all, regardless of race, sex, caste, or sinfulness. After the attainment of moksa no further practice of prapatti is required, although it may be done as an example for others to follow. Sin was seen simply as an occasion for God to give grace. Thus it was called the "cat school." Just as the mother cat does everything for the kitten, so the devotee has simply to surrender and God's grace does everything else. Even the act of prapatti itself is made possible by the grace of the Lord. The Tengalai school traces itself back to Pillai Lokacarya (1264–1369), who said that because the human soul is "owned by the Lord, it cannot take the initiative in actively seeking the Lord's protection. But the human being is urged to turn towards the Lord" and give assent to the grace of the Lord. Then the person's sinful faults will be accepted as if they were virtues.[42]

Leaving the Srivaisanava tradition, we shift to a very recent teacher of the bhakti marga—namely, Swami Bhaktivedanta (1896–1977),

founder of the International Society for Krishna Consciousness
(ISKCON), which he brought from India to New York City in 1965.
Swami Bhaktivedanta was initiated into the Gaudiya Vaisnava movement, which traces its heritage from Caitanya (b. 1486 CE) and ultimately from Lord Krishna himself. Baird notes that Bhaktivedanta takes
as his sources of authority the Vedic literature (including the Gita and
Puranas), all of which is taken to be authored by Lord Krishna.[43] Human nature is such that people, because of their karmic ignorance, are
unaware that they are really part of God, and this is the cause of their
personal and societal discontent. As Bhaktivedanta puts it, "Because of
this lack of Krishna consciousness in human society, people are suffering terribly, being merged in an ocean of nescience and sense
gratification."[44] Krishna created humans from his own nature and gave
them free will, which they have misused. Salvation requires that humans recover their forgotten true relationship with Krishna—thus
Bhaktivedanta's slogan "Back to Godhead," used for the title of the
ISKCON magazine. Krishna's grace is there waiting, but it is the duty
of the devotee to remove the obstacles to Krishna's grace so that Krishna
consciousness will result. One must surrender and engage in devotional
service, which consists of nine different activities: hearing, chanting,
remembering, serving, worshipping, praying, obeying, maintaining
friendship, and surrendering everything. Through such service together
with the mercy of the Lord, one's soul is cleansed of material karmic
contamination and rises to the level of pure, or "sattvic," consciousness
and then finally to Krishna's abode. Only the grace of the Godhead is
powerful enough to "neutralize," as Bhaktivedanta put it, the sinful
karma of the devotee and enable salvation to be realized.[45] The "Hare
Krishna" or ISKCON movement has had particular success in spreading
the bhakti marga to many Europeans and North Americans. In addition, it is now providing leadership in temple worship for many Hindus
in South Asian diaspora communities around the world.

KARMA MARGA

Karma marga may be described as the path of unselfish action—of
working without thought for fame or financial reward but simply as a
dedication to the Lord. The foundational scripture for this teaching is
Bhagavad Gita 2.47–48:

> Be intent on action,
> not on the fruits of action;
> avoid attraction to the fruits

and attachment to inaction!
Perform actions, firm in discipline,
relinquishing attachment;
be impartial to failure and success—
this equanimity is called discipline.[46]

In this passage of the Gita, Lord Krishna is teaching Arjuna, the soldier and protagonist of the epic poem, that he must do his duty (*dharma*) and go into battle to protect others in society. But the key point of Krishna's teaching is his focus on the motivation behind one's action. People lacking in wisdom cling to the Vedic scriptures and do the prescribed rituals merely to gain pleasure or power for themselves. Arjuna, however, is to act not for personal gain but simply to do his duty. He is to give up attachment to the "fruits of action" or its opposite, "attachment to inaction" (the attempt to live a life of contemplation without work). Maintain an equanimity of spirit regardless of success or failure, says Krishna, and get on with your work. The spiritual exercise of the soul is in working without thought that you will get some gain (fruit), for that is what keeps you in the karmic bondage of birth, death, and rebirth.[47] By doing one's daily duty with no thought for oneself but with intense dedication to the Lord, the intensity of one's dedication "burns up" the obscuring *karmas*, and when the last karma is burned up, perfection or moksa is realized. Ramanuja in his commentary on these verses of the Gita says that action associated with fruits is bondage, but action done for its own sake and in worship of the Lord becomes the means for the perfection of human nature. All action belongs to the Lord. One must do work thinking thus.[48] The renowned medieval commentator on the Gita, Jnaneshwar, adds, "Not by abstention from action does a man attain the state beyond *karma*, and not by renunciation alone does he approach perfection."[49]

Later, in chapter 3 of the Gita, the human dilemma is restated. However wise one may be or even if one withdraws from the world to sit in yoga, one is still stuck with one's body, which requires us to act even if only for its own maintenance. Since, then, every person necessarily has to act, and since all action binds us to the world and its cycle of rebirth, how is one ever to win moksa? Humans should imitate God, teaches the Gita (3.25), and do their duty in life—whatever it may be—in a totally detached spirit. The perfected person of action, like God, has nothing that needs to be done, but does his or her duty in life simply as a dedication to the Lord.

Many take Mahatma Gandhi to be a modern example of one who lived the karma marga. Certainly he was a man of action and called the

Gita his "spiritual dictionary." In his commentary Gandhi begins by noting that, like Arjuna, we cannot run away from our duty in life. No matter what, we are stuck with having to act. In Gandhi's commentary on Gita 2.47, the key passage teaching "desireless action" runs as follows: "Your right is to work, and not to expect the fruit . . . the reward of our work is entirely for [God] to give. Our duty is to pray to Him, and the best way we can do this is to work with the pickaxe, to remove scum from the river and to sweep clean our yards."[50] The duty to society and the work of the lowly cleaner (called the "sweeper" in India) is picked out by Gandhi as an example of the kind of work that, if done as a dedication to God, will burn up karma and lead one to release. Gandhi incorporated this emphasis into his teaching that humans are equal even though their *varna*, or caste duties, seemed to make some higher and some lower. To counter this he claimed that all occupations were of equal worth, as were all caste groups—which he took to be the teaching about caste in the Vedas. To demonstrate this in his own life, Gandhi championed the cause of the untouchables, who were consigned the dirty jobs in Indian society (removing human waste, cleaning floors and toilets, tanning animal skins, and so on), by seeking to include them among the Sudras, or servant class, renamed as Harijans (Children of God). In the early 1930s Gandhi dedicated himself to an all-India tour aimed at convincing caste Hindus to change their attitude and behavior toward untouchables and low-caste groups. Ambedkar, the untouchable leader of the day, sometimes supported but most often challenged Gandhi's attempt to change the behavior of caste Hindus, which ultimately failed. Together, however, they managed to have the Congress outlaw untouchability in 1948.[51] However, many caste Hindus have been slow to embrace this change in their daily lives. In his leading India to independence, Gandhi merged the principles of non-violence (*ahimsa*) and desireless or dedicated action into what he called *satyagraha* (truth force). By giving up one's own desires and dedicating one's nonviolent protests against various forms of British injustice, Indians would succeed in driving the British from India and winning independence.[52]

In Gandhi's view, for such "action campaigns" to succeed, they must be undertaken as a manifestation of spiritual discipline—as a dedication to God. Gandhi is a fine example of one who is dedicated to the path of perfecting himself through action (*karma*). For a person, like Gandhi, with the temperament of always planning, practicing, completing, failing, and starting over again, the karma marga of dedication to desireless action offers an attractive path to release from rebirth. In moments of repose such a person gains strength and direction for more activity. One should do one's work in the world but not allow the world to possess one. One must reach a state of desireless action that allows one to attain a liberation that transcends all karmas and dharmas (duties). Rabindranath Tagore, the Nobel laureate, captured this approach well in this comment on the *Isa Upanishad*: "Do your work, but let not your work cling to you. For work expresses your life so long as it flows with it, but when it clings, then it impedes, and shows, not the life, but itself."[53]

YOGA MARGA

Perhaps no other aspect of Indian culture is more widely known than yoga. From exercise programs to meditation training, yoga teachers abound in most communities of Europe and North America. And in bookstores, the self-help sections contain numerous yoga titles. In most cases these modern presentations of yoga are updated versions of some aspect of the Yoga Sutras of Patanjali (200 CE), described in chapter 6. Pulling together seed ideas of Yoga found in the *Upanishads* and the theoretical thinking of the Sankhya philosophers,[54] Patanjali outlined a psychological and spiritual discipline for perfecting oneself that when rigorously practiced would lead to release. Key commentaries filling out Patanjali's teaching were composed by Vyasa and Vacaspati Misra in the classical period shortly after the time of Patanjali and in the sixteenth century by Vijnanabhiksu.[55] New commentaries attempting to further develop Yoga thought and practice continue to be written both in India and the West.

An overview of Patanjali's eight practices for perfecting one's human nature is given in chapter 6 and will not be repeated here. Patanjali maintains that Yoga practice needs to be done under the guidance of a guru who has achieved perfection. It is a full-time occupation and thus is not possible for most people to take up until the second last stage of life—retirement from worldly affairs to live in a forest ashram.

One such ashram was established at Pondicherry, India, in the first half of the twentieth century by the contemporary Yogi Aurobindo Ghose (1872–1950 CE). Aurobindo, after studying Western psychology in England, revised Yoga thought and practice to include modern evolutionary theory while still remaining rooted in the Veda.[56] Through his major writings, such as *The Life Divine* and *The Synthesis of Yoga*, Aurobindo developed his own approach, which he called "Integral Yoga."

In Aurobindo's view human nature is at first entirely veiled by karma, but there is something within that survives death and draws the human to evolve upward. Yoga practices foster this development but alone cannot bring about the total transformation needed. For that to happen another power is required, which Aurobindo calls the Supermind. Only the Supermind, described as "self-achieving Truth-Consciousness," can descend without losing its full power of action and help us to achieve our upward spiritual evolution. As Aurobindo puts it, "For a real transformation there must be direct and unveiled intervention from above; there would be necessary, too, a total submission and surrender of the lower consciousness."[57] Aurobindo's system of Integral Yoga is complex and difficult to summarize. It is a theory of not just individual but cosmic perfectibility in which the paths to union with Brahman are two-way streets: enlightenment comes from above, while the spiritual mind, through yogic practice, strives to reach upward. When these two meet, an illumination arises that transcends both reason and intuition, and eventually frees the individual and by extension all humankind from the karmic bonds of individuality. Thus, Aurobindo's Yoga looks to a future evolution of consciousness that offers perfection to both individuals and all humans. Aurobindo attempted to express this complex vision through philosophical writings, plays, poetry, and the creation of a model spiritual community, Auroville, which attracted many devotees from the West.

The above four margas, or paths to release, represent the dominant Hindu thinking on perfection or moksa and how to reach it. Unlike Judaism, Christianity and Islam, not a lot of attention is given to heaven or the afterlife, since in the Hindu view the afterlife is composed of being reborn on earth over and over again until, through the practice of one of the above margas the obscuring karma is purged away and moksa is realized. This is perfection, and it will occur during life on earth (*jivanmukti*), after which one will not be reborn on earth but will enjoy eternal union or communion with the Divine. We conclude this chapter with a more detailed look at this unique Hindu idea of jivanmukti or embodied perfection.

JIVANMUKTI: PERFECTION DURING THIS LIFE

The idea that one could perfect one's human nature and reach release while still alive and embodied is found in seed form in the Upanishads. The Buddhists (see chapter 8) may well have been the first to suggest that release from karma could be attained while one is still alive, a living state they called *nirvana*. This helped foster a parallel development in Hindu thought, so that in the Gita's discussion of a sage endowed with firm wisdom (*sthita-prajna*) both Buddhist and Upanishadic influences may be seen. And, as Patricia Mumme notes, "The *Brahma Sutra* contributed the notion of *karma* which has already begun manifesting (*prarabdha-karma*), and the *Samkhya-Karika* (ca. CE 400) proposed the seminal analogy of the potter's wheel to help explain continued embodiment among the enlightened."[58] Just as when the potter puts the final finishing touch on a pot so that there is no longer a need for the wheel to turn, yet it continues a few more revolutions out of its own inertia, so also when the last obscuring karma has been purged away and enlightenment realized, the body stays with the Self (*atman*) for "a few more revolutions," as it were, until the body's inertia is exhausted and death of the perfected person finally occurs. It is that embodied interval between perfect enlightenment and death of the body that is referred to as the jivanmukti state. As a Hindu concept it is first given systematic development by Sankara. Vyasa, the author of the *bhasya* (commentary) on Patanjali's Yoga Sutras, gives an early description to the idea as well, but using different terminology. Ramanuja and the bhakti or devotional traditions offer a quite different view from that of Sankara, as does the neo-Vedanta viewpoint of Ramana Maharshi and Vivekananda. Let us begin with Sankara's understanding.

JIVANMUKTI FOR SANKARA

In his commentary on *Chandogya Upanishad* 6.14.2, Sankara states that a key need for the state of living liberation is to provide us with gurus or teachers. If no one has attained jivanmukti, then there would be no one who has perfected himself and remains alive long enough to teach the rest of us so that we too can attain release. Without teachers in the jivanmukti or living liberation state, we would be reduced to the blind leading the blind. Thus, while Sankara (ca. 700 CE) never explicitly claimed to be a jivanmukta, he was seen that way by his followers. Within Hindu philosophy and religion there is a strong tendency to see founding theologians, thinkers, or saints to be liberated while alive.

   To consider how Sankara describes liberation or moksa while living, it is first necessary to remind ourselves of his basic terms. The true Self (*atman*) is identical with Brahman, the ultimate reality and the single conscious, efficient, and substantial cause of the world. Brahman is free from all limitation and is the self-evident ever-shining inner light that makes all knowing, sensing, and acting possible. In our ordinary karmic existence, "The Self's light is confused with the intellect (*buddhi*) and body and sense activity...which causes the superimposition (*adhyasa*) of the unreal on the real (and vice-versa), which manifests as the name and form apparent to us."[59] In terms of the Hindu view of human nature, it is making the mistake of taking the karmic gross body and subtle body to be the true Self. Sankara defines moksa as the overcoming of this ignorance (*avidya*) or mistake by coming to the sudden realization that one's true Self (*atman*) is not one's body, mind, or intellect, but Brahman, the Divine. Liberation is the sudden flash of insight that one is nothing but Brahman, pure being, pure consciousness, and pure bliss. In this sudden realization there are no degrees, nor is moksa something to achieve, for it is something we have always been but just not known. All of this is given detailed description in the path of knowledge outlined earlier in this chapter.

Given this understanding of the knowledge path to perfection or moksa, how does Sankara describe the jivanmukti state of liberation while still living? In his commentary on the *Katha Upanishad* 6.1, Sankara says that one can be free from ignorance (*avidya*) and desires while still living—indeed, unless one is freed during this life one will be reborn. However, if one realizes moksa before the body falls off at death, one will not be reborn. Therefore one should strive for self-realization before dropping the body, "for here alone (i.e. while living *and* liberated) one sees the self as clearly as in a mirror."[60] Bhagavad Gita 5.28 says that one who has controlled his senses and realized his identity with Brahman is eternally liberated prior to release from the body. In addition a key emphasis of the Gita is that the enlightened atman will remain free from karma no matter how vigorously the body engages in work. In his commentary on the Gita, Sankara stresses that the sage gives up action because it is incompatible with knowledge (*jnana*). But in that state of living liberation, he is filled with compassion and acts for the good of the world. As the Gita 4.21 puts it: "The ascetic who . . . before undertaking action, has realized his self as Brahman, the actionless, inner Self that dwells in all . . . acting only for the maintenance of the body, abiding in knowledge, is liberated. . . . Because all his actions are burnt in the fire of knowledge, he is liberated without any obstacle."[61] Sankara agrees with the Gita's teaching that compassionate work for the welfare of the world is compatible with Self-knowledge in an embodied state. Nelson notes that Sankara suggests that "the jivanmukta has compassion and concern for others, that he is childlike, unostentatious, retiring and detached, and that he works for the well-being of the wider community."[62] Like the Gita, the *Brahma Sutra* at 3.4.51 teaches that one can realize perfecting knowledge in this life and that action or karma does not cling to one who is liberated while still in the body. "Sankara indicates that this is because the knower (*jnanin*) has realized that the Self is not the agent of action . . . certain realized saints may do more than merely remain alive. If God has given them a special office or mission (*adhikara*), they may retain their individuality after death and even return to earth to do good works by taking on additional bodies."[63] Sankara is clear that it is not the presence or absence of a body that indicates the attainment of moksa but rather knowledge that one's true Self is Brahman, or in the great words of the Upanishads, "That thou art." Nelson summarizes Sankara's position: "[T]he critical factor is not literal freedom from the body—that would make *jivanmukti* impossible. What is required is rather a figurative disembodiedness, the transcendence of body consciousness, the destruction of the unenlightened identification with the psycho-physical organism. This the *mukta* may achieve while living."[64] Sankara is quite clear that our goal for perfection is to realize our identity with Brahman and thus achieve moksa or release from rebirth while living in this very body.

But a technical question remains. If knowledge of the Self (*atman*) brings moksa or liberation thus apparently ending ignorance (*avidya*) and destroying karma (including the body), how then does embodiment continue? Sankara offers several responses. In his commentary on *Brahma Sutra* 1.1.4 Sankara concludes that one who reaches the knowledge that an embodied Self is a false notion is really bodiless while living. He explains using the metaphor of the skin shed by a snake. The perfected person's body, known not to be the atman or true Self, is to the person like the cast-off skin is to the snake. As Fort puts it, "When one thinks that the body, tied to desire and action [*karma*], is the self, one is embodied and mortal, but one is truly separate from the body and immortal."[65] Moksa is thus not physical death but mental detachment from the body. Moksa is the death of the process of rebirth, something gained by knowledge, not by physical death. While the perfected person's body, senses, and mind "remain until being permanently discarded at death, they have already 'disappeared' for him."[66] Sankara's technical explanation for how the karma of the body continues after one has realized knowledge of Brahman, while all other karma is canceled out, makes use of the idea of *prarabdha*, or already manifesting karma. While knowledge of Brahman immediately cancels out karmas that have not begun to manifest or produce fruit (action), it does not destroy karmas whose action or fruit is already manifesting itself—such as the karma making up one's body, sense, and mind. That karma will continue until it has fully manifested its fruit in the form of the body's life span, at which time the body will die. Once knowledge of Brahman is realized, the delay in death is only the time it takes for the body's karma to experience its already manifesting fruits. "The body is like an arrow once launched: its momentum both necessarily continues for a time and inevitably diminishes and ceases."[67] This is Sankara's description of prarabdha karma. All other karma that would require further births to manifest is burned up by the realization that one's atman is Brahman. After giving this technical explanation for the karmic possibility of the jivanmukti state, Sankara adds as a further argument the experience of the great gurus who have realized knowledge of Brahman while their embodiment has continued. As Fort puts it, "How can any other person contradict one convinced in his heart of hearts that he knows *brahman* while retaining a body? Sankara gives as an example the *Gita's* one with firm wisdom, the *sthita-prajna.*"[68] The point of all these explanations of the jivanmukti state by Sankara is the clear understanding that once one realizes knowledge of Brahman, perfection has been reached and one is released from further rebirths.

Isvara as the Jivanmukti Paradigm in the Yoga Sutras

In *Yoga Sutra* 1.24 the so-called Original Speaker, Isvara, is defined as a special kind of self or purusa that is beginninglessly untouched by the taints of karmas, or their fruition, or their latent impulses (*vasana*). The taints or hindrances of which Isvara is free include ignorance, ego-sense, desire, hatred, and clinging to life. Isvara has never been touched by any such experiences and thus is a unique purusa. While all other purusas have to break their bonds with such experiences to realize release, Isvara has always been and always will be perfect and free. Yet he is at the same time in the world, in prakrti, because, as Vyasa puts it, he has assumed a body of pure *sattva* (transparent consciousness). It is this pure sattvic body that enables Isvara to function as a mind in the world. Vacaspati Misra notes that Isvara takes on this pure sattva body due to this wish to help those purusas still in bondage. Unlike others whose sattva is tainted by admixtures of *rajas* (movement or passion) and *tamas* (dullness of consciousness), Isvara's sattva is free of other *guna*s (obscuring qualities of consciousness), and this enables him to be in the world, yet untouched by it. Vacaspati offers the analogy of the actor who takes on the role of Rama and yet does not confuse his identity as purusa with that of the worldly prakrti. In answer to the question as to what causes Isvara to take on this sattva body, the answer is given by Vacaspati that at the end of each cycle of creation Isvara thinks to himself, "[A]fter this period of latency finishes I must again assume a pure *sattva* body so as to continue to help the world." This thought lays down a seed or memory trace that causes Isvara to take on a sattva body at the start of the next creation cycle. Again Vacaspati offers an analogy. Isvara's action between the cycles of creation is like that of Chaitra who contemplates, "Tomorrow I must get up at daybreak" and then having slept gets up at that very time because of a *vasana* or habitual memory trace laid down by his contemplation.[69]

In answer to the question "What is the function of this sattva body that Isvara takes on at the start of each new creation cycle?" Vyasa replies that its function is to reveal the scriptures. Indeed, in response to an opponent who asks for proof of the existence of Isvara's special sattva body, the existence of the scriptures is cited. Furthermore, the authority of the scriptures comes from the fact that they are a manifestation of Isvara's sattva. Clearly this argument is circular, and Vyasa admits there is a beginningless relation between the scriptures (with their authority on spiritual matters) and Isvara's sattva body. This is the presupposition upon which the *Yoga Sutra* definition of scripture, with regard to supersensuous matters, is grounded. In his comment on Vyasa, Sankara takes the further step of arguing that all of this is established by inference as follows: because Isvara's sattva body has never been tainted, it is unique and therefore it is unsurpassed by any other power (all others have been tainted). Thus, the special sattva of Isvara and the scriptures it reveals can never be equaled. "Therefore this Lord is one whose power has none to equal or surpass it, and it is established that the Lord is a special *Purusa* apart from *pradhana* [the originator] and other *Purusas.*"[70]

Having established the existence of Isvara's special sattva body on the basis of testimony and inference, *Yoga Sutra* 1.25 goes on to examine its special quality of omniscience. Unlike our minds in which the proportion of tamas present prevents us from knowing supersensuous things, and thus restricts our use of *agama* (scripture) to words based on inference and sensuous perception, Isvara's pure sattva reflects all of reality, the sensuous and the supersensuous. "All certain knowledge, of past or future or present or a combination of them, or from extrasensory perception, whether that knowledge be small or great, is the seed of [Isvara's] omniscience."[71] The characterization of this omniscient knowledge in Isvara's sattva as a "seed" (*bija*) is consistent with the idea that it "sprouts" or manifests itself anew in the Vedas at the start of each cycle of creation. Out of all the purusas, only Isvara has the power to fulfill this crucial role beginninglessly, since he has a sattva that has never been tainted by karma. The great saints such as Buddhas or Jinas were all at one stage immersed in karma, and due to that limitation do not have the same fullness of omniscience as Isvara, since he has never been limited by karma. Thus, as Patanjali says, Isvara is the most perfect purusa in whom the seed of omniscience is at its utmost limit or excellence (*Yoga Sutra* 1.25).

The last part of Vyasa's commentary of *Yoga Sutra* 1.25 emphasizes the motivation of Isvara—to help the persons caught in the whirling vortex of samsara. Since the motivation is for others, and not for himself, Isvara remains free from the taint of karma. His freely chosen purpose, as explained in *Yoga Sutra* 1.26, is to give help by teaching knowledge and dharma. In doing this Isvara is the first or original speaker, who may be thought of as dictating the Vedas to the rsis at the start of each creation cycle. Chapple points out that it is Isvara's capacity for action untainted by karma that qualifies him as a jivanmukta. This ideal is put forward in the Yoga Sutras as the paradigm for others to follow so that success in *samadhi* (concentration) is guaranteed. Patanjali does not suggest that by Yoga practice all action comes to an end; just afflicted action ends. *Yoga Sutra* 4.30 says that by the practice of yoga afflicted action (*klesa karma*) ceases and an active clarified mode of perception (*citi sakti*) arises. In this way the yoga devotee approximates to the pure sattva state of Isvara (described above) and achieves a perfected or jivanmukti existence.[72]

Is Jivanmukti Possible in Ramanuja?

Unlike the Yoga Sutras and Sankara's Advaita Vedanta view that jivanmukti is not only possible but necessary for moksa, Ramanuja offers both rational and theoretical arguments for the impossibility of embodied liberation. Ramanuja develops his position over and against Sankara's earlier Advaita Vedanta perspective. For his rational critique Ramanuja focuses on scripture's teaching that moksa or release requires being without a body. Sankara, however, defines the state of jivanmukti as liberation while in a body. It is internally inconsistent to argue, as Sankara does, that the jivanmukta is in a state of moksa or by definition without a body and at the same time embodied. Thus, says Ramanuja, in his commentary on *Brahma Sutra* 1.1.4, Sankara's jivanmukti doctrine is self-contradictory and unacceptable from a logical perspective. In Ramanuja's view, as long as one is still embodied one is subject to the binding and contaminating qualities of karma—even if only prarabdha or manifesting karma. Only after death is one completely freed from the manifesting karma that composes one's body. Simply coming to know that one is never really entangled in karma (Sankara's self-realization experience) is not adequate for Ramanuja. If the world is real and a person is still in a body, then he or she is still entangled in its karma and is not fully free. Only by continued devotional practice (*bhakti*) will the last manifesting karma that binds the Self to the body be burnt up so that after death one is not reborn.[73]

Ramanuja's theological reasons for rejecting the possibility of jivanmukti rest on his disagreement with Sankara over the role of God.

For Ramanuja, moksa requires losing the physical body and allowing the Self to reach the abode of God and remain in an eternal state of separate but intimate communion with God. Only at death does one become completely free from the influences of good, bad, and manifesting karma so that such an intimate state of communion becomes possible. Ramanuja opposes Sankara not only in regard to the goal and nature of moksa or salvation, but also regarding the specific means to achieve it. For Ramanuja, attention to required devotional, social, and moral actions are necessary for liberation. Self-surrender to the Lord, not just the achievement of an epistemological state, is the key requirement. In response to acts of loving surrender from the devotee, God showers compassion and grace on the devotee's remaining karma, burning it up. Through such spiritual devotion eternal communion with God is attained at death as a gift from the Lord. In Ramanuja's view, liberation (living in the direct presence of God) is not possible until after death. Then one reaches the abode of God, the only place where divine communion (*sayujya*) is fully possible.[74] Thus, for both theological and rational reasons Ramanuja judged Sankara's supposed state of jivanmukti to be impossible. Although Ramanuja does accept the possibility of a final embodied state in which only the prarabdha or manifesting karma of one's body remains, this is not equated with the final perfection of moksa.

Within a century of his death Ramanuja's followers divided into two paths to perfection. "One is the path of devotion, *Bhakti Yoga*, which Ramanuja details in his *Brahma Sutra* and *Bhagavad Gita* commentaries and which is limited to twice-born males, because it uses Vedic rites and Upanisadic meditations (*vidyas*) as auxiliaries. The other is the simple path of surrender to the Lord, *prapatti*, which is open to all."[75] Some scholars suggest that bhakti yoga may be unable to produce a state where only prarabdha karma remains, thus delaying one's liberation until a subsequent lifetime when the remaining karmas can be burned up by additional devotion. By contrast, prapatti or surrender is held to purge away all but one's already manifesting prarabdha karma, and one is assured of full disembodied moksa at the end of this very lifetime.[76]

RAMANA MAHARSHI ON JIVANMUKTI

Many Hindus judged Ramana Maharshi (1879–1950, life described earlier in this chapter) to be a contemporary example of a jivanmukta. South Indian scholars like T. M. P. Mahadevan assume rather than argue for Ramana's status as a jivanmukta.[77] Ramana is held to exemplify the jivanmukta characteristics of karma free devotion and detachment in his life and teachings. When asked about the possibility of a released person still being embodied, Ramana apparently responded that a jivanmukta is one who realizes "I am not the body; I am *Brahman* which is manifested as the self . . . [and am] endowed with a mind that has become subtle [through prolonged meditation]."[78] Regarding currently manifesting karma, Ramana holds "that one remains embodied here due to *prarabdha karma* despite being a knower, and that *karma* alone is responsible for the activity or inactivity of the sages . . . the body of a Realized Man continues to exist until his destiny [*karma*] has worked itself out, and then it falls away."[79] He uses the same analogy as Sankara—namely, that the bodily continuity or manifesting karma of a jivanmukta is like an arrow released from its bow, continuing until it hits its mark. But in reality, the perfected or realized person "has transcended all *karma* and is bound neither by the body nor by its destiny."[80] On the scholarly arguments regarding the differences between embodied and bodiless moksa, Ramana denies any true distinction—there is not one stage of liberation with the body and another when the body has been shed. The apparent difference exists only for the onlooker. There are no degrees of liberation, although these may be different stages on the one path. The perfected knowledge of the Self as Brahman is, for the jivanmukta, the same before and after the body is dropped off at death.

VIVEKANANDA: THE JIVANMUKTA AND SOCIAL SERVICE

While Ramana follows Sankara in suggesting that the jivanmukta has transcended the realm of ethical responsibility, another contemporary Hindu, Swami Vivekananda (1863–1902), argues that a realized being's presence is a blessing bringing peace and social goodness wherever he goes. Vivekananda puts it as follows: "Even if he lives in the body and works incessantly, he works only to do good; his lips speak only benediction to all; his hands do only good works; his mind can think only good thoughts; his presence is a blessing wherever he goes. He is himself a living blessing. Such a man will, by his very presence, change even the most wicked persons into saints. Even if he does not speak, his very presence will be a blessing to mankind."[81]

In Vivekananda's view such a person cannot do any evil. Although Vivekananda takes seriously the world-devaluation of traditional Advaita thought, he does say that what is left to one who has realized the Self and seen Brahman is a good momentum from the remnant good karmic impressions of his past life—like the momentum of a potter's wheel that keeps it turning for a few revolutions after the pot is finished. But while Sankara restricts prarabdha or manifesting karma to one's body, senses, and mind, Vivekananda seems to interpret it more broadly so as to include manifesting karma from previous good actions or thoughts. The jivanmukta, says Vivekananda, continues living "until the momentum of past work is exhausted."[82] This is "living free"—living in this world without being attached (like the lotus that is water-borne but unwet) when one has realized oneness with Brahman. Vivekananda is convinced that the jivanmukta, although utterly free, will do no evil but only good. Indeed, Vivekananda goes so far as to say that "good is the inner coating of the Real Man, the Self."[83] Thus, while not extravagant, Vivekananda does make modest claims for the social service of the jivanmukta or embodied perfected person.

Let us conclude this discussion of the concept of jivanmukti or living liberation in Hinduism by noting that all schools that support the concept judge their founders to have been fully liberated while alive. Thus, the jivanmukti concept plays an important practical role in authorizing founding teachers and gurus. This is clear with Sankara and Patanjali, and in the case of the contemporary figures Ramana Maharshi and Swami Vivekananda. In the case of Ramanuja, his followers tend to see him not as a jivanmukta but as an *avatara* (a full or partial incarnation of Vishnu). This is generally true of the Vaisnava schools that take a strong stance against embodied moksa in this life. These schools tend to view their founders and gurus as avataras. By contrast, disciples in the Advaita and Yoga schools see their gurus as jivanmuktas.[84]

CONCLUSION

Hindu scriptures view human nature as composed of an eternal Self (*atman*) enclosed by various bodily layers or sheaths (*kosas*) including the body, breath, mind, and intellect. These layers are all understood to be composed of karma created by one's free choice in this and previous lives. Perfecting oneself requires the purging away of all of one's karma, for it is karma that causes one to be reborn. Once one has fulfilled one's duties (*dharma*) in the student and householder stages of life, then, if one has the desire to do so, one can move on to the final stages of seeking perfection or release from rebirth. Hindu scriptures such as Upanishads offer a very optimistic view regarding the perfectibility of human nature. The goal of moksa or release from rebirth is to find the atman or true Self within the layers of obscuring karma. While this spiritual quest may extend over many lifetimes, for Hindus it is the goal that each person must realize. Then the beginningless cycle of birth-death-rebirth (*karma-samsara*) will be ended and perfection or release from rebirth realized.

One of the strengths of Hinduism is that a variety of paths to this goal are offered (suited to our variety of temperaments and stations in life). For those with intellectual interest and ability there is the path of knowledge (*jnana marga*). For those who prefer to serve the community through some form of dedicated work there is the path of action (*karma marga*). Others may be drawn to the intense practice of daily devotion to the Lord in ritual, service, song or prayer meditation (*bhakti marga*). Then there may be those who wish to withdraw into esoteric yoga practice (*yoga marga*). Each of these paths, as outlined in the chapter, can enable one to perfect one's human nature and realize moksa or release from rebirth.

A special notion, that of the possibility of reaching perfection during this life (*jivanmukti*), is developed in systematic form in various Hindu schools from about the seventh century CE on. The jivanmukti or living liberation concepts of Sankara, the Yoga Sutras, Ramana Maharshi, and Swami Vivekananda were examined, along with the rejection of Ramanuja, in the final section of the chapter. Taken as a whole, the Hindu tradition offers a tour de force in its quest for the perfection of human nature. Arising out of early Hinduism, Gautama the Buddha turned his back on the Hindu context into which he was born and struck off to pioneer a new path for the perfection of human nature. It is to the Buddhist answer as to how to reach perfection that we now turn.

Chapter 8

The Perfectibility of Human Nature
in Buddhist Thought

Ancient India, where the Buddha (ca. 563–483 BCE) lived, was a land of large rivers. Sometimes these could be crossed by boats, but at other times, when the flow slackened, they had to be forded on foot. Crossing over such rivers was a major challenge for travelers and became a common metaphor for salvation in Buddhism. One of the titles given to the Buddha was that of "one who has crossed over the difficult current of suffering and rebirth, and shown a way for others to follow." It is a metaphor for escape from the miseries of *karma-samsara* (the "current" of birth, death and rebirth) to the far shore of freedom or release (*nirvana*). The term *nirvana* literally means the blowing out of a candle flame—in this case the "flame" of ego-selfish karmic desires that cause one to be trapped in the suffering of karma-samsara. To achieve this freedom or perfection Buddhists speak of taking refuge in the Three Jewels: the Buddha, the Dharma (his teaching) and the Sangha (the monastic community he established). The taking of these "refuges" is what defines a person as Buddhist.

When they speak of taking refuge in the Buddha, Buddhists are thinking of Gautama Buddha (Buddha is a title meaning "the Enlightened One" or "the Awakened One"). Gautama is the family name of a man who was born in the foothills of the Himalayas as the son of a father who ruled a small kingdom in Hindu society. Tradition has it that Gautama was married at a young age and had a son, but left home at age twenty-nine to find a new answer as to how to find release from suffering and rebirth (he did not find the Hindu answer satisfactory). After much rigorous trial and error, he reached enlightenment at age

An earlier version of this chapter appeared in Harold Coward, *Sin and Salvation in the World Religions* (Oxford: Oneworld, 2003).

thirty-five while seated in meditation beneath a tree at Bodh-Gaya in North India by realizing the truth (*dharma*). For Buddhists (as we saw for Hindus) truth is eternal but is blocked from realization by the karma we have created for ourselves through actions and thoughts in this and previous births. The cosmos has no beginning but goes through vast cycles. From time to time there arises a religious genius, a Buddha, who has purified himself of obscuring karma, has "seen" the truth or dharma and out of divine compassion teaches it to others so that they too may obtain enlightenment or release from suffering and rebirth. Buddhists think of Gautama as the most recent teacher in an infinite series of Buddhas. Gautama claimed to be only a human being having no special inspiration from any god. As Rahula puts it, "He attributed all his realization, attainments and achievements to human endeavor and human intelligence. A man and only a man can become a Buddha. Every man has within himself the potentiality of becoming a Buddha. . . ."[1] Buddhist perfection is open to anyone willing to follow the Buddha's example and strive for it. Why then is it so difficult?

THE HUMAN CONDITION

In his analysis of the human condition, Buddha adopted the same starting point that Hindus assumed—namely, that each of us is obscured by ignorance that results from the karma created by freely chosen actions and thoughts (especially our intentions) in this and previous lives. This karma, which we have created for ourselves, is stored up in our unconscious and acts as a veil of ignorance that keeps us from seeing the truth. It is this karma that causes us to be reborn and to repeat the beginningless and seemingly endless cycle of birth, death, and rebirth. But the Buddha differs sharply from Hindu teachers in the answer he gives as to how to get release from karma-samsara, this cycle of birth, death, and rebirth. However, before focusing on the Buddha's answer, let us examine some points of emphasis in the analysis of the human condition that are unique to Buddhism.

   First, based upon his own experience, the Buddha emphasized that each person has both the freedom and the responsibility to work out his or her own path to perfection or release. Indeed, we will keep on being reborn until we do. But each of us has the power to liberate his self or her self from ignorance and the suffering it causes us by his or her own personal effort and intelligence. Through the example of his own life the Buddha has shown us the way to liberation, yet we must each tread the path for ourselves. Because of this emphasis on indi-

vidual responsibility, the Buddha allows complete freedom to his followers. Nor did he try to control the Sangha (the order of monks and
nuns) or want the Sangha to depend on him. Nirvana, taught the
Buddha, comes with our own realization of truth and does not depend
on the grace of a god, nor is it a reward for good behavior or the blind
following of someone's teachings or scriptures as divine revelation.
Therefore, one's search for the path to perfection or release should
always begin with doubt, as did the experience of Gautama in question-
ing the Hindu teaching within which he had been raised. The Buddha
made this clear in his discussions with the inhabitants of the town of
Kalama. They told the Buddha that they were left in doubt and perplexity by the differing claims to truth of visiting holy men and Hindu
teachers (Brahmins). In his response the Buddha commended their
doubt in the face of such conflicting claims:

> Yes, Kalamas, it is proper that you have doubt . . . do not be
> led by reports, or tradition, or hearsay. Be not led by the
> authority of religious texts, nor by mere logic or inference,
> nor by considering appearances, nor by delight in specula-
> tive opinions . . . nor by the idea: 'this is our teacher.' But, O
> Kalamas, when you know for yourselves that certain things
> are unwholesome, and wrong . . . then give them up. . . . And
> when you know for yourselves that certain things are whole-
> some and good, then accept them and follow them.[2]

The Buddha rigorously extended this principle of doubting any teaching or teacher by applying it to himself. His teaching should only be
accepted and followed if it proved to be true and trustworthy when one
tested it out for oneself. But to even "try out" the Buddha's teaching
one must give it at least "provisional acceptance." It is rather like trying
to find one's way to an address in a foreign city. One asks directions of
a stranger who may reply, "Go three blocks straight ahead, at the stop-
light turn right, pass three more traffic signals and it will be on your
right." You follow these directions (give them "provisional trust") as
long as they seem to be taking you to where you want to go. But if they
do not pan out in experience you reject them as false and ask someone
else for new directions or simply search out the address on your own.
The spiritual quest is like that, said the Buddha: you have the freedom,
responsibility, and intelligence to test out each proposed answer for
yourself until the truth reveals itself to you in your own "testing-out"
experience. That was the way the Buddha reached his own enlightenment experience.

The fundamental characteristics of our ordinary human experience is that it is filled with ignorance and false views as to the truth. There is no sin in the sense of disobedience to God or to some blindly believed scripture. Rather, for Buddhism there is the karmic ignorance caused by the many false views that assail us on all sides. To overcome these false views one must begin by doubting them all. But one must not get trapped in doubt for that would be to give up the search for truth and end in nihilism. As Rahula puts it, "As long as there is doubt, perplexity, wavering, no progress is possible. It is also equally undeniable that there must be doubt as long as one does not understand or see clearly. But in order to progress further it is absolutely necessary to get rid of doubt. To get rid of doubt one has to see clearly."[3] To break out of this circle, one puts "provisional faith" in the Buddha and follows his teaching to see if it enables us to begin to see more clearly. Only if it does should one continue to follow it—but always testing it out as one goes. It was in this spirit of equally testing out all views that the Buddha exhibited an openness toward all other religions and their teachings— and urged his followers to do the same.

Another point of emphasis about our human condition is that the experience of being trapped by ignorance and within the confusion of conflicting views is one of *dukkha*—which in English includes suffering, frustration, and dissatisfaction. In his analysis of dukkha the Buddha is like a physician diagnosing a sickness from which we all suffer, although in our ordinary life we may not be aware that we are ill. The Buddha described the dukkha from which we all suffer in three ways.[4] First there is dukkha as ordinary suffering. This includes physical pain when we hurt ourselves, when a toothache starts, or when we are physically sick. It also includes the aches and pains of arthritis or other ailments that assail us as we age. The pain involved in giving birth to a baby, in sickness, and finally in death is an inescapable part of human experience. But this kind of ordinary physical pain is only the first kind of dukkha. The second, due to impermanence, is more psychological in nature and is characterized by feelings of frustration and unhappiness. This kind of dukkha occurs when an initial experience of pleasure changes to pain—as when we sit down to a banquet dinner of delicious food and overeat, ending up with a stomachache because we have taken too much. In our everyday experience, taught the Buddha, pleasure is pain in the making. Pleasure is insatiable, and therefore it always leaves a desire for more, which in itself is a kind of unquenchable pain. In sexual experience, for example, is one ever completely satisfied or sated so that no more sex is pursued? Or is one always left wanting more? This lack of lasting happiness or satisfaction is a major part of dukkha. And when it comes to clothes, houses, cars, computers—material possessions—we can always think of something else we need before we will be satisfied. The neighborhood we live in changes over time in ways we do not like. Unpleasant people move in next door. In our personal relationships a loved one may get sick or die. At work, the job we enjoy may be taken away and a new one given that does not seem so pleasant. In these and many other ways our everyday life, when we stop to analyze it, is full of frustration—mental suffering or dukkha. A third kind of dukkha is caused by the drives, lusts, greed, and so on that lead one to acts and mental states that cause suffering. For example, we become angry with our lover, mother, child, or sister, rupturing a relationship and leaving a deep unhappiness that fills our minds and hearts. Our selfish desires (karmic impulses) cause problems in our relationships with others, and even within ourselves leave us always wanting more or better than what we have.

With this diagnosis the Buddha leaves no doubt that our ordinary human condition is an existence filled with dukkha or suffering. The wise person recognizes this, the fool does not. Realization of this is the spiritual first step—the awareness that suffering is the universal human condition and that it cannot be cured by the world's medicine of wealth, fame, possessions, pills, and so on. We may try all these usual ways of dealing with our mental frustrations and physical pains, but eventually—even though it may take several lifetimes—we will get fed up with these alluring but ultimately false remedies and search for a new understanding that will take us out of this worldly ignorance and the seemingly endless suffering of birth-death-and-rebirth. That is when we are ready to seriously consider the path to perfection or release from suffering taught by the Buddha. The Buddha's role amounts to revealing the path and offering it to us. But then it is up to us. The way people respond divides them into two groups: the ordinary persons and those who become disciples (the *arya*). Buddhist scripture describes the ordinary person as the one who has not heard the Buddha's teaching or been changed by it, and identifies his self with an inner ego or soul. The other kind of person, the *arya* or disciple of the Buddha, recognizes dukkha or suffering for what it is and enters the path to release pioneered by the Buddha.[5] In Buddhist teaching much emphasis was put on changing from being an "ordinary person" satisfied with the everyday experience of the human condition to being an *arya*, one who is installed in the Buddha's family and whose eyes are being opened. Enlightenment or release from ignorance is described by the Buddha as like being "awakened" or "having one's eyes opened." Like the Hindu moksa, it is an experience of "inner intuition" of knowing by direct acquaintance rather than knowing by description.

In summary, the Buddha's diagnosis of the human sickness (karmic ignorance) in which we are all trapped through repeated rebirths is that it is composed of dukkha or suffering of two kinds: (a) wanting things you don't have; and (b) wanting to get rid of something you are currently stuck with—for example, an unhappy marriage. It is our mental attitude, not the experience itself, that causes our sense of suffering; it is our desires, our anxieties. Nor should we think that science or technology will get us over our suffering. It may help to postpone disease, but it cannot stop the process of aging and the ultimate prospect of death. The Buddha's prescription for this illness of the human condition that we all experience is nothing less than a complete change in our mental attitude and our self-understanding that comes when our eyes are opened to the karmic ignorance of the false views in which we have lived for many lifetimes—and look to continue living for lifetimes into the future. This radical change in lifestyle and self-perception is available to all, regardless of gender, age, caste group, or life stage, and whether we are educated or uneducated. This is a remarkable basis for religion in that it involves no authoritative scripture or doctrine, no divine grace, and no dependence on a God or divine being. Perfection is realized simply by one's own effort. What the Buddha offers is a path, based on his own experience, that led him to enlightenment and that one can try out for oneself. This path is offered in his teaching of the Four Noble Truths and the Middle Way, which together form the foundation of Buddhist scripture and the path to perfection.

PERFECTIBILITY IN BUDDHIST SCRIPTURE

Buddhist scripture, the Tripitaka (Three Baskets), is composed of the Sutra Pitaka (Basket of sayings of the Buddha), the Vinaya Pitaka (Basket of rules for the monasteries established by the Buddha), and the Abhidharma Pitaka (Basket of commentaries on the teachings of the Buddha composed by the Buddha's followers). The canon was established by the monastic orders, first in oral and later in written form following the Buddha's death. These scriptures are preserved in many different language collections, including Pali, Sanskrit, Tibetan, and Chinese. As mentioned above, scripture in Buddhism is not considered to be divine revelation but rather a human record of the Buddha's enlightenment and the path to it for those who want to follow him. The Buddha's followers did split into various schools or denominations to which we will refer later. All schools accept a core collection of a Sutra Pitaka and a Vinaya Pitaka but differ in regard to the Abhidharma

Pitaka; each school offered its own commentaries as to the meaning of the Buddha's sayings. The relation between the Buddhist scriptures and salvation for monks is well stated by the contemporary scholar Yun-Hua Jan: "Through a regulated life in accordance with the *Vinaya* rules, to study doctrinal statements attributed to the Buddha as presented in the *sutras*, to practice the teaching and to reflect on some of the points in the light of the commentaries are the consistent directives in Buddhist tradition. It is only through the threefold effort, the religious goal of Buddhahood or *Nirvana* might be attainable."[6] Rather than speaking in Sanskrit, the elite language of the Hindu Brahmins and the Vedas, the Buddha taught in the language of the common people of his day. He made his teaching of the path to perfection open to all regardless of caste or gender.

A study of the Sutra Pitaka or basket of sayings, the original teachings of the Buddha, indicates that he had definite views regarding the Vedic revelation of the Hindus.[7] In the Buddha's view, none of the teachers of the Hindu Vedic tradition, not even the original rsis, have experienced a direct vision of Brahman. Thus, the Vedic claim to scriptural knowledge of Brahman is not trustworthy, because it is not founded on direct experience of Brahman. The Veda, therefore, cannot be accepted as a revelation of truth. In his own religious experience, Gautama rejected a faith acceptance of the Veda and went out in search of a direct personal experience of reality. The words he spoke, which became the Buddhist scriptures, were a description of his experience of striving for and finally achieving the state of nirvana. Having had the direct personal experience face-to-face, as it were, the Buddha had none of the doubts that had worried him regarding the experience of the Hindu rsis. The words be spoke (e.g., the "Four Noble Truths") were intended to exhort and instruct others to enter this same path and also to realize release. Buddha's followers judged him to speak with an authority that arose from his own enlightenment experience, yet there seemed to be no thought that his words represented divine revelation or that they were dictated by a god. Rather, as Lancaster puts it, his "teaching arose from insights achieved in a special state of development, a state open and available to all who have the ability and desire to carry out the tremendous effort needed to achieve it."[8] For Buddhism, as for Hinduism, the truth taught by the scriptures is beginningless and eternal. Like the rsis (as they are understood within Hinduism), Gautama acts to clear away karmic obstructions that obscure the eternal truth. Other Buddhas have done this before him, and will do it again after him. Revelation in this Buddhist sense is *parivartina*—turning something over, explaining it, making plain the hidden. This is the

role of the Buddhas: to make visible the timeless truth to the unenlightened; to point the way to nirvana. In the Buddhist view, each of us is
a potential Buddha; we live in karmic ignorance, but with the possibility
for perfection or enlightenment within. This the Buddha offers to us
in his teaching of the Four Noble Truths.

Preached as the first teaching following his enlightenment experience on the outskirts of the city of Banaras, the Middle Way and the
Four Noble Truths are judged to contain the essence of the Buddha's
vision of release. The Middle Way is held to be a middle path between
the extreme of luxury on the one hand, and the extreme of asceticism
on the other. The Middle Way is reflected in the Vinaya and identified
with the Eightfold Noble Path, the fourth truth of the Four Noble
Truths. The Four Noble Truths should be taken like the mahavakyas or
summary sentences of the Upanishads, not as the premises for a deduc-
tive system of logic or doctrine, but as teachings to be meditated upon
until the learner, in a flash of insight (like the cartoon "lightbulb"
experience), suddenly catches on and breaks through to another level
of knowledge and experience. Thus, the Buddha often said while teaching, "So-and-so has caught on!" The Buddha's teaching of the Four
Noble Truths is as follows:

> The First Noble Truth of suffering (*dukkha*) is this: Birth is
> suffering; aging is suffering; sickness is suffering; death is
> suffering; sorrow and lamentation, pain, grief, and despair
> are suffering; association with the unpleasant is suffering;
> dissociation from the pleasant is suffering; not to get what
> one wants is suffering—in brief, the five aggregates of at-
> tachment are suffering.
>
> The Second Noble Truth of the origin of suffering is
> this: It is this thirst (craving) which produces rebirth and re-
> becoming, bound up with passionate greed. It finds fresh
> delight now here and now there, namely, thirst for sense-
> pleasures; thirst for existence and becoming; and thirst for
> non-existence (self-annihilation)....
>
> The Third Noble Truth is the cessation of suffering
> which is Nirvana which we must realize.
>
> The Fourth Noble Truth is the Noble Eightfold Path
> leading to the realization of Nirvana, namely right view; right
> thought; right speech; right action; right livelihood; right
> effort; right mindfulness; right concentration.
>
> As long as my vision of true knowledge was not fully clear in
> these three aspects, in these twelve ways, regarding the Four

Noble Truths, I did not claim to have realized the perfect Enlightenment. . . . But a vision of true knowledge arose in me thus: My heart's deliverance is unassailable. This is my last birth. Now there is no more re-becoming (rebirth).

This the Blessed One said. The group of five bhikkhus was glad, and they rejoiced at his words.[9]

In the Buddha's teaching, thirst (craving or desire) is the key component of our karma that causes rebirth. By understanding and enacting his teaching of the Four Noble Truths, the Buddha escapes the process of rebirth. His craving is gone, he is no longer reborn, he has realized release or nirvana.

The First Noble Truth is that all existence, when carefully analyzed, turns out to be suffering. As outlined in section 1 above, this dukkha includes the physical pain involved in being born, getting sick or hurt, and growing old and dying. It also includes the frustrations that arise when pleasure turns to pain or when desires, lusts, and so on lead one to acts and mental states that cause suffering. In ordinary life we are unconscious or unaware of the suffering our daily existence entails—we are like worms in the gutter who do not know where they are. But when we become aware of our suffering and of the possibility of release, then it is as if we have only one foot in the gutter. The Second Noble Truth is that this suffering is caused by one's own acts, one's own karma, one's own ignorance, anger, lust, and desire. It cannot be blamed on anyone or anything else—not on nature, on God, or on one's parents or society. The root case of dukkha is one's notion of "I" or "me" and the selfish desires that our sense of "I-ness" produces. The Third Noble Truth is that there is a way to end this dukkha or suffering in which we seem to be trapped. There is a way to achieve freedom from slavery to one's desires, frustrations, and anxieties. Buddha freed himself through his enlightened discovery that the "I," "me," or "ego" is an illusion that does not ultimately exist. When we realize that there is no permanent ego inside us, then we are freed from the selfish desires and frustrations that our illusory ego generated—desires and frustrations that caused our life to be experienced as dukkha. Minus ego and its selfish desiring, our life is free of dukkha or suffering, and that is the perfection realized by the Buddha—nirvana, consciousness in which the flame of desire has been blown out. Thus, nirvana is not some far-off heavenly or otherworldly state: it is simply this life in this place minus selfishness. In the Buddha's experience, once selfishness and the dukkha it causes are removed, the reality that is revealed is beautiful, harmonious and compassionate. Just as the

Buddha realized nirvana through his own systematic endeavor, so he has opened the path to nirvana for others.

The Fourth Noble Truth is really a practical path explaining how to actualize the teachings of the first three truths. After showing that our ordinary or samsara experience of life is one of suffering or frustration, that the cause of this suffering is desire or selfishness, and that this selfishness can be got rid of, the Buddha goes on in the Fourth Truth to outline the means to achieve this: the Eightfold Path. "The Eightfold Path is equivalent to a shorter formula, the Threefold Training, namely morality (right speech, action and livelihood), wisdom (right views and intention) and concentration (right effort, mindfulness and concentration)."[10] Morality goes beyond mere self-mortification, because it focuses on the effects of one's acts on others. Wisdom is the understanding of the teaching that results from hard study and meditation. Study of the scripture is more demanding than just the physical yogas of controlling one's breath or posture; it requires a discipline of the mind. Concentration (*samadhi*) is achieved by the cultivation of the specific skills that the Buddha learned from various teachers during his search for release. The Middle Way resulting from the Threefold Training is itself a yoga, a stringent discipline that engages the whole person and causes one to turn away from the worldly life. Because the selfish karmic patterns are so deeply entrenched through repeated lifetimes, the Buddha created the monasteries as places of retreat from ordinary life where monks who were serious about changing these selfish patterns by following the Eightfold Path of the Buddha would be surrounded by and have the support of like-minded colleagues. Within the monastery they would also have the benefit of teachers—those who were more advanced in the practice of the Eightfold Path. The Buddha clearly outlined the basis for life in the monastery in the Vinaya. Among other things, these rules allowed for only one meal per day (today often two meals are allowed, but they both must be taken before noon) to be obtained from the householders of a nearby town by going door-to-door with one's begging bowl. Vinaya rules also specified no sexual activity in thought, word, or deed so as to overcome the deeply rooted karmic patterns of sexual desire built up through lifetimes of repeated sexual activity.

Since scripture records the Eightfold Path and the rules for the Order, Buddhist scripture may be said to provide the pathway from samsara (rebirth) to nirvana (release). Scripture both points to the revelation experience of the Buddha and provides a path by which others may obtain perfection or enlightenment. The Buddha, like Jesus, wrote nothing himself, and his teachings were not written down for hundreds of years. Buddhist scripture attempts to express in language the "vision" or "intuition" of reality experienced by the Buddha. Scholars differ as to what degree the scriptural descriptions can be taken as adequate verbalizations of reality or the divine. Schmithausen, for one, maintains that "[i]n the case of Early Buddhism, most of the sources referring to Liberating Insight or Enlightenment . . . do not seem to indicate that there was any problem in verbalizing experience. Therefore, these sources would seem to refer either to experiences not felt to be in conflict with concepts or to theories of Liberating Insight or Enlightenment."[11] Robinson adds that although later Buddhist (Mahayana) doctrine elaborates the idea of the silence of the Buddha and maintains that nirvana is indescribable, "nowhere does the early Canon say that the content of the Enlightenment is nonintellectual, or that it is inexpressible."[12] For the early Buddhist communities (e.g., the Theravada school), the Buddha's enlightenment consisted in the discovery of an experience that could be communicated via scripture, and commented upon. Yet when a seeker approached the Buddha and asked a series of questions about ultimate truth—for example, "Are the world and souls eternal, noneternal, neither, or both?"—the Buddha, in some scriptures, is said to remain silent (although explaining his silence afterward to a disciple). Buddha's point would seem to have been that the language categories for existence or nonexistence do not obtain at the level of nirvana—it is not so much a question of whether such ideas are true or false, but rather that nirvana transcends them.[13] Cessation of suffering is not annihilation but the overflowing of transcendence— the Buddha's experience of nirvana, which he hinted at as being beautiful, harmonious, and compassionate.

Buddha's parable of the poisoned arrow provides a helpful illustration. A man has been struck by a poisoned arrow and a doctor has been brought to the scene. But before the man will allow the doctor to remove the arrow he wants to know: who shot the arrow, to what clan he belongs, what wood the arrow was made from, what kind of feathers were used on the arrow, and what kind of poison was on the tip. Just as the man would die, before his questions were answered, said the Buddha, so also a person wishing to know the nature of his beginningless karmic ignorance and the nirvana experience in words will die before the Buddha would be able to describe it to him (*Majjhima Nikaya Sutra*, 63).

The different schools of Buddhism, especially the major division into Theravada and Mahayana, established themselves on the basis of different commentaries written to bring out the meaning intended by the Buddha in his sutras. As mentioned, philosophical schools accept a core collection of sutras and the Vinaya, but focus, in their commentaries, on different sayings of the Buddha as key to the realization of perfection. Let us now examine these differing systematizations of the Buddha's teaching of release.

PHILOSOPHICAL DEBATE OVER HOW TO
REALIZE PERFECTION

Whereas Hinduism understood karma simply in terms of the action or thought itself, the Buddha emphasized the motivation behind the action as the key thing. Indeed, from the Buddha's perspective what caused one to be reborn in dukkha was not the memory traces of the actions or thoughts themselves, but rather the memory traces of the motivations attached to these actions or thoughts. In fact, one could say that the Buddha boldly reinterpreted karma as motivation: "It is intention that I call *karma*," he stated.[14] This had the radical effect of shifting the doctrine of karma away from its categorization in terms of the actions proper to one's caste, such as one's dharma or duty to society as described in the Hindu Bhagavad Gita, to an ethical dualism of right or wrong action as determined by one's intentions that applied equally to all, whether Brahmins, kings, servants, or untouchables. As Gombrich comments, "This single move overturns brahmanical, caste-bound ethics. For the intention of a brahmin cannot plausibly be claimed to be ethically of quite a different kind from the intention of an outcaste. Intention can only be virtuous or wicked."[15] The Buddha took the term "pure" as applying to the intention rather than just to the action itself. From the Buddha's perspective what makes an action good or bad is a matter of intention and choice. Actions motivated by greed, hatred, and delusion are bad, while actions motivated by nonattachment, benevolence, and understanding are good. Good actions must be pure also in doing no harm to oneself or others. Thus, it is the "purely motivated" action or thought that brings the Buddhist rewards in this and future lives. And since it is the mental motivation of the action that is key, the Buddha turned the focus of karma to meditation—the action of purifying one's state of mind, including one's intentions. Further, such mental purification of motivations can be done directly through meditation, without any accompanying action.

Consequently, in Buddhism, morality in the world and the meditation one does in retreat are seen to be directly connected. This is reflected in the pattern the Buddha established for his monks. Two-thirds of the year they were to be out in the world teaching, healing, and solving disputes, while during the rainy season they were to withdraw into the monastery for meditation. The Buddhist prescription as to how one realizes release from rebirth is seen to require both of these activities. Good (purely motivated) deeds and a virtuous life are required but alone are not enough. Leading a moral life is only one part of the requirement for nirvana. The other component required is wisdom (*prajna*). Wisdom in Buddhism involves a profound philosophical understanding of the human condition, an understanding that arises only through long reflection and deep thought. As Keown puts it, "It is a kind of *gnosis,* or direct apprehension of truth, which deepens over time and eventually reaches full maturity in the complete awakening experienced by the Buddha."[16] Perfection (*nirvana*), then, is realized through a fusion of pure action or virtue and wisdom. An early Buddhist text describes virtue and wisdom as two hands that wash and purify each other.[17] Buddhist ritual actions, as in the Tibetan Buddhist use of the scepter with the bell in formal chanting, symbolize this same relationship. In philosophy, however, differences arise over the analysis of human nature and the reality that makes up the wisdom side of the nirvana equation. We will turn now to a brief overview of these philosophical differences and their impact on how to realize nirvana. First, we will look at the Theravada approach, and second, the Mahayana.

THE THERAVADA PRESCRIPTION FOR
REALIZING PERFECTION

The Theravada or Early Buddhist approach is dominant in Sri Lanka and Southeast Asia (e.g., Thailand and Cambodia). The Theravada scholars commented on all the scriptures but focused on the Buddha's sutras dealing with "no-soul" (*anatman*), the "things" or "elements" (*dharma*s) that make up a person and the fact that all of reality is impermanent and in a state of constant change. Using these ideas of the Buddha, they developed a systematic philosophical description of what composed a person. The purpose of this philosophical analysis was the therapeutic goal of convincing one that there is no permanent self, "I-ness" or "ego" inside one's personality, but that the idea of a self within is a delusion and part of the ignorance we all share in our ordinary experience. Getting rid of this delusory notion of self via the process of a philosophical analysis has the important therapeutic purpose of removing one's belief in a permanent self, a belief that, according to the Buddha's teaching of the Four Noble Truths, is the cause of the selfish desiring and frustration that is turning our experience of the world into dukkha or suffering and preventing us from experiencing nirvana.

The false notion of soul, the Hindu idea of a permanently existing self or atman, is countered by the Buddha's teaching of *anatman* or
"no-soul." A major aspect of the Buddha's enlightenment experience
was the realization that everything is impermanent. This condition of
impermanence applies not only to mundane things around us and our
bodies, but also to our sense of soul. Consequently, there is no unchanging self at the center of our human nature and therefore no basis
for the notion of ego and the selfishness it produces, which turns our
life into dukkha. We, like all other beings in the universe, are transitory
and doomed to pass away in time—as we all realize when we think of
ourselves as aging and finally dying. This analysis of human nature,
however, gives rise to the question, "If there is no soul or self, then what
is reborn?"—for Buddha did accept the Hindu idea of samsara or rebirth. The Theravada analysis answers this question by developing the
Buddha's teaching of the dharmas into a comprehensive theory of
human nature.

In response to the question "If there is no soul what is reborn?"
the Theravada scholars outlined a view of human nature as composed
of a series of dharmas or elements. These dharmas are the "bits and
pieces," as it were, that make one up. There are dharmas of body,
feelings, perceptions, thoughts or ideas, and consciousness that, when
taken together, account for our whole personality and our daily experience.[18] Just as when a mechanic takes all the bits and pieces apart that
make up an automobile, there is no "car-essence" found at the center—
the car is created by all the "bits and pieces" smoothly working together—so when a human person is "dissected," as it were, all the
dharmas or "bits and pieces" that make one up are laid out on
the "operating table" there is no self or soul found at the center. The
notion of a self, "I," or "ego" is a delusion created by the smooth
functioning of all the parts or dharmas of body, feelings, perceptions,
ideas, and consciousness that make one up. The whole person is simply
the sum of its parts. Nothing more, no self or ego, is found or is
necessary. But if these dharmas that make one up are impermanent,
just like everything else in reality, then how can they carry forward our
identity as an individual person from moment to moment, let alone
from this life to the next?

To answer this question the Theravada philosophers evoke the
Buddha's teaching of "dependent arising" (*pratityasamutpada*).[19] The
dharmas that make us up as bits of body, feeling, perception, ideas, and
consciousness, like all the rest of reality, are constantly changing. The
idea of "dependent arising" is an explanation of how identity is maintained through this process of constant change. The arising of a dharma

(a part that makes one up) at this moment is only possible because of its existence in a previous moment of existence. That is, its arising now is dependent on its having existed previously. And its possibility for arising as a dharma in a future moment is dependent on its existence in this present moment. Thus, even though each dharma "dies or disappears" as the present instant of time passes, its "dying" provides the occasion for the arising of a new dharma in the next moment in time. But this new dharma is as it were "in series with" and made possible by the arising and subsiding of the previous dharmas in the series. It is this "series connection" or "arising" that is dependent on previous "point-instants" of existence (going backward beginninglessly) that creates our experience of identity in the midst of constant change. The identity created by the continuity of the series of changing dharmas of body, feelings, and so on that make us up as persons is all that is needed to give us our sense of identity from moment to moment, day to day, or life to life. The existence of a permanent soul or self is shown to be unnecessary and therefore a delusion.

Once this incorrect sense of self is removed from our self-perception, the basis for selfish desiring for things and experiences is also removed, and our life is no longer colored by dukkha. The sufferings and frustrations caused by selfish desire vanish with the disappearance of the delusory notions of ego and self. And with the removal of the obstructing ignorance of a permanent self, and the suffering and frustration it generates, the experience of nirvana (reality minus the desires of ego-selfishness) arises. This, from the beginning, was the therapeutic goal of the philosophical analysis of the human person by the Theravada philosophers. When the illusion of self and the flame of selfish desiring it produced was "blown out," through the twin processes of moral living and philosophical meditation on the constituent parts of human nature, the desire that pushes forward the dependently arising series of the dharmas disappears and the cause for rebirth is removed. Perfection or enlightenment is realized. A Buddhist scholar summarizes the gaining of enlightenment as follows:

> Ignorance refers to the absence of correct knowledge. An ignorant person does not know that impermanent phenomena are, in fact, impermanent. He is unable to see things as they actually are. Ignorance is not an active quality. Rather, various delusions are produced when other mental activities are influenced by ignorance. . . . However, just as a dream ceases as soon as a person realizes that it is a dream, so does ignorance disappear as soon as a person realizes that it is

ignorance. Consequently, the purpose of the doctrine of Dependent Arising is fulfilled with the discovery of ignorance. Because ignorance is the cause of mental formations, the cessation of ignorance results in the cessation of consciousness and so on until the process results in the cessation of old age and death.[20]

The process of birth, death, and rebirth, and the constant suffering it produced, is ended, and perfection, or nirvana, is realized.

ARHAT

In the Theravada tradition, a person who reached this level of nirvana realization is called an *arhat* (saint). An arhat imitates the example of the Buddha who, following his realization of enlightenment, devoted the remainder of his life on earth to teaching, healing the sick, and stopping conflicts between people. In the Theravada view, an arhat through self-effort has purged all impurities such as desire, hatred, ill-will, ignorance, pride, and conceit, and has attained the perfection of nirvana. An arhat is described as full of wisdom and compassion and after death will not be reborn.[21] From the Theravada perspective once the Buddha or an arhat has died they can have no more influence on those who are still living.

Except under extraordinary circumstances a man or woman can become an arhat only while living in a monastery. The arhat was supposed to be an enlightened one "knowing" what the Buddha knew. As Klostermaier notes, the Buddha was a kind of primus inter pares; he became to others the occasion to gain enlightenment; his status was not qualitatively different from that of an arhat. An arhat is a perfected person. For Theravada Buddhists it is the highest ideal; everything else is, at best, preparatory. The arhat embodies the highest qualities of mind and heart so that all actions are selfless, compassionate, right, and universally helpful. Klostermaier concludes, "Liberation meant the freeing of one's energies from their fixation on an imagined self, and a radiating of friendliness, compassion, joy and equanimity into the world just as the sun, while transforming helium into hydrogen and thereby generating heat[,] does not intentionally 'do good,' but by radiating light and warmth into the universe, it benefits planet earth and the myriads of living beings on it."[22] Recognition of the difficulty in reaching the level of perfection of an arhat led the Buddhists of Sri Lanka to believe, for several centuries, that arhatship was no longer attainable.

Realizing the perfection of an arhat does not come easily but is the fruit of a long process of meditation and selfless action that fully transforms one to be like the Buddha.

To this point we have emphasized that to become serious about reaching nirvana, a Buddhist should leave worldly life and join a monastery where the time and quiet needed for meditation would be provided. In the Theravada view, meditation is essential to the realization of enlightenment, and in the South Asian social environment, the peace and privacy required for meditation is generally not available. The Buddha did not consider it impossible for a layperson to attain enlightenment, and a few cases are recorded in Buddhist scriptures, including the case of the Buddha's own father. Tradition also suggests that should a layperson become enlightened, such a person would find it impossible to go on living in a worldly environment and would enter a monastery within the day—as the Buddha's father was said to have done.[23] However, laypeople are said to have made much spiritual progress, even to the point of living religious lives close to those monks or nuns, but without joining the Sangha or monastic order. They followed the same basic vows as those adopted by the Sangha, including the renouncing of sexual and economic activity. But the Buddha's general expectation was that the role of those in the householder stage of life was to provide food and economic support to the monks and nuns, and to follow a less stringent practice than was required for the attainment of salvation. Laypeople were to observe five precepts: abstention from killing, stealing, sexual misconduct, false speech, and intoxicants.[24] Nor, in traditional Theravada society, did laypeople have full access to all of the Buddha's teachings. In general the Buddha's view seems to have been that the full teaching was reserved for those who were seriously enough interested in attaining perfection that they would give up the householder life to become monks or nuns. Only then would they have the time, privacy, quiet, and support needed for serious meditation on the key teachings.

The rules and organization for the Sangha were given by the Buddha in his Vinaya teaching. Persons over twenty years old could receive full ordination and become monks or nuns. Those below the age of twenty could be initiated and enter the Sangha as male or female novices, with a usual minimum age of fourteen (in special cases it might be lowered to seven). Of the 250 or so rules in the Vinaya the most important (four for monks, eight for nuns) deal with abstention from sexual intercourse, stealing, taking human life, and lying about one's spiritual achievements. Commission of any of these acts meant lifelong expulsion from the order. Next in importance came a second set of thirteen rules for monks and seventeen for nuns dealing with such things as sexual offenses, false accusations against another monk or nun, and attempts to cause schisms in the order. If a person commits any of these acts, he or she is required to go before a meeting of the Sangha and confess his or her wrongdoings. Then for seven days the sinner must live apart from the order and do penance. Then the order may meet and readmit the person if they are satisfied with his or her penance. A third set of rules dealt with offenses of undetermined seriousness (i.e., with the seriousness determined by the evidence given by witnesses) of monks found with women. A fourth set gives thirty rules for monks and nuns relating to such matters such as possession of robes (only three are allowed), begging bowls, gold, silver, jewelery and medicine. If these rules are violated, the items in question must be surrendered and the person must confess his or her wrongdoing. A fifth set of rules, numbering about ninety-two for monks and two hundred for nuns, concern minor offenses such as speaking harshly or lying, and these require confession. Three other sets of rules deal with acceptance of inappropriate food, procedures for begging, eating, and preaching, and finally there are rules for the resolution of disputes within the order.[25]

Life within the monastery was designed to help monks and nuns curb their desires and thus make progress toward nirvana. A typical day would involve rising early and meditating. Later in the morning one would go out to beg for one's food and then return to eat with the other monks or nuns before noon (only one meal a day was generally allowed and nothing was to be eaten after noontime). In the afternoon one could visit the homes of lay believers or go to the forest to meditate. In the evening group discussions might be held in the monastery focused on the Buddha's teachings or one might have a meeting with one's teacher. Finally, one would withdraw to one's own room for more meditation and go to sleep late at night. Six times each month laypeople would come to the monastery and the monks would preach the teachings of the Buddha to them. Twice each month the monks or nuns would gather to do this for themselves and to chant together the rules for monastic life established by the Buddha—the *pratimoksa*. If this seems a very austere and ascetic monastic practice, one should remember that from Buddha's perspective this was a "middle way" between the extreme of rigorous asceticism, such as was practiced by the Jain monks of his day, and the luxuries of worldly life. It was a path that would simply sustain bodily life in such a way that the time and support for the virtuous living and meditational practice needed for the realization of nirvana were provided to the serious searcher.

THE MAHAYANA PRESCRIPTION FOR
REALIZING PERFECTION

The Mahayana approach to perfection develops in conflict with the interpretation of the Buddha's teaching by the Theravada or Tradition of the Elders. The evolution of the Mahayana began after the time of Buddha's death, continued through the Second Council during Asoka's reign, and was almost complete by the first century BCE.[26] Mahayana scholars in their commentaries focus on such passages in the sutras as the silence of the Buddha in response to questions of a metaphysical nature (e.g., Is the world eternal or not? Will the Buddha exist after death or not? Is the soul or self identical to or different from the body?) or the Buddha's parable of the wounded man who wanted to know all about the poisoned arrow stuck in his chest before he would allow it to be removed. Early on the advocates of Mahayana teachings were few in number and were branded as heretics by the Theravadins. However, by about the beginning of the Common Era the Mahayana had become dominant, spreading from Northern India to China, and later to Tibet, Korea, and Japan.[27] Major points of difference (or "heresy" from a Theravada perspective) included a desire to extend the Buddhist canon of scripture to include new sutras or sayings of the Buddha, a change in understanding of the nature of the Buddha himself, and the attributing of imperfections to the arhats.[28]

The arhats, the enlightened saints who have realized nirvana, were described by one early teacher, Mahadeva, as open to ignorance, seduction, doubt, and so on. Parallel to this lowering of the arhat's status is a raising of the status of the Buddha to something more than just a purely human being. Although he was born in this world, he was, it is suggested, not tainted by it. The popular literatures that grew up after the Buddha's death recounts his many virtuous deeds in previous lives as a bodhisattva—one on the path to Buddhahood. Because of the merit the Buddha built up in previous lives, his birth and life take on suprahuman qualities: he is conceived without sexual intercourse; he emerges from his mother's right side without pain; and, as the text of the *Mahavastu* puts it, he merely appears to wash, eat, sit in the shade, take medicine, and so on, out of conformity to the ways of the world.[29] The Buddha is said to be omniscient, never to sleep, and to be always in meditation. This finally leads to the teaching of some Mahayana scholars that the Buddha's death was also a mere appearance—in reality he remains present in this world out of compassion for suffering humanity. Following this new image of the Buddha, the goal for humans to strive toward is not to become an arhat but to take the bodhisattva vow (not to go into nirvana until all other beings have realized release) and to "embark on the long path to a supreme, totally superior Buddhahood."[30]

The claim of the continued presence of the Buddha after his death allowed Mahayana monks to associate the Buddha's name with sutras composed after his death—and therefore outside the closed canon of the earthly utterances of the Buddha held to by the Theravada tradition. Thus, around the first century BCE the above developments resulted in the appearance of a new literature, the Mahayana sutras, which claim to be the word of the Buddha himself composed in his lifetime but concealed until later. These new sutras arose from different groups of monks, nuns and sometimes laypersons practicing within existing Buddhist traditions. These sutras focus on the supremacy of the Buddha, the path of the bodhisattva and concern for the well-being of all. These monks, nuns and perhaps a small number of householders who accepted this new literature formed a series of cults that were probably based on the different sutras. Some "may have felt themselves in direct contact with a Buddha who inspired them in meditation or in dreams. Sometimes they proclaimed the Doctrine itself, embodied in the text, as the body of the Buddha,"[31] his ever-present "Dharma-body," which was judged much superior to the relics of the historical Buddha (such as a tooth) that had been placed in stupas or burial mounds and used as a focus for Theravada worship. Although a minority within Indian Buddhism, their numbers increased as time passed until they identified their approach to perfection as a Mahayana or superior way.

According to Williams the key characteristic of the Mahayana sutras is that "the *sutra* is not one object among others, but rather is the body of the Buddha, a focus of celebration and worship on the model of relic worship."[32] As such, the Mahayana sutras are sacred books that are not only memorized by repeated chanting, copied, and studied, but are also themselves objects of worship. Each monk or nun probably owned no more than one or two sutras, which would be rapidly learned by heart through repeated chanting and through use as a focus for meditation. These texts were used as a basis for exposition by teachers in terms of their own experience and their lineage of previous teachers traced back to the Buddha himself. In this way the Mahayana sutras, or sacred texts, provided a basis for teaching, study, meditation, and worship by which one could realize nirvana. The sacred texts still function this way in traditional Mahayana cultures such as Tibetan Buddhism, where the sutras also serve as the basis for the sacred art of the tradition.

The Mahayana *sutras* vary in length from a few words to over 100,000 verses in one of the Prajnaparamita (Perfection of Wisdom) sutras, with the longer ones likely having grown and developed over the centuries in different countries (such as China). The earliest Mahayana sutras seem to be the Prajnaparamita sutras, which probably originated in central or southern India and became quite influential in northwest India during the first century CE. Conze has distinguished four phases in the development of the Prajnaparamita literature, beginning about 100 BCE and stretching over one thousand years.[33] These texts seem to provide the foundations for much Mahayana philosophical thought. The concept of *prajna* (wisdom) and its perfection, developed in these texts, refers to a combination of conceptual and nonconceptual understanding gained through meditation—such as the nonconceptual and direct awareness of *sunyata* (the universal absence of any ultimate existence as the true characteristic of all dharmas). Ultimate prajna, as understood by Mahayana and the Prajnaparamita sutras, refers to a number of perfections to be mastered by the bodhisattva as he or she follows the long path to perfect Buddhahood. They include giving (*dana*), morality (*sila*), patience (*ksanti*), effort (*virya*), meditative concentration (*dhyana*), and wisdom (*prajna*). Wisdom is often given the primary emphasis, and within that the extension of the Buddha's teaching of no-self to no-essence is key. The central critique is of the Theravada claim to have found some things that really ultimately exist—that is, dharmas. The radical Mahayana critique meant that anyone attempting to practice these teachings in meditation had to engage in a complete "letting go" of all conceptual belief and discursive analysis, a giving up of all intellectual attachment. That could be achieved, according to Williams, only as the truth of emptiness was realized.[34] This teaching, as basic to the practice of the bodhisattva in the perfection of nirvana, provided ample grounds for a different philosophical interpretation to develop. In the Tibetan Buddhist tradition a distinction is made between knowing something by description or by acquaintance. We may know someone by external description or by knowing the person intimately by acquaintance—knowing at a deeper than merely conceptual level. The Buddhist claim here is that through deep meditative analysis one can come to know things as they really are. Prajna or wisdom, says Williams, is in this sense sometimes understood as "a meditative absorption the content of which is the ultimate truth, the way things really are . . . a *prajna* [that] is non-conceptual and non-dual. . . ."[35]

The great Indian philosopher Nagarjuna (second century CE) is taken to be the founder of the Madhyamaka school (within the Mahayana tradition) with his great work the *Mulamadhyamakakarika*. In it Nagarjuna develops a critique of the Theravada theory of dharmas as the elements or parts that make up the whole person. Basing himself on the silence of the Buddha in response to the unanswerable questions such as "Does the self or soul exist after death or not?" Nagarjuna criticized the Theravada philosophers' confidence that we could conceptually know things just as they are. This approach, as we saw above, was to analyze phenomena (e.g., a person) in terms of the dharmas or essences (*svabhava*) that made them up. Such an analysis, said the Theravadas, resulted in an absolutely true view of things, which they termed ultimate truth (*paramarthasatya*), in contrast to the relative, commonsense beliefs of the less insightful, which were termed relative truth or worldly convention (*samvrtisatya*).[36] The aim was to come to understand and accept the correct view; then, through meditation, one could actualize its meaning in one's daily life. Through this "philosophical therapy" the Theravada path aimed at a final awakening through a step-by-step process of understanding, meditation, and practice. The difficulty with this from Nagarjuna's critical perspective was that the Theravada approach put conceptual knowledge at the center. Unless one had an ultimately true view of things, one could not hope to follow a meditation that would lead to release. Nagarjuna deconstructed this Theravada approach. In reaction to the Hindu belief in an atman (a self that is ultimately real), the Theravada Buddhists had made the mistake of swinging the pendulum to the opposite extreme and adopting a dharma view that the parts that make up the person are ultimately real. Like the silence of the Buddha, Nagarjuna's aim is to show the hollowness of all viewpoints and put an end to all attempts to conceptualize reality through language, leaving only silent meditation as the path to perfection or release.

Nagarjuna's critique rests on the perceived discontinuity between the way the world is and what philosophy thinks the world to be. Suspicious of any absolute claim made about the nature of reality (such as the Hindu and Theravada claims), Nagarjuna shows "that the philosopher engaged in such metaphysics is living a sick form of life, infecting others who take him seriously."[37] The only cure for this disease is to demonstrate the utter hollowness of all metaphysical claims through the deconstructive analysis offered by reductio ad absurdum argument. Nagarjuna develops this approach in his *Mulamadhyamakakarika*.[38] Nagarjuna's four-pronged negation shows the futility of attempting to take any sort of ultimate philosophical position. Conceptual language is useful for everyday purposes such as buying a loaf of bread, but when it is used to make ultimate claims it becomes deceptive and entrapping: saying "*x* exists" becomes the basis for the belief that "*x* actually exists." Psychologically, one has fallen into the trap of becoming ego-attached to one's own philosophical or theological worldview. This is not simply a case of falling in love with the theory we have created or adopted; it also plays the role of providing for us a shelter from the anxiety and insecurity faced by the ego when the partiality and ultimate emptiness of all worldviews is realized. But Nagarjuna's aim is not nihilism and the psychological depression it might induce. Rather it is the freeing of one from seeing everyday reality through "philosophical or theological glasses" that give only a partial and distorted perception. Nagarjuna's *catuskoti* technique is a method for deconstructing our distorting "philosophical or theological glasses" so that reality is no longer experienced through the subject-object and subject-predicate filtering of language. Once this enlightened state is realized, the application of the *catuskoti* is no longer necessary—the philosophical disease has been overcome and the patient is cured.[39] The need, both psychological and epistemological (for a worldview we can put our trust in as absolute truth), has been totally overcome. Reality is immediately experienced just as it is, and that is perfection or nirvana—this world minus ego-selfish desiring and philosophizing. Thus Nagarjuna's famous dictum "samsara is nirvana." Nirvana is not the end of rebirth as the Hindus and Theravadas taught, but a rebirth in which each life is lived in compassion for others, without trace of selfish desires or the distorting worldviews that turn life into dukkha or suffering.

Madhyamaka Buddhism sees language, with its construction of the forms of subject and object, as ontologically empty—as unable to encapsulate the truth of ultimate reality—as the Buddha's silence signified.[40] Rather than making us self-aware, these imaginary constructions act as obstacles to the clear perception of reality. Thus the need for the negation of the structures of language for the spiritual realization of perfection to proceed. Even the oral and written scriptures of Buddhism must eventually be transcended if nirvana is to be realized. Seen from an ultimate (*paramartha*) perspective, all words, even those of the Buddha, are empty (*sunya*) of reality.[41] The goal of Nagarjuna's deconstructive critique of language (his catuskoti) is not to reduce the holders of a philosophical or theological viewpoint (*drsti*) to nihilism, but to sensitize them to the interdependent (*pratityasamutpada*) universe of which they are merely a part, and to act in conformity to its inherent compassion—which the Buddha's enlightenment has revealed. For Nagarjuna, the subject-object separation, which language necessarily seems to create, prevents one from reaching the spiritual goal while under its sway. As long as one approaches reality through the viewpoints of language, *pratityasamutpada* and one's necessary place within it will never be seen. Thus the necessity to go beyond language through the silence of meditation into direct experience in which no subject-object duality is present. For Nagarjuna, language, even the sacred words of scripture, does not seem able to participate in the final spiritual goal.

But this very negative critique of language as a means to salvation seems tempered by some Mahayana scholars and traditions (e.g., Zen). A contemporary Mahayana scholar, David Loy, offers a more positive assessment of the role of language and cites Nagarjuna in support. Loy points out that the assumption that a distinction can be made between an "apparent world" mediated by language and the "real world" unmediated by language is inconsistent with the fundamental tenet of Nagarjuna that "samsara is nirvana" (language being very much part of samsara). Sunyata, says Loy, referencing *Mulamadhyamakakarika* 13.7–8 and 22.11, is intended by Nagarjuna to be a therapy to get one to release; it is not an ultimate truth or an ontological category. "In other words, emptiness, the relativity of all things, is itself relative; the ultimate truth, like the conventional, is devoid of independent being."[42] The end of views such as "ultimate" and "conventional" leaves the world as it really is—an empty or nondual world in which there is no philosophical or theological meddling but in which language still participates. We speak, just as we act; but we do not cling to any action or conceptual system. "If there is no subject-object separation between language and object, between signifier and signified, then all phenomena, including words, are *tatha*, 'thusness.' That is why, as we clearly see in the Zen tradition, language too participates in the reality it manifests . . . [otherwise] how could so many Zen dialogues have led to a realization on the part of the student?"[43] This makes clear Loy's different interpretation of Nagarjuna as ending in a spiritual realization that is in one sense beyond language, but in which language still participates—as we see in Zen koan practice and some Tibetan or Japanese Jodo-Shinsu mantra chanting.

The above is only a brief and incomplete outline of Nagarjuna's teaching with regard to release. A more complete summary can be found in Paul Williams's *Mahayana Buddhism* along with references to other Madhyamaka scholars we have not mentioned. Williams also offers a good treatment of the Yogacara or "Mind Only" school that developed as a response to Nagarjuna and the Madhyamaka school, along with other Mahayana developments such as the *tathagatagarbha* (Buddha-essence/Buddha-nature), the Chinese Hua-yen (Flower Garland tradition), the *Lotus Sutra*, and Tibetan Tantric Buddhism.[44] While these developments were important to the philosophically minded nirvana seekers, the larger number of Mahayana followers sought perfection through religious practices based on the bodhisattva path.

BODHISATTVA

During the early centuries the bodhisattva model was worked out in some detail. First must come a strong motivation to become a bodhisattva in order to save others—the "thought of enlightenment" (*bodhicitta*) experience. The person then seeks initiation as a bodhisattva and takes a vow to save all beings by leading them to nirvana no matter how long it takes. The aspiring bodhisattva practices the six Mahayana virtues mentioned earlier (generosity, morality, patience, courage, meditation, and wisdom) and progresses through a system of ten *bhumis* (stages). On reaching the seventh stage it is held to be certain that one will reach nirvana and that it is impossible to fall back.

Bodhisattvas who had reached the higher stages were visualized as very powerful and virtually equivalent to the Buddha in his ever-present or heavenly form. One who has attained such a high status is Avalokitesvara (the Lord who looks down in compassion), of whom the Tibetan Dalai Lamas are said to be incarnations. Avalokitesvara is depicted with many arms reaching out to help those who are suffering. In East Asia he changed sex and became Kwan-yin in China, Kannon in Japan. Manjusri, another such bodhisattva of high attainment, carries the flaming sword of wisdom that cuts through ignorance. Over the centuries a vast pantheon of Buddhas and bodhisattvas "is conceived of as inhabiting a majestic unseen universe. Just as our own world system was graced by a Buddha, it seemed not unreasonable to suppose that others had been too. The Mahayana therefore proceeded to invent names and characteristics for these fictional Buddhas and located them in magnificent Buddha-realms."[45] A common depiction shows a group of five Buddhas in the circular pattern called a mandala. These mandalas can be focused upon, painted or drawn in the sand as forms of meditation. A typical arrangement places the historical Buddha at the center with four celestial Buddhas seated around him: Amitabha ("Infinite Light") to the west; Aksobhya ("the Imperturbable") to the east; Ratnasambhava ("the Jewel Born," representing Buddha as giver of gifts) to the south; and Amoghasiddhi ("Infinite Success," Buddha's miraculous power to save) to the north. Some depictions show various bodhisattvas seated on petals in between.[46] Amitabha, the western Buddha, became the focus of a popular East Asian cult that formed around the idea of a "Pure Land" he was thought to inhabit. Amitabha (Amida in Japan) took a vow that he would help anyone who called upon him with true faith and would ensure that they would be reborn in his Pure Land (*sukhavati*). In contrast to the Theravada tradition where the most the Buddha offered was his teaching and personal example and it was up to the person to make his or her own effort to follow, we find in Mahayana practice the suggestion that salvation in the form of rebirth in the Pure Land can be attained through faith in Amitabha and the grace he will give. But even in this tradition some individual effort is still required, for the Pure Land or western paradise of Amitabha is not the same as nirvana. A person reborn there would still need to make a final effort to gain full perfection or enlightenment. The geographical and artistic representations of the Pure Land as a magnificent western paradise may use notions of faith and grace to begin with, but they are designed to eventually give one the insight that "[i]f there are mountains in this world, and all is flat in the Pure Land, that is because there are mountains in the mind." This impure world is indeed the Pure Land. It only appears impure because of the impurities in our minds. "Thus the real way to attain a Pure Land is to purify one's own mind. Put another way, we are already in the Pure Land if we but knew it. . . . The Pure Land is truly, therefore, not a 'heavenly abode' but enlightenment itself."[47] This is the result of the final self-effort that has to be made. In the Japanese Jodo Shinshu tradition, it is the "far end" of the simple congregational and individual chanting of the name of the Buddha (*nembutsu*). The formula *namu amida butsu*, "I surrender myself to Amida Buddha," is something that the most simple layperson can recite.[48] The Jodo Shinshu tradition, which with its clergy, laity, and congregational worship looks thoroughly "Protestantized," offers a devotional practice for purifying the mind that the most lowly layperson can follow and yet, with sufficient sincerity of surrender, reach Nagarjuna's realization that "samsara is nirvana"—that one's own impure mind of this world, when purified, is the Pure Land of nirvana. As Williams notes, this is only "a short step from the Ch'an (Zen) notion that the Pure Land is the tranquil, clear, radiant, pure Mind,"[49] but in the case of Zen it is a realization to be reached by rigorous meditation (*zazen*) on the flow of one's breath. In this great variety of ways, Mahayana Buddhism offers paths to perfection that serve monks, nuns, and laypeople alike.

As the Prajnaparamita sutras show, the concern of the bodhisattva is with perfection or full Buddhahood not just for one's own self but for all sentient beings.[50] The bodhisattva thus generates infinite compassion. This total selflessness is well illustrated in the following passage from the *Diamond Sutra*: "As many beings as there are in the universe of beings . . . all these I must lead to Nirvana. . . . And yet, although innumerable beings have thus been led to Nirvana, no being at all has been led to Nirvana. . . . If in a Bodhisattva the notion of 'being' should take place, he could not be called a 'Bodhi-being.' "[51] Being selfless, the bodhisattva turns over all the spiritual merit accumulated from past good deeds so that they can be used for the benefit of others. "He develops 'skill-in-means' (or 'skilful means'—*upaya*), the ability to adapt himself and his teaching to the level of his hearers, without attachment to any particular doctrine or formula as being necessarily applicable in all cases."[52] In the Mahayana scriptures the compassion and wisdom of the bodhisattvas is both descriptive and inspirational. Not only have they progressed far along the path to Buddhahood themselves, but they are also willing and able to help other sentient beings progress along their paths toward perfection. So Mahayana devotees are invited to take the stories of the bodhisattvas as models and to take the bodhisattva vow themselves.

CONCLUSION

Buddhism, like Hinduism, assumes that each of us is obscured by ignorance that results from the karma created by freely chosen actions and thoughts (especially our intentions) in this and previous lives. The Buddha emphasized that each person has both the freedom and the responsibility to work out his or her own path to purification or release from rebirth. Through his own life the Buddha offers us an example to emulate. He found that ordinary human experience is filled with false views. Trapped within these false views one experiences human life as dukkha or suffering of three types: physical pain, mental frustration, and unhappiness caused by selfish desires. The ordinary person is one who has not heard the Buddha's teaching and been changed by it. By contrast, the arya, or disciple of the Buddha, recognizes dukkha for what it is and enters the path to purification pioneered by the Buddha. This radical change in lifestyle and self-perception is available to all regardless of gender, age, caste group, or life stage, and whether they are educated or uneducated. This path, based on the Buddha's own experience that led him to perfection or nirvana, is offered to all in his teaching of the Middle Way and the Four Noble Truths that together form the foundation of Buddhist scripture. Developed by Buddha's followers, the different schools of Buddhism all accept a core collection of his sayings and his rules for the monasteries (the Vinaya), but focus in their commentaries on different sutra sayings of the Buddha as key to the realization of perfection.

The Theravada or early Buddhist approach, as we saw, focuses on the Buddha's sutras dealing with "no-soul," the elements or dharmas that make up human nature, and the fact that all of reality is in a state of constant change. Using these ideas of the Buddha, the Theravada philosophers developed a philosophical analysis of what composed a person; the purpose of the analysis was the therapeutic goal of removing one's false belief in a permanent self, which is the cause of selfishness that is turning our experience of the world into dukkha and preventing us from experiencing it as nirvana. A correct understanding of the constantly changing dharmas that make up our human nature reveals that there is no permanent self and thus no basis for the selfish desiring of things and the dukkha or sufferings that result. With the illusion of self and the resulting flame of selfish desiring "blown out" through the twin processes of moral living and philosophical meditation on the constituent parts of human nature, perfection is realized. One who has reached this goal is called by the Theravada school an arhat, a perfected person who embodies the highest qualities of mind and heart so that all actions are selfless and compassionate. An arhat is not reborn.

The Mahayana approach develops later and in conflict with the Theravada interpretation of the Buddha's teaching. Instead of "no-soul" and the dharmas, Mahayana scholars focus on the silence of the Buddha in response to questions of a metaphysical nature such as "Is the world eternal or not?" and the Buddha's parable of the wounded man who wanted to know all about the poisoned arrow stuck in his chest before he would allow it to be removed. The Mahayana sutras, as we noted, develop the teaching of a nonconceptual understanding (*prajna*) gained through meditation—a direct awareness of sunyata or the universal absence of any essence. This is a key critique of the Theravada claim to have found some things that ultimately exist, namely, dharmas. It meant that anyone engaging in meditation had to completely "let go" of all conceptual belief—only by giving up such intellectual attachment could human nature be purified of ignorant desiring and realize the perfection of emptiness or sunyata. This is the achievement of the bodhisattva. As the Prajnaparamita sutras show, the focus of the bodhisattva is with perfection not just for one's own self but for all sentient beings. Thus, the initiation vow of the bodhisattva to save others by leading them to nirvana. Through this vow a perfection is developed that is said to be totally selfless and filled with infinite compassion.

Chapter 9

Conclusion

The chapters of this book offer an introduction to the ideas and practices regarding the perfectibility of human nature found within philosophy, psychology, and the major world religions. By way of conclusion, let us briefly review the findings of the preceding chapters.

We began by surveying some of the views of human nature and its perfectibility found in Western philosophy and psychology. While there is considerable diversity in the understanding of human nature, there is general agreement that while progress may be made toward perfection, the limitations inherent within it make the full realization of perfection unlikely. For example, although Plato allowed that one might perfect oneself in the performance of the role in life to which one is called, he held that that is not sufficient by itself to ensure one's perfection as a human being. This view was adopted by other Western thinkers, including Luther, Calvin, and Duns Scotus. Aristotle's more complex idea of "teleological perfection" argues that every form of activity is directed toward reaching its natural end, which for humans is "happiness" or "well-being." This way of thinking was picked up and given further development by Aquinas and Kant. Kant, as we saw, thought of one's natural goal in terms of unrealized potentialities and "becoming perfect" as the actualizing of one's inherent potentialities—although this cannot be fully achieved in this life, thereby necessitating additional time to work at it in the afterlife. Augustine solves the problem presented by negative elements within human nature (e.g., lying, stealing, or bigotry) by suggesting that such negative behaviors are not the actualization of one's true potentialities but rather the result of their absence. Descartes and Leibnitz seem to follow Augustine in their understanding of evil as the absence of good. In Western philosophy Plato seems to have started the speculation regarding human perfectibility by introducing the idea of a metaphysical good as the ideal to be achieved and the idea of evil as the lack of good, with the human

condition being the tension between the two and the struggle to re-
solve it. To help in this struggle an ideal is often conceived for humans
to emulate—for Plato (in the *Theaetetus*) and Aquinas, God is adopted
as the metaphysical ideal of perfection upon which humans must model
themselves. However, in other dialogues Plato identifies perfection with
order and harmony in society. As we saw in chapter 2, this idea that
society has a role in enabling humans to progress toward perfection is
given further exploration in later Western philosophy and psychology.

In the chapter on Judaism we saw that there is no single answer
to our question regarding the perfectibility of human nature. Although
within Jewish thought there is no single answer, there is general agreement that humans are created in the image of God and have a role to
play in the work of creation. Unlike the dualistic Greek view of human
nature as composed of a separate soul weighted down by a materialistic
body, Hebrew thought (especially in the Hebrew Bible) conceives of
the person as a psychosomatic unity composed of many parts. Because
they are created in God's image, humans are seen to have been given
both authority and responsibility as established by God's covenant with
Moses at Mount Sinai, later reaffirmed by God speaking through the
prophets. Israel's failure to live up to the covenant revealed other aspects of human nature, namely, its sinfulness that obstructs progress
toward perfection. The Psalmists also point out that as constituted from
dust humans are subject to disease, diminution, and death. This inherent frailty, taken together with human sinfulness, works to prevent the
actualization of the image of God within, but does call forth God's
mercy, which makes progress toward a perfect covenant relationship
possible. While the priests focused on holiness and the prophets focused on righteousness as the path to perfection, for the rabbis it is the
observance of commandments and the study of Torah that is required.
Observance of the commandments is seen by the rabbis not only as the
path to perfection but also as an act of cocreation with God.

Turning to the Jewish philosophers, we observed that while they
ground themselves in biblical and rabbinic thought, they evidence varying degrees of Greek influence in their understanding of human nature
and the role of reason in the pursuit of perfection. Maimonides, as we
saw, adopts a dualistic Greek view of human nature as having a soul
separate from the body. But Maimonides follows Aristotle more closely
than Plato and holds that to make progress toward perfection humans
must overcome their finite material natures via metaphysical and scientific
studies that give one an "acquired intellect." According to Maimonides it
is the "acquired intellect" that enables one to transcend bodily desires
and at death achieve immortality. But just as God's intellect, as the Torah

reveals, involves both knowledge ("theoretical perfection") and ethical action ("practical perfection"), so also human perfection is understood as a perfection of the intellect together with ethical action—the latter made possible by God's divine "overflow" or "emanation." Thus, even for a philosopher like Maimonides, some element of God's mercy or spirit (*ruach*) is required along with reason and ethical activity (required by the Torah's commandments) for the realization of perfection, which will not be complete until after the body drops off at death.

Developing alongside Jewish philosophy during the medieval period, the Kabbalists (the mystical tradition of Judaism) held that the unity of God's good creation, symbolized in the ten sefirot, has been broken apart by human sin. Perfection comes with the restoration of unity and harmony among the sefirot. We focused on the thought of Isaac Luria, for whom perfection is found in the restoration of a state in which the breaking of vessels (caused by the inrush of divine light at the time of creation) is completely mended and the originally intended harmony of the sefirot is realized. Although the Messiah will, in the end, come and restore harmony to all of creation, people as well as nature, it is up to humans to take the lead in restoring the cosmos with all of its peoples to its original perfection. With the possible exception of the thought of the kabbalists, Jewish thought sees human nature as so limited by human sinfulness and frailty that it is unable to reach perfection without God's help.

In the Christianity chapter we saw that New Testament thought adopted the Hebrew Bible's understanding of human nature as a psychosomatic unity of body, mind, and spirit—evident in the adoption of the Jewish teaching of the resurrection of the body. The New Testament describes human nature as having intelligence, emotions, free will, moral responsibility and the possibility of eternal life. Jesus describes the goal for Christians in terms of perfection when he says, "Be ye perfect even as your heavenly Father is perfect" (Matt. 5:48). Paul, like Jesus, says humans are created by God as a mind-body-spirit unity and in the image of God. Yet in spite of this there is some inherent perversity within human nature that causes people to sin. So Paul says, "I do not do the good I want, but the evil I do not want" (Rom. 7:19). Salvation is made possible by God's grace given through Jesus Christ, which enables Paul to strive on toward the goal of perfection.

Among the many Christian theologians, the teachings of Augustine, Aquinas, Luther, and Reinhold Niebuhr on human nature and its perfectibility were surveyed. Augustine combined Greek and biblical thought in his understanding of human nature. He introduced the idea of "original sin," namely, that humans had fallen from their original

188 The Perfectibility of Human Nature

good and loving nature by an act of their own will. This fall cannot be reversed by a similar exercise of human will but only by God's grace. Only then, said Augustine, can progress be made toward perfection, but full perfection will not be realized until the resurrection of the body occurs in the afterlife. Aquinas offers a blending of Aristotle, biblical thought, and the theology of Augustine. Full perfection belongs to God alone, but a lower perfection, "evangelical perfection," is open to humans and incumbent upon them. This involves removing all mortal sin and cultivating the love of God and one's neighbor. Although humans must cultivate sinlessness, even with the help of God's grace they can never live a wholly perfect and sinless life in this world. Aquinas follows Aristotle in maintaining that perfection requires not only sinlessness but also the rational contemplation of God until a vision of God is achieved. But, like sinlessness, this highest seeing of God can only occur in the afterlife. However, Aquinas does propose a hierarchy of perfection with bishops at the top, followed by religious orders and parish priests, with laypersons at the bottom.

Luther rejects Aquinas's hierarchy of perfection and his emphasis on free will. Like Paul, Luther found himself a sinner no matter how hard he tried to do the good. Freedom came, not from trying to perfect oneself by overcoming sin, but by admitting one's sinfulness, repenting, and having faith in God—a faith made possible by God's grace through Christ, namely, the Holy Spirit, to which humans must surrender. No one can hope to achieve perfection in this life. While human nature cannot perfect itself, it can be made holy when God's word is united with the soul until it glows as if on fire with God's love. But perfection can only occur in the afterlife. Niebuhr agrees with much of Luther's teaching but is strongly influenced by Kierkegaard in identifying existential anxiety resulting from the refusal to accept the finiteness of human nature as the root cause of sin. Only by surrender to God's grace is there hope of escaping the anxiety of finitude and, with it, sin. The idea that humankind can perfect itself by its own efforts through science, technology, or progress is the essence of sinfulness and the refusal to acknowledge human finiteness. Nevertheless Niebuhr remains optimistic about human destiny, which is to be realized in the resurrection and the world to come.

The Islamic chapter found that Muslims view human nature as a unity of body, mind, and spirit. In the Qur'an it is the entire person in all of his or her physical, emotional, and spiritual capacities that is created, dies, and will be resurrected on Judgment Day. Nor is there any notion of original sin; rather, the Qur'anic concept of fitra argues for a human nature that, in its primordial state, is sound, sinless and capable of progressing toward perfection in this life and the next. To achieve this goal, God's guidance is given in the Qur'an and in the shari'a. But human effort is required to actualize human nature's inherent capacities by following the guidance offered in scripture and law. Sin occurs when a person uses free choice to follow his or her base desires and go against the guidance given by God. But the possibility of actualizing the inherent goodness in human nature by following God's guidance is always present and is exemplified by Muhammad, who is seen as the "Perfect Man."

Our survey of Islamic thinkers on human nature and its perfectibility included the views of al-Ash'ari, al-Ghazali, and Ibn 'Arabi. Al-Ash'ari focused on the tension between the Qur'an's teaching of God's omnipotence in relation to human free will. Although he argued that God's powers were absolute, he attempted to present a middle position between complete human free will and divine predestination through his theory of the acquisition of God's actions by humans using their human choice to follow God's teachings in the Qur'an. Perfection in this approach seems to be more a result of God's action rather than of human effort. Al-Ghazali opposed the dominant Neoplatonic Muslim thinking of his day, which focused on contemplation of the perfections of the world to come. Instead, al-Ghazali found that careful observance of religious law and ritual, together with intellectual knowledge and contemplation, is the way to perfect human nature for this world and the next. With Ibn 'Arabi we saw a Sufi mystic who holds the perfecting of human nature to be made possible by the outpouring of God's love present in the Qur'an. God's motive in creating the universe is love and a desire to be known. Adam, the "Perfect Man," created in God's image, is the paradigm of creation and embodies all the perfection of the universe. Muhammad is such a Perfect Man, one who has realized all the possibilities inherent in our original human nature and thus is the model for each of us to follow. To do this one must perfect one's human nature through a series of journeys: from God when we are born into the world, toward God with the help of a guide, and finally within God—the journey which has no end. In this last journey, although one is externally performing shari'a and living in society, internally one is dwelling with God and sharing with God the direct experience of all creation and of God himself. It is this intimate knowledge achieved in the state of human perfection that qualifies humans to be God's khalifah or vice-regents on earth. The Sufi view of human nature and its perfectibility offers an inspiring vision that is open to all to follow.

In part 2 our focus shifted to Eastern thought, particularly as found in Indian philosophy, traditional Yoga psychology, and the Hindu and Buddhist religious traditions. We saw in chapter 6 that the Astika and Nastika schools of Indian philosophy adopt a common worldview marked by the basic presuppositions of anadi, karma, and samsara and the release from rebirth as a result of having perfected oneself by purging the obscuring karma from one's nature. Ignorance replaces the Western ideas of sin, disobedience, or personal limitation as the basic human condition that needs to be overcome for perfection to be realized. Rather than salvation or redemption from sin with the help of God's grace, release from rebirth is the spiritual goal of perfection—usually envisaged as enlightenment that extinguishes the karmic ignorance that is causing us to be reborn. The various philosophical schools and religious traditions offer different answers as to how to realize this goal. But all agree that we will be born over and over again until each of us perfects himself or herself—not in the afterlife, as is often suggested in Western thought, but here on earth. In chapter 6 we sampled the approaches of the Mimamsa, Grammarian, and Sankhya-Yoga schools in this regard. Sankhya-Yoga, as we saw, develops traditional psychological theory and specific yoga practices for the perfection of human nature. This traditional Yoga psychology is seen to function in common for all schools of Indian philosophy and religion at the level of physical and mental practice in spite of major disagreements at the level of metaphysical beliefs. We also observed that the philosophy of language developed by the Grammarian school provided an approach to the understanding and use of mantra chanting as having the power to purify and perfect human nature. With these basic assumptions and approaches in mind we then turned to the specific Hindu and Buddhist ideas of how to perfect human nature and realize release from rebirth.

In the Hinduism chapter we saw that the Vedas view human nature as composed of an eternal self (*atman*) enclosed by various bodily layers (*kosas*), including the body, breath, mind and intellect. These layers are understood to be composed of karma created by one's free choice in this and previous lives. Perfecting oneself requires the purging of one's karma, for it is karma that causes one to be reborn. Hindu scriptures such as the Upanishads offer an optimistic view regarding the perfectibility of human nature by revealing the atman or true self within the layers of obscuring karma. This spiritual quest may extend over many lifetimes, but it is understood by Hindus to be the goal that each person must realize. Then the beginningless cycle of birth-death-rebirth (*karma-samsara*) will be ended and perfection or release from rebirth realized. As we saw, Hinduism offers a variety of paths (suited to the variety of human temperaments) to this goal: the path of knowledge, the path of action, the path of devotion, and the path of esoteric yoga practice. Each path can enable one to perfect one's human nature and realize release (*moksa*) from rebirth.

Hinduism developed a special concept of living liberation (*jivanmukti*) or perfection while living from the seventh century CE on. We surveyed the *jivanmukti* concepts of Sankara, Patanjali's Yoga Sutras, Ramana Maharshi, and Swami Vivekananda and found much in common between them. Each of these founders is judged to have been a jivanmukta by his followers. Each develops a particular way of dealing with the problem of prarabdha karma, or karma that is manifesting as one's own body and mind in this life. Ramanuja, however, concludes that only after death is one completely freed from the manifesting karma that composes one's body. Consequently, to propose perfection (i.e., the complete purging of all karma) while still in a living body, as the jivanmukti doctrine requires, is impossible. Thus Ramanuja rejects the jivanmukti idea and argues that, after a life of devotional surrender, only at death does one become completely free from all karma (including the parabdha) and reach an eternal state of separate but intimate communion with God—perfection and release for Ramanuja. For Ramanuja and his followers, the simple path of surrender to the Lord (*prapatti*—open to all regardless of caste or gender) is held to purge all but one's already manifesting or parabdha karma and one is assured of full disembodied perfection or *moksa* at the end of this very lifetime.

In the Buddhism chapter we saw that, like Hinduism, Buddhism assumes that each of us is obstructed by ignorance that results from the karma created by freely chosen actions and thoughts (especially our intentions) in this and previous lives. The Buddha emphasized that each person has both the freedom and the responsibility to work out his or her own path to purification or release from rebirth. Through his own life the Buddha offers us an example to emulate. He pioneered a path by which the ordinary human experience of life as dukkha or suffering can be transformed into the perfection of nirvana. The followers of the Buddha, as we saw, divided into two schools, each with its own model for the perfected human being: the arhat for the Theravadins, and the bodhisattva for the Mahayana.

Focusing on the Buddha's teachings of "no-soul" (*anatman*), the elements or dharmas that make up human nature, and the fact that all reality is in a state of constant change, the Theravadin philosophers developed a philosophical analysis of what composed a person with the therapeutic purpose of removing one's false belief in a permanent self—the cause of selfish desiring and frustration that is turning our experience of the world into dukkha and preventing us from experiencing it as nirvana. One who has reached this goal is called by the Theravada school an arhat, a perfected person who embodies the highest qualities of mind and heart so that, as was the case with the Buddha, all actions are selfless and compassionate. An arhat after death is not reborn. Focusing on the silence of the Buddha in response to questions of a metaphysical nature, the Mahayana scholars developed a deconstructive critique of language and offered a nonconceptual understanding (*prajna*) gained through meditation as the path to perfection. In this approach one has to give up intellectual attachment to philosophical or theological belief systems so that human nature can be purified of ignorant desiring and the perfection of emptiness or sunyata be realized. This the bodhisattva manifests by living a vow of perfection that is held to be totally selfless and filled with infinite compassion for all beings in the cosmos. Bodhisattvas, at this highest level of realization, are seen to be very powerful and virtually equivalent to the Buddha in his ever-present or heavenly form—as visualized in Mahayana sutras and mandalas. As we saw, one such bodhisattva, Amitabha (Amida in Japan) became the basis of Chinese and Japanese devotional practice toward perfection and nirvana. In the Mahayana scriptures the compassion and wisdom of the bodhisattva is both descriptive and inspirational. Not only have they progressed along the path of Buddhahood themselves, but they show themselves devoted to helping all other sentient beings progress along their paths toward perfection. So Mahayana devotees, monks, nuns, and laypeople are invited to take stories of the bodhisattvas as models, and to take the bodhisattva vow themselves.

Having reviewed and summarized our findings regarding human nature and its perfectibility, let us conclude with an overview of similarities and difference between Eastern and Western thought. Let us begin with similarities. Terence Penelhum observes that at a very general level, both Eastern and Western traditions tell us that each of us inherits a spiritual condition from the past within human nature.[1] In the West, for example, the Christian view of human beings is that their nature is corrupted through sin, which entered the world at the onset of human history through the disobedience of Adam and which manifests in us in a strong tendency to follow our temptations rather than the good that we know. In Judaism, also, humans are thought of inheriting a constitutional frailty (being composed of dust), which, taken together with human sinfulness (but not original sin), works to prevent the actualization of the image of God within. The parallel in Indian philosophy and psychology and in Hindu and Buddhist thought is the fundamental notion of karma-samsara. As we have seen, karma-samsara embodies the belief that each of us in our human nature inherits the consequences of our past actions and thoughts, and that this inheritance forms the major obstacle to our perfection. In this view, I am born with a long (beginningless) legacy of karmic dispositions stored up from the choices made by my karmic forebearers or previous selves, which I am individuating in this life by my choices made in the physical and social circumstances in which I find myself. This karmic aspect of my human nature determines what sort of individual I begin life as. The karmic dispositions created by my choices in previous lives are reborn or relocated "in the physical embryo that most appropriately embodies how it was when the body in which it was last expressed came to its end. We live in a world that has a justice-system built into its biology."[2] This is not fatalism, for the choices I made in previous lives created my karmic inheritance, and the same applies to the new life I am now living. The main similarities between the karma-samsara doctrine and Western thought are two. First, there is the common insistence on an inheritance that ensures none of us starts life with a clean slate, but with a human nature containing "a set of circumstances and inner dispositions with which we have to contend and for which we carry responsibility."[3] Second, there is, in each of these perspectives, the idea that there are also opportunities for spiritual progress within our nature. If we use our free will to pursue these opportunities, they place us on the path to perfecting ourselves. All agree that this process may be aided by a source of spiritual power that, while available from within, transcends our selves as individually and ordinarily conceived.

It is when one asks what perfection itself consists of that clear differences emerge between traditions. First, the obstacle in human nature to be overcome for perfection to be realized is differently conceived. In the West it is sin and human frailty—a weakness of will and constitution. In the Eastern thought grounded in India, with its traditions of enlightenment, the ultimate obstacle to be overcome is ignorance. This is why the teachings of figures such as Gautama or Sankara, rather than their persons, occupy the central place in their traditions. So Penelhum remarks, "In this respect the great enlightenment religions of the Eastern world are more like the secular philosophical traditions of the West that come down to us from Socrates, than they are like the Semitic religious traditions [of Judaism, Christianity and Islam]."[4] This leads to a second major difference that we have observed in our analysis: the degree to which the perfection of human nature can be achieved. In Western philosophy, psychology, and the Jewish, Christian and Islamic religious traditions, it is generally maintained that due to our limited, flawed, and/or sinful natures, perfectibility cannot be realized in this life. At best, it may be achieved in the afterlife but then only with the help of God's grace (possible exceptions here are the Kabbalists and the Sufis). By contrast, in Indian thought, perfectibility of one's nature is achievable by all, and one will continue being reborn until success is realized. All of the Indian philosophies, traditional psychologies, and religious traditions are simply different paths to perfection. This major difference in the Indian and Western assessments of the limits (or lack thereof) of human nature strikes me as being most significant. Too often, Western scholars have not been willing to treat this difference with the seriousness it deserves. For example, the psychologist Carl Jung, when confronted by the claims of Patanjali's Yoga psychology that the individual ego could be (and spiritually needed to be) totally transcended, concluded that the yogis had been meditating in the Indian sun too long and that such a transcendent state was psychologically impossible.[5] Another example is found in the philosopher John Hick's *The Fifth Dimension: An Exploration of the Spiritual Realm.* In it Hick argues that claims of "union with the ultimate in this life" (exactly the claim of the Yoga Sutras, the Hindu jivanmukta or the Buddhist bodhisattva) must be understood "metaphorically" rather than "literally."[6] In my mind the evidence reviewed in part 2 of this book is simply too detailed and too substantial an exploration of the perfectibility of human nature to be so dismissed. Our study leaves us with the clear dilemma that while Western thought largely judges the perfectibility of human nature in life to be impossible, the evidence of the Eastern traditions arising in India is that not only is it possible, but we will each be reborn until it is realized. Is it the case that roughly one half of humanity is misled as to the philosophical, psychological, and spiritual limits of human nature?

Perhaps this apparent impasse between Eastern and Western views of human nature and its perfectibility can be overcome through the contemporary challenge offered by our increasing scientific and moral awareness of the intimate relationship we humans have with the world of animals, plants, sun, earth, air, and water that makes life possible. In this book we have attempted to understand human nature and its perfectibility in the context of human thought and institutions as differently developed East and West. What is now needed, it seems, is an assessment of human nature in the context of the natural ecosystems of which it is but a small interdependent part. Paul (in Romans 8), the kabbalists and Sufis in the West, and the Hindus and Buddhists in the East offer hints as to what such as assessment might look like. Such future study will likely bring us closer to the quest for "the still point of the turning world" (Eliot) and the sense of our "wider selves" (James) that drives my scholarly curiosity.

Notes

CHAPTER 1. INTRODUCTION

1. T. S. Eliot, "Burnt Norton," in *A Little Treasury of Modern Poetry*, ed. Oscar Williams (New York: Scribners, 1952), p. 29.

2. Keith Ward, *Religion and Human Nature* (Oxford: Clarendon Press, 1998), pp. 1–9.

3. Ibid., p. 1.

4. For a detailed presentation of the Yoga view, see my *Yoga and Psychology* (Albany: State University of New York Press, 2002).

5. Ward, *Religion and Human Nature*, p. 3.

6. Ibid.

7. Ibid., p. 4.

8. Ibid., p. 8.

CHAPTER 2. PERFECTIBILITY IN WESTERN PHILOSOPHY AND PSYCHOLOGY

1. John Passmore, *The Perfectibility of Man* (New York: Charles Scribner's Sons, 1970), p. 11.

2. Ibid., p. 13.

3. Ibid., p. 18.

4. As quoted by Passmore, *Perfectibility of Man*, p. 18.

5. Augustine, *The City of God*, trans. Gerald Walsh et al. and abridged by Vernon Bourke (New York: Image Books, 1958), bk. 11, p. 217.

6. Passmore, *Perfectibility of Man*, p. 19.

7. Ibid., p. 20.

8. Ibid.

9. Immanuel Kant, *Groundwork of the Metaphysic of Morals*, trans. H. J. Paton (New York: Harper Torchbooks, 1956), p. 76.

10. As quoted by Passmore, *Perfectibility of Man*, p. 23.

11. Passmore, *Perfectibility of Man*, p. 23.

12. Ibid., p. 25.

13. Ibid., p. 27.

14. Ibid., p. 147.

15. Ibid., p. 149.

16. Ibid., p. 150.

17. Ibid.

18. *New Encyclopedia Britannica*, 15th ed. s.v. "Locke, John."

19. Gordon Allport, *Becoming* (New Haven, CT: Yale University Press, 1955), p. 7.

20. As stated by Passmore, *Perfectibility of Man*, p. 161.

21. Ibid., p. 163.

22. *The Encyclopedia of Philosophy*, ed. Paul Edwards (New York: Macmillan, 1972), s.v. "Rousseau, Jean-Jacques."

23. As quoted by Passmore, *Perfectibility of Man*, p. 178.

24. *Encyclopedia of Philosophy*, s.v. "Rousseau, Jean-Jacques."

25. Ibid.

26. Passmore, *Perfectibility of Man*, p. 180.

27. Ibid., p. 173.

28. Ibid., p. 174.

29. Ibid., p. 193.

30. As stated by Erich Fromm in *Marx's Concept of Man* (New York: Frederick Ungar, 1966), p. 26.

31. Passmore, *Perfectibility of Man*, p. 236.

32. Ibid., p. 237.

33. *Encyclopedia of Philosophy*, s.v. "Marx, Karl."

34. Passmore, *Perfectibility of Man*, p. 238.

35. Ibid., p. 187.

36. Ibid., p. 189.

37. Gordon Allport, *Becoming: Basic Considerations for a Psychology of Personality* (New Haven, CT: Yale University Press, 1955), p. 8.

38. Ibid., p. 9.

39. Edwin Boring, *A History of Experimental Psychology* (New York: Appleton-Century-Crofts, 1950), p. 644.

40. Passmore, *Perfectibility of Man*, p. 168.

41. Boring, *History of Experimental Psychology*, p. 650.

42. B. F. Skinner, *Walden Two* (New York: Macmillan, 1962), p. 194.

43. B. F. Skinner, "A Case History in Scientific Method," in *Psychology: A Study of a Science*, ed. Sigmund Koch (New York: McGraw-Hill, 1959), 2: 378.

44. Passmore, *Perfectibility of Man*, p. 169.

45. Allport, *Becoming*, pp. 12ff.

46. Passmore, *Perfectibility of Man*, p. 215.

47. Kant, as quoted by ibid., p. 216.

48. Ibid.

49. Immanuel Kant, *Religion within the Limits of Reason Alone*, trans. Theodore M. Greene and Hoyt Hudson (New York: Harper Torchbooks, 1960), pp. 46–47.

50. Boring, *History of Experimental Psychology*, p. 334.

51. Ibid., pp. 356–61.

52. Calvin S. Hall, *A Primer of Freudian Psychology* (New York: Mentor, 1958), p. 37.

53. Sigmund Freud, "Beyond the Pleasure Principle," trans. J. Strachey in *The Standard Edition of the Complete Psychological Works of Sigmund Freud*, ed, J. Strachey (London: Hogarth Press, 1957), 18: 42.

54. Passmore, *Perfectibility of Man*, p. 291.

55. Sigmund Freud, *Civilization and Its Discontents*, trans. James Strachey (London: Hogarth Press, 1975).

56. C. G. Jung, *Memories, Dreams, Reflections*, ed. Anelia Jaffe (New York: Vintage Books, 1963), p. 161.

57. C. G. Jung, *The Archetypes and the Collective Unconscious*, trans. R. F. C. Hull (Princeton, NJ: Princeton University Press, 1969).

58. See Harold Coward, *Yoga and Psychology: Language, Memory and Mysticism* (Albany: State University of New York Press, 2002), pp. 73 ff.

59. C. G. Jung, *Psychological Types*, trans. R. F. C. Hull (Princeton, NJ: Princeton University Press, 1971), pp. 10–11.

60. C. G. Jung, *Letters*, ed. G. Adler (London: Routledge, 1973), 1: 236.

61. Allport, *Becoming*, p. 90. See also Harold Coward, *Jung and Eastern Thought* (Albany: State University of New York Press, 1985).

62. William James, *Psychology* (New York: Henry Holt, 1893), pp. 151ff.

63. William James, *The Varieties of Religious Experience* (New York: Mentor, 1958).

64. Ibid., p. 42.

65. Ibid., p. 61.

66. Ibid., p. 290.

67. Ibid.

68. Ibid.

69. Gordon Allport, *The Individual and His Religion* (New York: Macmillan, 1960), p. 76.

70. Ibid., p. 78.

71. Ibid., p. 80.

72. Ibid., p. 82. See also Paul Tillich's argument for the necessity of doubt if faith is to flourish and psychological development to occur. Tillich, *Dynamic of Faith* (New York: Harper Torchbooks, 1958).

73. Abraham Maslow, *The Farther Reaches of Human Nature* (New York: Viking, 1973), p. xv.

74. Ibid., p. xvi.

75. Ibid., p. xvii.

76. This and the following description of the self-actualization process is taken from ibid., pp. 43–50.

77. Ibid., p. 48.

78. Ibid., p. 49.

79. Ibid., p. 50.

80. Michael Washburn, *The Ego and the Dynamic Ground* (Albany: State University of New York Press, 1988).

81. Ibid., p. v.

82. Charles Tart, ed., *Transpersonal Psychologies* (New York: Harper Colophon, 1975).

83. Ibid., p. 2.

84. Robert Ornstein, ed., *The Nature of Human Consciousness* (San Francisco: W. H. Freeman, 1973), p. xi.

85. In Tart, *Transpersonal Psychologies*, p. 244.

86. Ibid., p. 262.

CHAPTER 3. PERFECTIBILITY IN JEWISH THOUGHT

1. *The Interpreter's Dictionary of the Bible* (New York: Abingdon Press, 1962), s.v. "Man, Nature of in the OT."

2. Arthur Hertzberg, ed. *Judaism* (New York: George Braziller, 1962), p. 178.

3. Personal communication from Eliezer Segal, University of Calgary, Nov. 6, 2005.

4. Isidore Epstein, *Judaism: A Historical Presentation* (New York: Penguin, 1987), pp. 16, 108.

5. The following is based on H. Wheeler Robinson, "Hebrew Psychology," in *The People and the Book*, ed. Arthur S. Peake (Oxford: Clarendon Press, 1925), pp. 252–382; and Hans Walter Wolff, *Anthropology of the Old Testament* (London: SCM Press, 1974). See also E. E. Urbach, *The Sages: Their Concepts and Beliefs*, trans. I. Abrahams (Jerusalem: Magnes Press, Hebrew University, 1975), pp. 214–54. Wolff notes that the Bible does not present a unified doctrine of human nature for the biblical words examined are used as poetic metaphors (*Anthropology*, pp. 7–9).

6. Robinson, "Hebrew Psychology," p. 355.

7. Ibid., p. 362.

8. Ibid., p. 363.

9. Ibid., p. 366

10. Millar Burrows, *An Outline of Biblical Theology* (Philadelphia: Westminister Press, 1946), p. 141.

11. *Interpreter's Dictionary of the Bible*, s.v. "Man, Nature of in the OT."

12. *The Concise Encyclopaedia of Living Faiths*, ed. R. C. Zaehner (New York: Hawthorn Books, 1959), s.v. "Judaism," by R. J. Zwi Werblowsky.

13. J. Kenneth Kuntz, *The People of Ancient Israel* (New York: Harper & Row, 1974), p. 356. See also Lamentations 2:4; Psalsms 137; Ezekiel 1–24.

14. *Interpreter's Dictionary of the Bible*, s.v. "Man, Nature of in the OT."

15. Ibid.

16. Jacob Neusner, *The Way of Torah: An Introduction to Judaism* (Belmont, CA: Dickenson, 1974), p. 12.

17. *The Oxford Dictionary of the Jewish Religion*, ed. R. J. Zwi Werblowsky and G. Wigoder (Oxford: Oxford University Press, 1997), s.v. "Holiness."

18. Ibid.

19. *Interpreter's Dictionary of the Bible*, s.v. "Priests and Levites."

20. Ibid., "Priests and Levites."

21. Epstein, *Judaism*, p. 60.

22. Ibid., p. 61.

23. Urbach, *Sages*, p. 214.

24. Ibid., p. 215.

25. Ibid., p. 217.

26. Ibid., p. 218.

27. Ibid., p. 221.

28. Ibid., p. 222.

29. As quoted by J. Saldarini and Joseph Kanofsky, "Religious Dimensions of the Human Condition in Judaism," in *The Human Condition*, ed. Robert Neville (Albany: State University of New York Press, 2001), p. 118.

30. Urbach, *Sages*, p. 334.

31. Ibid., p. 339.

32. Ibid., p. 342.

33. Ibid., p. 667.

34. Ibid., p. 671.

35. Louis Finkelstein, *Akiba: Scholar, Saint and Martyr* (New York: Atheneum Books, 1971), p. 259.

36. Urbach, *Sages*, p. 679.

37. Ibid., p. 683.

38. Ibid.

39. *Encyclopaedia Judaica* (Jerusalem: Keter Publishing House, 1971), s.v. "Philosophy, Jewish."

40. Ibid.

41. Edward Milton, "The Nature and Destiny of Man in Alexandrian Judaism" (PhD diss., McMaster University, 1983), p. 38.

42. Ibid., p. 42.

43. Ibid., p. 47.

44. Ibid., p. 65.

45. As quoted by ibid., p. 74.

46. Milton, "Nature and Destiny of Man," p. 74.

47. *Encyclopaedia Judaica*, s.v. "Philosophy, Jewish."

48. Ibid.

49. *Encyclopaedia Judaica*, s.v. "Redemption."

50. Howard Kreisel, *Maimonides' Political Thought: Studies in Ethics Law, and the Human Ideal* (Albany: State University of New York Press, 1999).

51. Ibid., pp. 126ff.

52. Ibid., p. 131.

53. As quoted by ibid., p. 135.

54. Kreisel, *Maimonides' Political Thought*, p. 136.

55. As quoted by ibid., p. 136.

56. Kreisel, *Maimonides' Political Thought*, p. 137.

57. Ibid., pp. 149–50.

58. Taken from *The New Encyclopaedia Britannica*, 15th ed., s.v. "Judaism," p. 465

59. *Encyclopaedia Judaica*, s.v. "Redemption."

60. Ibid., p. 6.

61. Gershom G. Scholem, *On the Kabbalah and Its Symbolism* (London: Routledge and Kegan Paul, 1965), p. 46.

62. *New Encyclopaedia Britannica*, s.v. "Judaism," p. 467.

63. Elliot R. Wolfson, "Light through Darkness: The Ideal of Human Perfection in the Zohar," *Harvard Theological Review* 81 (1988): 76.

64. Ibid., p. 88.

65. Epstein, *Judaism*, p. 245.

66. *Encyclopaedia Judaica*, s.v. "Redemption."

67. Epstein, *Judaism*, p. 245.

68. For more on this fascinating rebirth idea that bears some resonance with the ideas of the Buddhist bodhisattva (one who has realized enlightenment or perfection but stays behind to help others reach the same state rather than going off into nirvana) and the Hindu *rsi* (one who has reached perfection and release from rebirth in a previous life but is reborn at the start of each cycle of the universe to speak the Hindu scripture, the Veda, so as to help others realize the same goal), see ibid., pp. 246ff.

69. Luria, as summarized by ibid., p. 246.

70. Epstein, *Judaism*, p. 246.

71. Lawrence Fine, *Physician of the Soul, Healer of the Cosmos* (Stanford, CA: Stanford University Press, 2003).

72. Ibid., p. 151.

73. Ibid., pp. 151–52.

74. Ibid., p. 152.

75. Ibid., p. 313.

76. Ibid., p. 155. The following analysis of Luria's body-letter correspondence is based upon pp. 155–60.

77. Ibid., p. 155.

78. Ibid.

79. Ibid., p. 156.

80. Ibid., p. 157.

81. Ibid., p. 163.

82. Ibid., p. 166.

83. Ibid., p. 167. Luria claimed the ability to cleanse the soul of stains from sinful or polluting acts such as improper sexual activity, failing to recite the daily Shema prayer, and thinking about committing a transgression (see ibid., pp. 167–80).

84. Ibid., p. 179.

85. Ibid., p. 313.

86. Urbach, *Sages*, p. 683.

CHAPTER 4. PERFECTIBILITY IN CHRISTIAN THOUGHT

1. A notable exception in this regard was Pelagius (c. 400 CE), an Irish or British monk who came to Rome maintaining that Jesus would not have

commanded humans to become morally perfect if they were incapable of doing so. Therefore, humans must be able to perfect themselves. But Pelagius has almost unanimously been condemned as a heretic. Mainstream Christianity has held that sinlessness is impossible in this life. W. Walker, *A History of the Christian Church* (New York: Charles Scribner's Sons, 1959), pp. 168–69.

2. Immanuel Kant, *Critique of Practical Reason*, trans. L. W. Beck (New York: Bobbs-Merrill, 1956), p. 127.

3. *The Encyclopedia of Philosophy*, ed. Paul Edwards (New York: Macmillan, 1972), s.v. "Perfection."

4. Reinhold Niebuhr, *The Nature and Destiny of Man*, vol. 1 (New York: Charles Scribner's Sons, 1964).

5. *The Interpreter's Dictionary of the Bible*, vol. 3 (New York: Abingdon Press, 1962), s.v. "Man, Nature of, in the NT."

6. Ibid.

7. Ibid.

8. Ibid.

9. Ibid.

10. *Encyclopedia of Philosophy*, s.v. "Perfection."

11. *Encyclopedia of Religion and Ethics* (Edinburgh: T & T Clark, 1917), s.v. "Perfection (Christian)."

12. *Dictionary of the Bible*, ed. James Hastings (New York: Scribner's Sons, 1963), s.v. "Perfection."

13. H. Fernhout, "Man: The Image and Glory of God," in *Towards a Biblical View of Man*, ed. A. De Graaff and J. H. Olthius (Toronto: Institute for Christian Studies, 1978), p. 27.

14. *Dictionary of the Bible*, s.v. "Perfection."

15. Margaret R. Miles, "The Body and Human Values in Augustine of Hippo," in *Grace, Politics and Desire: Essays on Augustine*, ed. H. A. Maynell (Calgary: University of Calgary Press, 1990), p. 55.

16. Augustine, *The Confessions*, trans. Rex Warner (Toronto: Mentor-Omega, 1963).

17. Miles, "Body and Human Values," p. 57.

18. Augustine, *The Confessions*, 8:5, as paraphrased by ibid., p. 58.

19. Augustine, *Confessions*, 13:6.

20. Miles, "Body and Human Values," p. 60.

21. Although Augustine was influenced by Plotinus's view of human nature, Miles shows how in *The Confessions* Augustine presents a perspective that gives more weight to the Hebrew biblical conception of human nature—especially in regard to the body.

22. This summary of Plotinus is based on John Passmore, *The Perfectibility of Man* (New York: Charles Scribner's Sons, 1970), pp. 64–67. See also *New Encyclopaedia Britannica*, 15th ed., s.v. "Platonism after Plato."

23. Miles, "Body and Human Values," p. 61.

24. Ibid., p. 60.

25. Ibid., p. 62.

26. Ibid., p. 63.

27. Augustine, *The City of God*, trans. C. G. Walsh et al. (New York: Image Books, 1958).

28. Miles, "Body and Human Values," p. 64. See also Mark 12:18–27.

29. Miles, "Body and Human Values," p. 65. Augustine's view of sex bears similarities to the Yoga view we will encounter in chapters 6 and 7—namely, that sexual desire in human nature is the result of a habit humans have developed over the generations, a habit that, for perfection, needs to be overcome.

30. As quoted from Augustine's sermons by Miles, "Body and Human Values," p. 65.

31. *New Encyclopaedia Britannica*, 15th ed., s.v. "Augustine."

32. See Passmore, *Perfectibility of Man*, pp. 94–99.

33. Robert Pasnau, *Thomas Aquinas on Human Nature* (Cambridge: Cambridge University Press, 2002), p. 3.

34. *Encyclopedia of Philosophy*, s.v. "Aquinas, Thomas."

35. Pasnau, *Thomas Aquinas on Human Nature*, p. 9.

36. Ibid., p. 20.

37. R. Newton Flew, *The Idea of Perfection in Christian Theology* (Oxford: Oxford University Press, 1968), p. 225.

38. The following description of Aquinas's view of human nature is based on F. C. Copleston, *Aquinas* (Markham, ON: Penguin, 1975), pp. 156–98.

39. Ibid., p. 160.

40. Ibid., p. 163.

41. Ibid., p. 164.

42. Ibid., p. 168.

43. Ibid., p. 170.

44. Ibid., p. 175.

45. Ibid., p. 186.

46. Ibid., p. 187.

47. Flew, *Idea of Perfection in Christian Theology*, p. 235.

48. Passmore, *Perfectibility of Man*, p. 71.

49. Ibid., p. 101.

50. Ibid.

51. Ibid., pp. 102–3. Aquinas's emphasis on ultimate perfection as being a "vision of God" is in some ways very close to the Hindu view we shall encounter in chapter 7, and the *Yoga Sutra* test for mastery of Isvara Pranidhana (being "like God") in chapter 6.

52. Passmore, *Perfectibility of Man*, p. 121. Passmore points out some hermits and monks held that the elite, if only for passing moments, could "see God face to face" and thus temporarily achieve perfection in this life (ibid., p. 121).

53. Flew, *Idea of Perfection in Christian Theology*, pp. 230–43.

54. Ibid., p. 242.

55. Passmore, *Perfectibility of Man*, p. 130.

56. Ibid., p. 92.

57. Ibid., p. 93.

58. *Encyclopaedia of Religion and Ethics* (Edinburgh: T & T Clark, 1915), s.v. "Luther."

59. *Martin Luther: Selections from His Writings*, ed. John Dillenberger (New York: Anchor Books, 1961), p. 53.

60. Ibid., p. 55.

61. Ibid., p. 60.

62. Ibid., p. 68.

63. Ibid., p. 85.

64. *Encyclopaedia of Religion and Ethics*, s.v. "Luther."

65. Gerhard Ebeling, *Luther: An Introduction to His Thought* (Philadelphia: Fortress Press, 1977), p. 157.

66. As quoted by Passmore, *Perfectibility of Man*, p. 105.

67. Passmore, *Perfectibility of Man*, p. 105.

68. As quoted by ibid., p. 106.

69. Passmore, *Perfectibility of Man*, p. 106.

70. Flew, *Idea of Perfection in Christian Theology*, p. 250.

71. *The Encyclopedia of Religion*, ed. M. Eliade (New York: Macmillan, 1987). s.v. "Perfectibility."

72. Reinhold Niebuhr, *An Interpretation of Christian Ethics* (New York: Meridan Books, 1963), p. 59.

73. Reinhold Niebuhr, *The Nature and Destiny of Man*, vols. 1 and 2 (New York: Charles Scribner's Sons, 1964).

74. Ibid., 1: viii.

75. Ibid., p. 122.

76. William John Wolf, "Reinhold Niebuhr's Doctrine of Man," in *Reinhold Niebuhr: His Religious, Social and Political Thought*, ed. C. W. Kegley and R. W. Bretall (New York: Macmillan, 1961), pp. 229–50.

77. Ibid., p. 238.

78. Gordon Harland, *The Thought of Reinhold Niebuhr* (New York: Oxford University Press, 1960), pp. 68–69.

79. Ibid., p. 77.

80. Niebuhr, *The Nature and Destiny of Man*, 1: 182.

81. Ibid.

82. Ibid., p. 182 n. 2.

83. Passmore, *Perfectibility of Man* , p. 112.

84. Ibid.

85. Niebuhr, *Nature and Destiny of Man*, 2: 99.

86. Harland, *Thought of Reinhold Niebuhr*, pp. 81–82.

87. Ibid., p. 82.

88. *New Encyclopaedia Britannica*, 15th ed., s.v. "Neibuhr, Reinhold."

CHAPTER 5. PERFECTIBILITY IN ISLAMIC THOUGHT

1. *Encyclopaedia of the Qur'an*, ed. Jane D. McAuliffe (Boston: Brill, 2002), s.v. "Ethics and the Qur'an."

2. As quoted by Frederick Denny in "Salvation in the Qur'an," in *In Quest of an Islamic Humanism*, ed. A. H. Green (Cairo: The American University of Cairo Press, 1984), p. 206.

3. Muhammad Abul Quasem, *Salvation of the Soul and Islamic Devotions* (London: Kegan Paul), 1981, p. 19.

4. William C. Chittick, "The Islamic Concept of Human Perfection," in *Jung and the Monotheisms*, ed. J. Ryce-Menuhin (London: Routeledge, 1994), p. 164.

5. Muddathir 'Abd al-Rahim, *Human Rights and the World's Major Religions*, vol. 3: *The Islamic Tradition* (London: Praeger, 2005), pp. 20–23; see also p. 157.

6. Ibid., p. 22.

7. Ibid., p. 23.

8. S. Normanul Haq, "The Human Condition in Islam," in *The Human Condition*, ed. Robert Neville (Albany: State University of New York Press, 2001), p. 171.

9. A. Ezzati, *Islam and Natural Law* (London: Islamic College for Advanced Studies Press, 2002), p. 93.

10. *Encyclopaedia of Islam* (Leiden: Brill, 1965), s.v. "Fitra."

11. Frederick Denny, "God's Friends: The Sanctity of Persons in Islam," in *Sainthood: Its Manifestations in World Religions*, ed. R. Kieckhefer and G. D. Bond (Berkeley and Los Angeles: University of California Press, 1988), p. 71.

12. Ibid., p. 72.

13. Ezzati, *Islam and Natural Law*, p. 93.

14. Ibid.

15. *Encyclopaedia of Islam*, s.v. "Fitra."

16. Ezzati, *Islam and Natural Law*, p. 95.

17. Ibid., p. 96.

18. Ibid., pp. 100–1.

19. Ibid., p. 101.

20. Ibid.

21. Ibid., pp. 101–2.

22. Ibid., p. 104.

23. Ibid., p. 105.

24. Annemarie Schimmel, "Sufism and the Islamic Tradition," in *Mysticism and the Religious Traditions*, ed. Steven Katz (Oxford: Oxford University Press, 1983), p. 131.

25. Henry Corbin, *History of Islamic Philosophy* (London: Kegan Paul, 1996), pp. 97–98.

26. Mary Pat Fisher, "The Ideal Individual, as Described by All the Prophets," in *Dialogue and Alliance* 10, no. 2 (1996): 56.

27. Fazlur Rahman, *Major Themes of the Qur'an* (Minneapolis: Bibliotheca Islamica, 1994), p. 88; see also pp. 161–62.

28. Ezzati, *Islam and Natural Law*, p. 134.

29. Ibid., p. 135.

30. Ibid., p. 144.

31. Ibid. p. 108.

32. Rolland Miller, "The Muslim Doctrine of Salvation," *Bulletin of Christian Institutes of Islamic Studies* 3, nos. 1–4 (1980): 150.

33. Ibid., p. 151. See also W. Montgomery Watt, *Islamic Philosophy and Theology* (Edinburgh: Edinburgh University Press, 1985), p. 66.

34. As quoted by Miller, "Muslim Doctrine of Salvation," p. 151.

35. As quoted by Miller, "Muslim Doctrine of Salvation," p. 153.

36. Corbin, *History of Islamic Philosophy*, p. 117.

37. Miller, "Muslim Doctrine of Salvation," p. 154.

38. *New Encyclopaedia Britannica*, 15th ed., s.v. "Al-Ghazali."

39. Hava Lazarus-Yaleh, "The Place of the Religious Commandments in the Philosophy of Al-Ghazali," *Muslim World* 51 (1961): p. 173.

40. Ibid., p. 174.

41. Al-Ghazali, as quoted by Eric L. Ormsby, *Theodicy in Islamic Thought* (Princeton, NJ: Princeton University Press, 1984), p. 32.

42. Ormsby, *Theodicy in Islamic Thought*, p. 49.

43. From al-Ghazali's *Ihya* (*The Revival of the Religious Sciences*) 4: 373, as quoted by ibid., p. 51.

44. *Encyclopaedia of the Qur'an*, ed. Jane D. McAuliffe, vol. 5 (Boston: Brill, 2006), s.v. "Soul."

45. Majid Fakhry, *A Short Introduction to Islamic Philosophy, Theology and Mysticism* (Oxford: Oneworld, 1998), pp. 71–72.

46. Ibid., p. 78.

47. As quoted by ibid..

48. Fakhry, *Short Introduction*, p. 79.

49. As quoted by ibid., p. 79.

50. Ibid., p. 79.

51. Montgomery Watt, *The Faith and Practice of Al-Ghazali* (London: Allen & Unwin, 1963), p. 11. See also *Encyclopaedia of Islam*, s.v. "Al-Ghazali."

52. Watt, *Islamic Philosophy and Theology*, p. 14.

53. Ibid., p. 91.

54. Ibid., pp. 86–152.

55. Al-Ghazali, "Faith in Divine Unity and Trust in Divine Providence," in *The Revival of the Religious Sciences*, trans. David Burrell (Louisville: Fons Vitae, 2001), p. xii.

56. The following is based on Lazarus-Yaleh "Place of the Religious Commandments," p. 175.

57. Lazarus-Yaleh, "Place of the Religious Commandments."

58. Ibid., p. 177.

59. Ibid., p. 178.

60. Ormsby, *Theodicy in Islamic Thought*, p. 52.

61. Ibid., p. 79.

62. Ibid., p. 80.

63. Ibid., p. 253.

64. Annemarie Schimmel, *Mystical Dimensions of Islam* (Chapel Hill: University of North Carolina Press, 1975), p. 263.

65. Seyyed Hossein Nasr, *The Heart of Islam* (New York: Harper Collins, 2002), p. 213.

66. Fakhry, *Short Introduction*, p. 82.

67. Ibid., p. 81.
68. Ibid.
69. Ibid., p. 82.
70. Schimmel, *Mystical Dimensions of Islam*, p. 272. See also John T. Little,
"The Perfect Man According to Ibn 'Arabi," *Muslim World* 77.01 (2004): 43–54.
71. Corbin, *History of Islamic Philosophy*, p. 293.
72. Schimmel, *Mystical Dimensions of Islam*, p. 268.
73. Ibid., p. 270.
74. Ibid.
75. Ibid., pp. 271–72.
76. Ibid., p. 272.
77. *Encyclopaedia of Islam*, s.v. "Ibn 'Arabi."
78. Ibid.
79. Ibid.
80. Fakhry, *A Short Introduction*, p. 81.
81. Ibid., pp. 81–82.
82. Ibid., p. 82.
83. *Encyclopaedia of the Qur'an*, vol. 5, s.v. "Soul."
84. Al-Rahim, *Human Rights*, p. 163.
85. Ibid.

CHAPTER 6. PERFECTIBILITY IN INDIAN PHILOSOPHY
AND YOGA PSYCHOLOGY

1. *Yoga Sutras* 2.12–14, 4.7–9. For an English translation see *The Yoga System of Patanjali*, trans. J. H. Woods, Harvard Oriental Series, vol. 17 (Varanasi: Motilal Banarsidass, 1966). For a detailed analysis of the passages in question, see Harold G. Coward, "Psychology and Karma," *Philosophy East and West* 33 (1983): 19–60.

2. See Ellison Banks Findly, "Mantra kavisasta: Speech as Performative in the Rgveda," in *Understanding Mantras*, ed. Harvey Alper (Albany: State University of New York Press, 1989), p. 18.

3. Rudolf Otto, *The Idea of the Holy* (New York: Oxford University Press, 1958), pp. 4–7.

4. Jan Gonda, "The Indian *Mantra*," *Oriens* 16 (1963): 247.

5. Aurobindo Ghose, *The Secret of the Veda* (Pondicherry: Sri Aurobindo Ashram Press, 1956), p. 6.

6. See Thomas B. Coburn, "Scripture in India," *Journal of the American Academy of Religion* 52 (1984): 447.

7. Findly, "Mantra kavisasta," p. 17. For dates of the Vedas, see David Kinsley, *Hinduism* (Englewood Cliffs, N.J.: Prentice-Hall, 1982), p. 12.

8. Paul Hacker, "Notes on the Mandukyopanisad and Sankara's Agamasastravivarana," in *India Maior: Congratulatory Volume Presented to J. Gonda*, ed. J. Ensink and P. Gaefke (Leiden: Brill, 1972), p. 118.

9. Findly, "Mantra kavisasta," p. 20.

10. Ibid., pp. 21–22.

11. Ibid., p. 26.

12. J. L. Austin, "Performative Utterances," in *Philosophical Papers* (Oxford: Oxford University Press, 1961), pp. 220–39.

13. S. J. Tambiah, *Culture, Thought and Social Action* (Cambridge, MA: Harvard University Press, 1985), pp. 17–59.

14. Findly, "Mantra kavisasta," p. 28.

15. Ibid., p. 43.

16. George Weston Briggs, *Gorakhnath and the Kanphata Yogis* (Delhi: Motilal Banarsidass, 1982).

17. As quoted by T. R. V. Murti in the foreword to *The Sphota Theory of Language,* by Harold Coward (Delhi: Motilal Banarsidass, 1986), p. viii.

18. See Frits Staal, "Oriental Ideas on the Origin of Language," *Journal of the American Oriental Society,* 99 (1979): 9.

19. See Gonda, "Indian Mantra," pp. 261–68.

20. Staal, "Oriental Ideas," p. 10.

21. This presentation of the Mimamsa school's position is based on P. T. Raju, *Structural Depths of Indian Thought* (Albany: State University of New York Press, 1985), pp. 40–77.

22. Shashi Bhusan Dasgupta, "The Role of the Mantra in Indian Religion," in *Aspects of Indian Religious Thought* (Calcutta: Firma KLM, 1977), p. 25.

23. Mircea Eliade, *Yoga: Immortality and Freedom* (Princeton, NJ: Princeton University Press, 1971), p. 212.

24. For a detailed and comprehensive presentation of the Grammarian school's position, see Harold Coward and K. Kunjunni Raja, *Philosophy of the Grammarians* (Princeton, NJ: Princeton University Press, 1990).

25. *The Vakyapadiya of Bhartrhari,* trans. K. A. Subramania Iyer (Poona: Deccan College, 1965), 1.1, 1.9; hereafter cited as *Vak.*

26. *Vak.* 1.5.

27. *Vak.* I.123.

28. *Vak.* 1.1.

29. *Vak.* 1.126.

30. *Vak.* 1.332.

31. *Vak.* 1.124.

32. T. R. V. Murti, "Some Comments on the Philosophy of Language in the Indian Context," *Journal of Indian Philosophy* 2 (1974): 322.

33. *Vak.* 1.51.

34. *Vak.* 1.52, *Vrtti.* Bhartrhari's philosophy presented in the next three pages previously appeared in Harold Coward, "The Meaning and Power of Mantras . . ." *Studies in Religion* 11, no. 4 (1982): 370–74.

35. *Vak.* 1.23–26, 1.122–23.

36. *Vak.* 1.84, *Vrtti.*

37. *Vak.* 2 in which Bhartrhari establishes the vakya-sphota or sentence-whole over against the view of the Mimamsakas.

38. *Vak.* 1.24–26, *Vrtti.*

39. See Wade Wheelock, "A Taxonomy of the Mantras in the New- and Full-Moon Sacrifice," *History of Religion* 19 (1980): 358.

40. W. T. Stace, *Mysticism and Philosophy* (London: Macmillan, 1961), p. 15. This is, of course, exactly the opposite of the common modern interpretations given to the term "mystical"—such as vague, mysterious, and foggy.

41. *Vak.* 1.142. Note that in *Vrtti*, sounds of cart-axle, drum, and flute are all forms of manifested *vak*, and therefore potentially meaningful mantras.

42. *Vak.* 1.152–54.

43. Gonda, "Indian Mantra," p. 271.

44. *Vak.* 1.89.

45. For a more complete analysis, see Harold Coward, "The Yoga of the Word (Sabdapurvayoga)," *Adyar Library Bulletin* 49 (1985): 1–13.

46. Gerald Larsen, *Classical Samkhya* (Delhi: Motilal Banarsidass, 1979), chap. 1.

47. See Woods, *Yoga System of Patanjali*, p. xix for the date offered by Woods. Cites below to the Yoga Sutras are to this volume.

48. Jadunath Sinha, *Indian Psychology: Cognition* (Calcutta: Sinha Publishing House, 1958), pp. 334–66.

49. See Mircea Eliade, *Yoga, Immortality and Freedom*, trans. W. R. Trask (Princeton, NJ: Princeton University Press, 1971), p. 5; and T. H. Stcherbatsky, *The Conceptions of Buddhist Nirvana* (London: Mouton, 1965), pp. 16–19.

50. Woods, *The Yoga System of Patanjali*. A good recent secondary source on the Yoga school is Ian Whicher, *The Integrity of the Yoga Darsana* (Albany: State University of New York Press, 1998).

51. Yoga Sutras 1.24–29.

52. Yoga Sutras 1.5.

53. Yoga Sutras 2.44.

54. *Bhasya* or commentary on Yoga Sutras 1.28 as rendered by Rama Prasad, *Patanjali's Yoga Sutras* (Delhi: Oriental Reprint, 1978), p. 51.

55. In making these parallel comparisons between Patanjali's Yoga and Bhartrhari's Grammarian philosophy a technical qualification must be made. It must be realized that at the highest level of basic presuppositions, there are fundamental differences between the two philosophies. Bhartrhari offers an absolutism of word-consciousness or sabdabrahman while the Yoga system is ultimately a duality between pure consciousness (*purusa*) and nonintelligent matter (*prakrti*). Consequently, Isvara's *sattva* (transparent mind) as itself a part of prakrti does not have the power of consciousness (Yoga Sutras 1.24, *tika*). Since our concern here is not with the ultimate nature of the metaphysics involved, the discussion has proceeded as if the sattva aspect of prakrti were indeed real consciousness. This is in accord with the Yoga view of the nature of the psychological processes. The sattva aspect of *citta*, insofar as it is clear, takes on or reflects the intelligence (*caitanya*) of purusa. For practical purposes, therefore, no duality appears, and prakrti may be treated as self-illuminating (see *tika* in Yoga Sutras 1.17).

56. Yoga Sutras 2.45.

CHAPTER 7. PERFECTIBILITY IN HINDU THOUGHT

1. Gregory P. Fields, *Religious Therapeutics: Body and Health in Yoga, Ayurveda and Tantra* (Albany: State University of New York Press, 2001), p. 23.

2. Ibid., p. 24.

3. John M. Koller, "Human Embodiment: Indian Perspectives," in *Self as Body in Asian Theory and Practice*, ed. T. P. Kasulis (Albany: State University of New York Press, 1993), p. 47.

4. Wilhelm Halbfass, *Tradition and Reflection: Explorations in Indian Thought* (Albany: State University of New York Press, 1991), pp. 269–73.

5. See S. Radhakrishnan, *The Principal Upanisads* (London: Allen & Unwin, 1968), pp. 541ff. The dating of the various layers of the Vedas vary greatly. The dates given are taken from David Kinsley, *Hinduism* (Englewood Cliffs, NJ: Prentice-Hall, 1982), p. 12.

6. Fields, *Religious Therapeutics*. p. 25.

7. *Chandogya Upanishad* 7.25.2, trans. Robert E. Hume, *Thirteen Principal Upanisads*, p. 261.

8. *Isa Upanishad*, verse 9 trans. S. Radhakrishnan, *Principal Upanisads*, p. 573.

9. *Mundaka Upanishad* 3.2.3, trans. Radhakrishnan, in Radhakrishnan, *Principal Upanisads*.

10. Ibid., 3.1.9.

11. Ibid., 3.2.1.

12. *Chandogya Upanishad* 8.4.2. (trans. Hume).

13. *Maitri Upanishad* 4.4. (trans. Radhakrishnan).

14. *Brhad-Aranyaka Upanishad* 5.14.8, trans. Robert Hume, *Thirteen Principal Upanisads*.

15. Ibid., 4.3–4.

16. Ibid., 4.3.6.

17. Other mahavakayas or "great summary sentences" of the Upanishads include: *aham brahma asmi* (I am Brahman); *ayam atma brahma* (This atman is Brahman); and *prajnanam brahma* (Consciousness is Brahman).

18. *The Bhagavad-Gita*, trans. R. C. Zaehner (Oxford: Clarendon Press, 1969), pp. 132–33.

19. Ibid.

20. *The Bhagavad Gita*, trans. Barbara Stoler Miller (New York: Bantam, 1986), 12.6–8, p. 112.

21. For example, see Zaehner's translation and commentary.

22. *Bhagavad Gita* (trans. Zaehner) 2.39.

23. For a readable English translation see *Patanjali's Yoga Sutras*, trans. Rama Prasada (New Delhi: Oriental Books, 1978).

24. *The Brahma Sutra*, trans. by S. Radhakrishnan (London: Allen & Unwin, 1960).

25. See Wimal Dissanayake, introduction to part 2, "The Body in Indian Theory and Practice," in Kasulis, *Self as Body in Asian Theory and Practice*, pp. 41–42.

26. Anantanand Rambachan, "Hinduism," in *Life after Death in World Religions*, ed. Harold Coward (Maryknoll, NY: Orbis Books, 1997), p. 73.

27. Ibid., p. 74.

28. *Brahma-Sutra Bhasya of Sankaracarya*, trans. Swami Gambhirananda (Calcutta: Advaita Ashrama, 1977).

29. R. Balasubramanian, "Two Contemporary Exemplars of the Hindu Tradition: Ramana Maharsi and Sri Candrasekharendra Sarasvati," in *Hindu Spirituality: Vedas through Vedanta*, ed. Krishna Sivaraman (New York: Crossroad, 1989), pp. 361–91.

30. Ibid., p. 364.

31. *Brhad-Aranyaka Upanishad* 2.4.5 (trans. Hume).

32. As quoted by Balasubramanian, "Two Contemporary Exemplars," p. 366.

33. Ibid., p. 372. Other scholars (e.g., Anatanand Rambachan) challenge this interpretation by arguing that it is not the world but ignorance (*avidya*) that disappears.

34. Ibid., p. 374.

35. The following presentation of the Srivaisnava tradition is based largely on Vasudha Narayanan, "*Karma*, Bhaktiyoga and Grace in the Srivaisnava Tradition: Ramanujya and Karattakvan," in *Of Human Bondage and Divine Grace*, ed. John Carter (La Salle, IL: Open Court, 1992), pp. 57–94.

36. Ibid., p. 58

37. Ibid., p. 60

38. Ibid., p. 60–61.

39. Ibid., p. 62.

40. Ramanuja's commentary on the Bhagavad Gita 10.10 and 10.11 and 13.6 and 13.7 as quoted by Narayanan, "*Karma*, Bhaktiyoga and Grace," p. 63.

41. Ibid., p. 69.

42. Vasudha Narayanan, "Bondage and Grace in the Srivaisanava Tradition: Pilai Lokacharya and Vedanta Desika," in Carter, *Of Human Bondage and Divine Grace*, p. 83.

43. Robert Baird, "Swami Bhaktivedanta and Ultimacy," in *Religion in Modern India*, ed. Robert Baird (Delhi: Manohar, 1995), p. 516.

44. As quoted by ibid., p. 522.

45. Ibid., p. 527.

46. Bhagavad Gita 2.47–48 (trans. Miller), p. 36.

47. Bhagavad Gita 2.42–69.

48. *The Gitabhasya of Ramanuja*, trans. M. R. Sampatkumaran (Madras: Ramacharya Memorial Trust, 1969), p. 55.

49. *Jnaneshwar's Gita*, trans. Swami Kripananda (Albany: State University of New York Press, 1989), p. 34.

50. M. K. Gandhi, *The Bhagavadaita* (Delhi: Orient, n.d.), p. 14.

51. See Harold Coward, "Ambedkar, Gandhi and the Untouchables," in *Indian Critiques of Gandhi*, ed. Harold Coward (Albany: State University of New York Press, 2003).

52. Troy Organ, *The Hindu Quest for the Perfection of Man* (Athens, Ohio: Ohio University, 1970), p. 239.

53. As quoted by ibid., p. 246.

54. See Gerald Larson, *Classical Sankhya* (Delhi: Motilal Banarsidass, 1979).

55. A recent translation is by Jean Varenne, *Yoga and the Hindu Tradition* (Delhi: Motilal Banarsidass, 1989).

56. Aurobindo Ghose, *On the Veda* (Pondicherry: Sri Aurobindo Ashram Press, 1956). For a good overall study of Aurobindo, see Robert Munor, *Sri Aurobindo: The Perfect and the Good* (Calcutta: Minerva, 1978). The ashram that Aurobindo created is critically examined by Robert Minor, *The Religious, the Spiritual and the Secular: Auroville and Secular India* (Albany: State University of New York Press, 1999).

57. As quoted by Sisirkumar Ghose, "Sri Aurobindo: The Spirituality of the Future," in *Hindu Spirituality: Postclassical and Modern*, ed. K. R. Sundararajan and Bithika Mukerji (New York: Crossroad, 1997), p. 387.

58. Patricia Mumme, "Living Liberation in Comparative Perspective," in *Living Liberation in Hindu Thought*, ed. Andrew Fort and Patricia Mumme (Albany: State University of New York Press, 1996), p. 247.

59. Andrew O. Fort, *Jivanmukti in Transformation: Embodied Liberation in Advaita and Neo-Vedanta* (Albany: State University of New York Press, 1998), p. 32.

60. Ibid., p. 34.

61. As quoted by Lance Nelson, "Living Liberation in Sankara and Classical Advaita," in Fort and Mumme, *Living Liberation in Hindu Thought*, p. 22.

62. Ibid., p. 18.

63. Ibid., p. 22.

64. Ibid., p. 23.

65. Fort, *Jivanmukti in Transformation*, p. 36.

66. Ibid.

67. Ibid., p. 38.

68. Ibid., p. 39.

69. See Vachaspati Misra's gloss on *Yoga Sutra* 1.24 in *Patanjali's Yoga Sutras*, trans. Rama Prasada (Delhi: Oriental Books, 1978), pp. 42–45.

70. *Sankara on the Yoga Sutra*, trans. Trevor Leggett (London: Routledge and Kegan Paul, 1981), p. 89.

71. *Vyasa* on 1.25 as quoted in Sankara's *Vivarana* and translated by Trevor Leggett in Leggett, *Sankara on the Yoga Sutra*, p. 89.

72. Christopher Key Chapple, "Living Liberation in Samkhya and Yoga" in Fort and Mumme, *Living Liberation in Hindu Thought*, p. 124.

73. This presentation of Ramanuja's position is based on Kim Skoog, "Is the *Jivanmukti* State Possible?" in Fort and Mumme, *Living Liberation in Hindu Thought*, pp. 63–90.

74. Ibid., p. 83.

75. Mumme, "Living Liberation in Comparative Perspective," p. 259.

76. Ibid.

77. Fort, *Jivenmukti*, p. 146.
78. Ibid., p. 147.
79. As quoted by ibid.
80. Ibid.
81. Swami Vivekananda, *The Yogas and Other Works* (New York: Ramakrishna-Vedanta Center, 1953), pp. 334–35.
82. Fort, *Jivenmukti*, p. 178.
83. As quoted by ibid.
84. Mumme, "Living Liberation in Comparative Perspective," pp. 263–64.

CHAPTER 8. PERFECTIBILITY IN BUDDHIST THOUGHT

1. Walpola Rahula, *What the Buddha Taught* (New York: Grove Press, 1974; Oxford: Oneworld, 1977), p. 1.
2. As quoted by ibid., p. 3.
3. Rahula, *What the Buddha Taught*, p. 3.
4. The following is based on ibid., pp. 19ff.
5. Alex Wayman, "Buddha as Saviour," in *Salvation in Christianity and Other Religions* [no editor given]. (Rome: Gregorian University Press, 1980), p. 196.
6. Yun-Hua Jan, "Dimensions of Indian Buddhism," in *The Malalasekera Commemoration Volume*, ed. O. H. de A. Wijesekera (Colombo, Sri Lanka: 1976), p. 162.
7. The following is based upon K. N. Jayatilleke, *Early Buddhist Theory of Knowledge* (Delhi: Motilal Banarsidass, 1980), pp. 183ff.
8. Lewis Lancaster, "Buddhist Literature: Its Canons, Scribes and Editors," in *The Critical Study of Sacred Texts*, ed. Wendy Doniger O'Flaherty (Berkeley, CA: Berkeley Religious Studies Series, 1979), p. 216.
9. As quoted by Malcolm David Eckel, "Beginningless Ignorance," in *The Human Condition*, ed. R. C. Neville (Albany: State University of New York Press, 2001), pp. 50–51.
10. Richard Robinson, *The Buddhist Religion* (Belmont, CA.: Dickenson, 1970), p. 28.
11. L. Schmithausen, "On Some Aspects of Descriptions or Theories of 'Liberating Insight' and 'Enlightenment' in Early Buddhism," *Studien zum Jainismus und Buddhismus* 23 (1983): 200–201.
12. Robinson, *Buddhist Religion*, p. 19.
13. Ibid., p. 31.
14. As quoted by Richard Gombrich, *Theravada Buddhism: A Social History from Ancient Benares to Modern Colombo* (London: Routledge & Kegan Paul, 1988), p. 67.
15. Gombrich, *Theravada Buddhism*, p. 67.
16. Damien Keown, *Buddhism: A Very Short Introduction* (Oxford: Oxford University Press, 1996), p. 47.

17. Ibid.

18. See N. R. Reat, *Buddhism: A History* (Berkeley. CA: Asian Humanities Press, 1994), p. 37.

19. For a clear presentation of the theory of "dependent arising," see Hirakawa Akira, *A History of Indian Buddhism*, trans. Paul Groner (Honolulu: University of Hawaii Press, 1990), pp. 51ff.

20. Akira, *History of Indian Buddhism*, p. 53.

21. Rahula, *What the Buddha Taught*, p. 8.

22. Klaus Klostermaier, *Buddhism: A Short Introduction* (Oxford: Oneworld, 1999), p. 117.

23. Gombrich, *Theravada Buddhism*, p. 73.

24. Akira, *History of Indian Buddhism*, p. 62.

25. The above listing of rules is taken from ibid., pp. 62–66.

26. T. R. V. Murti, *The Central Philosophy of Buddhism* (London: Allen & Unwin, 1960), p. 77.

27. Ibid.

28. The following outline of the origins of Mahayana Buddhism is based on Paul Williams, *Mahayana Buddhism: The Doctrinal Foundations* (London: Routledge, 1989), pp. 16ff.

29. Williams, *Mahayana Buddhism*, p. 19.

30. Ibid., p. 20.

31. Ibid., p. 33.

32. Ibid., p. 37.

33. Edward Conze, *Selected Sayings from the Perfection of Wisdom* (London: Buddhist Society, 1968), pp. 11ff.

34. Williams, *Mahayana Buddhism*, p. 49.

35. Ibid., pp. 43–44.

36. *L'Abhidharmakosa de Vasubandu*, trans. Louis de la Vallee Poussin (Paris: Paul Geuthner, 1923–35), 6:139.

37. Jeffrey R. Timm, "Prolegomena to Vallabha's Theology of Revelation," *Philosophy East and West* 38, no. 2 (1988): 109.

38. See Mervyn Sprung, *Lucid Exposition of the Middle Way* (London: Routledge & Kegan Paul, 1979). This deconstructive approach is nicely exemplified in the analysis of the statement, "the human soul is eternal" offered by Nagarjuna and his commentator, Candrakirti. Candrakirti asks what the relationship is between the subject "the human soul" and the predication "is eternal." Are the two terms identical or different? If the two terms are identical, we are left with a tautology: the eternal human soul is eternal. If they are different and distinct, what could possibly justify the claim that they are related? See Timm, "Prolegomena," p. 109; and Sprung, *Lucid Exposition of the Middle Way*, pp. 165–86.

39. Gadjin M. Nagoa, "From Madhyamika to Yogacara: An Analysis of MMK XXIV.18 and MV 1.1–2," *Journal of the International Association of Buddhist Studies* 2 (1979): 32.

40. Richard H. Robinson, *Early Madhyamika in India and China* (Delhi: Motilal Banarsidass, 1978), p. 49.

41. See the discussion of nirvana, in ibid., pp. 46–47.

42. David Loy, "How Not to Criticize Nagarjuna: A Response to L. Stafford Betty," *Philosophy East and West* 34, no. 4 (1984): 443.

43. Private correspondence from David Loy, September 29, 1989.

44. Williams, *Mahayana Buddhism*, chaps. 3–9.

45. Keown, *Buddhism*, p. 67.

46. *New Encyclopedia Britannica*, 15th ed. s.v. "Buddhism," pp. 268–315.

47. Williams, *Mahayana Buddhism*, p. 227.

48. For an illustration of how this "Pure Land" practice has adapted to a Canadian setting, see David Goa and Harold Coward, "Sacred Ritual, Sacred Language: Jodo Shinshu Religious Forms in Transition," *Studies in Religion* 12, no. 4 (1983): 363–79.

49. Williams, *Mahayana Buddhism*, p. 227.

50. Ibid., p. 49.

51. As translated by Conze and quoted by ibid., pp. 50–51.

52. Williams, *Mahayana Buddhism*, p. 51.

CHAPTER 9. CONCLUSION

1. Terence Penelhum, *Christian Ethics and Human Nature* (London: SCM Press, 2000), pp. 64–66.

2. Ibid., p. 65.

3. Ibid., p. 66. We should note here that the Islamic view is alone in allocating to human nature a clean slate at birth with positive potentials to be actualized by following God's commands.

4. Ibid., p. 68.

5. See Harold Coward, *Yoga and Psychology* (Albany: State University of New York Press, 2000), p. 61.

6. John Hick, *The Fifth Dimension: An Exploration of the Spiritual Realm* (Oxford: Oneworld, 1999), p. 141. The Yoga Sutras anticipate Hick's "metaphorical rather than literal" move and explain it as the psychological state of one who has not seriously taken up the practice of Yoga under a qualified teacher. Such a person, claims Yoga, is in no position to pass judgment on whether or not states of egolessness are psychologically possible.

Index

www.ingramcontent.com/pod-product-compliance
Lightning Source LLC
Chambersburg PA
CBHW030320270326
41926CB00010B/1438